Judy Ff......

11 95

Stratford-upon-Avon
Second Series

General Editor: Jeremy H:
Professor of Modern British Literatu
University of Trondheim, Norway

Documentary and the Mass Media

Editor: John Corner

Edward Arnold
A division of Hodder & Stoughton
LONDON NEW YORK MELBOURNE AUCKLAND

© 1986 Edward Arnold (Publishers) Ltd

First published in Great Britain 1986
Reprinted 1990

Distributed in the USA by Routledge, Chapman and Hall, Inc.
29 West 35th Street, New York, NY 10001

British Library Cataloguing in Publication Data

Documentary and the mass media.—(Stratford-
upon-Avon studies. Second series)
  1. Mass media
  I. Corner, John   II. Series
  302.2'34   P90

  ISBN 0–7131–6493–X

Acknowledgements

The editor and publishers would like to thank BBC TV for permission
to use the stills from their video of *Horizon – A New Green Revolution*
and the video hard copies from their programme *Brass Tacks – A Fair
Day's Fiddle*, © BBC 1984.

Editor's Note

The film which Bill Nichols discusses at some length in Chapter 6, *Roses in
December* (1982), is available for hire in Britain from Contemporary Films
(c/o Harris Films Ltd, Glenbuck Road, Surbiton, Surrey).

Typeset in 10/11 pt Garamond Compugraphic by
Colset Private Ltd, Singapore.
Printed and bound in Great Britain for Edward Arnold, the educational,
academic and medical publishing division of Hodder and Stoughton
Limited, Mill Road, Dunton Green, Sevenoaks, Kent TN13 2YA by
J. W. Arrowsmith Ltd, Bristol

Contents

Select Bibliography

Eric Barnouw, *Documentary: A History of Non-Fiction Film* (New York, OUP, 1974).

Richard Barsam, *Non-Fiction Film* (London, Allen & Unwin, 1974).

Andrew Goodwin *et al*; eds., *Drama-Documentary: BFI Dossier 19* (London, British Film Institute, 1983).

Forsyth Hardy, ed., *Grierson on Documentary* (London, Faber & Faber, rev. edn. 1979).

Lewis Jacobs, ed., *The Documentary Tradition: From Nanook to Woodstock* (New York, Hopkinson & Blake 1971).

G. Roy Levin, *Documentary Explorations* (New York, Doubleday, 1971).

Alan Lovell and Jim Hillier, eds., *Studies in Documentary* (London, Secker & Warburg, 1972).

Rachel Low, *Documentary and Educational Films of the 1930s* (London, Allen & Unwin, 1979).

Don Macpherson, ed., *Traditions of Independence* (London, British Film Institute, 1980).

Bill Nichols, *Ideology and the Image* (Bloomington, Indiana University Press, 1981).

Alan Rosenthal, *The New Documentary in Action* (Berkeley, University of California Press, 1971).

Paul Rotha, *Documentary Diary* (London, Secker & Warburg, 1973).

Roger Silverstone, *Framing Science: The Making of a BBC Documentary* (London, British Film Institute, 1985).

William Stott, *Documentary Expression and Thirties America* (New York, OUP, 1976).

Elizabeth Sussex, *The Rise and Fall of British Documentary* (Berkeley, University of California Press, 1976).

Dai Vaughan, *Portrait of an Invisible Man* (London, British Film Institute, 1983.

Thomas Waugh, *'Show us Life': Towards a History and Aesthetics of the Committed Documentary* (London, The Scarecrow Press, 1984).

John Wyver, ed., *Nothing But The Truth: Cinema Vérité and the Films of the Roger Graef Team* (London, Institute of Contemporary Arts/British Film Institute, 1982).

Preface

The collection of essays presented here has been commissioned and edited
with a guiding idea very much in mind. This idea is that close examination
of the forms, circumstances and historical development of 'documentary'
work in the media can be of quite central importance to an understanding
both of the representational conventions of media imagery and language
and the relationship of public communication systems to the societies
within which they are set and within which their messages are circulated.

It would be hard to find a category of media output where the technological, the aesthetic, the social and the political have impinged so directly
on one another for so long, and in such complexity of combination, as in
the various forms of the documentary account. It would also be hard to find
another media category in which the practitioners so routinely displayed
anxieties as to methods and to aims, and felt the need to define both
against past and current practice, as is the case here. Documentary-making
has perennially been regarded as a problematic, if also a necessary and
exciting, use of media possibilities.

But to talk of a 'category' like this might seem immediately to beg too
many questions. What is the definition of documentary? Where exactly are
the frontier lines with current affairs journalism, with types of realist drama
and with a range of recreational, educational and promotional uses of
media technologies and formats? Although it is possible to trace the use of
the word itself back to John Grierson's adaptation of a French term for
travelogue – *documentaire* – in the 1920s,[1] too much emphasis on the
etymology will miss the point that the project of attempting somehow to
'document' real events and circumstances through mechanically recorded
images is as old as the technologies themselves.[2]

---

[1]The term is said to have been first used of Flaherty's *Moana* in 1926. See, for instance,
Grierson's comments in Forsyth Hardy, ed., *Grierson on Documentary* (London, Faber &
Faber, rev. edn 1979), p. 35.
[2]As well as the obvious, earlier example of still photography, the work of the pioneer cinema-
photographer Louis Lumière in the 1890s is often cited in this connection, much of it being
short 'actuality' sequences. See the discussion in chapter 1 of Eric Barnouw, *Documentary*
(New York, OUP, 1974).

It is perhaps not surprising that a few commentators have decided, after deliberation, that the term is simply too all-embracing adequately to serve as any sort of classication and have suggested other terms which might do the job better, being either less ambitiously generic (e.g. 'non-fiction film') or else used in differentiating combination with each other.[3]

The definitional problems are real ones, and they connect up with those more fundamental questions (discussed in many of the following essays) about the criteria, techniques and kinds of status applicable to the production and use of recorded representations.

However, the documentary notion seems to me to be helpful in organizing the kind of studies collected here because for over 50 years it has served to reference, for practioners, public and critics alike, an area of media work – a type of enterprise – with a surprising degree of continuity in its ambitions, problems and terms of internal debate and practice. This is so whatever the definitional untidiness thrown up in the consideration of specific developments in photography, film, radio and television.

I think it is possible to get a good preliminary sense of this area by examining three of its dimensions – the *technological*, the *social* and the *aesthetic*. It may be useful to give some attention to each one in turn.

Technological factors lie at the root of the documentary enterprise because it is the technological capacity to record the visual and / or aural elements of a particular piece of the world which provides the primary *evidential* quality sought by documentary accounts, a quality which has variously excited the imagination of documentarists towards more expansive and ambitious goals. In this sense, documentary projects not based on the direct referentiality of recording technologies (e.g. written accounts, certain types of theatre production) are of a rather different, displaced, kind from the mainstream of work self-identified under the heading.

All sorts of questions are immediately raised, of course – for instance, about how the *local* relationship between particular physical entity or sound and the recording of it is supposed to match up with the *general* relationship between, say, 'youth unemployment in Merseyside' and the edited assemblage of a 30-minute television programme. Even the primary veracity of images and recorded sounds themselves may be open to both a technical and a philosophical scepticism (as symbols they connect with more than directly referential meanings) whilst, at the other end of the scale, the introduction of any idea of 'reconstruction' immediately ushers in a whole realm of potential duplicity. Nevertheless, it remains the case that the imaginative and informational potency of most documentary work has been premised, however artfully, on the powerful way in which recording apparatus can certify the independent existence of that which is recorded (the 'that' in question being indispensible to the very process of the recording), and, moreover, can do so by reproducing an engaging

[3] See, for instance, chapter 1 of Richard Barsam, *Nonfiction Film* (London, Allen & Unwin, 1974).

likeness. At times, consideration of this aspect of the technological capacity to produce 'traces' of reality, and thus, in some eyes, to offer secure ground for a representational realism, attains to a mystical level of awe. Here, the French film-maker and critic Andre Bazin, with his talk of the 'virginal purity' of real objects being captured by the 'impassive lens' and his historical analogy with the direct physical imprint of the face evidenced by death-masks, provides an imaginatively stimulating if also a rather eccentric example.[4] However, most of us know very well both the force of witness and the special fascination which recorded images and perhaps certain kinds of sound recording can exert.

The *sociological* dimension of documentary not only follows from its important and sensitive positioning within the political and social structures of 'public communication', 'public knowledge' and 'public opinion', but is also a result of the self-proclaimed purposes which documentary work has frequently espoused and the social character of so many of its topics (e.g. social and occupational change, social problems, the lives and circumstances of various 'others'). John Grierson's own commentaries on his aims and aspirations for the British documentary film movement of the 1930s, particularly for the group closely associated with him in the film units successively of the Empire Marketing Board and the General Post Office between 1926 and 1939, cannot be simply read as some manifesto of common purpose for all documentary activity in that period[5] but they do seem to indicate elements in a broader agenda. It is interesting that, in Grierson's view, the origins of documentary lay in ideas of 'national education' and in 'sociological rather than aesthetic ideas'.[6] Within the perspective of Grierson's brand of social democratic politics, documentary films were to be given the function of providing the public with something akin to a regularly updated 'civic education' programme. Through this, citizens would be better equipped to participate in a rapidly changing, industrialized democracy thought to be displaying increased enthusiasm for efficiency and greater equality. Such a programme of national improvement (comparison with Reith's philosophy of public service broadcasting is inviting, though beyond the scope of this preface)[7] would not only provide

[4]See the discussion and references around the idea of the image as an 'index' in the articles by Richard Collins and by Dai Vaughan in this volume.
[5]For a useful and provocative criticism of received wisdom in this area, see Annette Kuhn, 'British Documentary in the 1930s and "Independence": Recontextualising a Film Movement' in Don Macpherson, ed., *British Cinema: Traditions of Independence* (London, British Film Institute, 1980). Another forcefully argued reappraisal which gives detailed attention to sociological and political factors is to be found in Stuart Hood, 'John Grierson and the Documentary Film Movement' in James Curren and Vincent Porter, eds., *British Cinema History* (London, Weidenfeld & Nicolson, 1983). A good, general discussion of the Grierson philosophy in a developed historical context is Robert Colls and Philip Dodd, 'Representing the Nation: British Documentary Film 1930–45', *Screen* 26.1 (1985).
[6]Hardy, ed., *Grierson on Documentary* p. 78.
[7]But see the articles by Paddy Scannell and by Elaine Bell in this volume for an analysis of the role of documentary within the formative phases of radio and of television.

information but would, imaginatively, put people 'in touch' with one another by revealing infrastructural relations of interdependence and also by seeking in some measure to extend the mutuality and trust depicted in the films across the separate regions, classes, workplaces and lives of the nation/audience.

This 'radical revelatory' aspect to documentary film-making appears to be a common theme underlying a number of different political approaches and different applications. In the more committedly critical type of work, the images and sounds might be used as witness for the prosecution in the case against 'things as they are', as documents in the cause of change, rather than elements in some celebratory revelation of community or nationhood (as, for understandable reasons, they often became in the films produced during the Second World War).[8]

Within the very different conditions of modern television production and scheduling, the 'socially revelatory' ambitions of documentary are equally apparent, and have a whole new range of technologically grounded possibilities to exploit in the construction of immediacy and presence, including of course that sense of 'live' occurrence which can be used to enhance even recorded programme material. Work subsumed under the documentary label includes many programmes in regular slots (e.g. *Panorama*, *World in Action*, *TV Eye*, *Brass Tacks*, *Forty Minutes*), some of which, by sheer audience size and composition and by spread of influence on a range of public issues, have to be considered as part of popular rather than minority television and as an important input into popular knowledge. The documentary enterprise in its dominant modern manifestation within broadcasting systems is not only at some remove from the terms of Grierson's own version of its 'mission to inform' – the centrality, scope and power of its contemporary character far exceed the scale on which even his sense of its social possibilities was framed.

Consideration of forms and of formal developments leads on to the final dimension of documentary which I want to consider here – the *aesthetic*. The word is a troublesome one in the history of documentary debates, smacking to some directors and critics of precisely that 'artiness' and consequent artificiality to which they see themselves as most firmly opposed in their quest for the raw substance of reality. Nevertheless – and here we touch on one of the central problem areas for documentary practice, to be addressed many times in different ways in the following pages – documentaries must necessarily be *organized* according to compositional principles, using material (film and soundtrack) itself produced by countless processes of construction and selection.[9] Protestations of 'innocence' are therefore

[8]On the wartime films, see Bjorn Sorenssen in this volume, the valuable account in Dai Vaughan, *Portrait of an Invisible Man* (London, British Film Institute, 1983) and chapters 10 and 11 of Anthony Aldgate and Jeffrey Richards, *Britain Can Take It* (Oxford, Blackwell, 1986).

[9]Grierson's felicitously accommodating remarks about documentary being the 'creative interpretation of reality' are often quoted in discussion of this general point. As a committed

completely out of order in the light of this fact, despite the continuing allure of supposing oneself to be simply 'telling it like it is' or, perhaps more potently still, '*showing* it like it is'.[10] Aesthetic factors, in respect at least of the principles for producing convincing and pleasing representations, have always played a key role in the devising of the various rhetorical possibilities out of which the range of documentary discourse has been developed. Each set of devices within the range (e.g. forms of shot, forms of voice-over, conventions of interview method, the combinations of vision and sound in editing, *vérité* sequences, use of music, use of reconstructions) tends to bring with it both a new potential for imaginative engagement, for immediacy and perhaps for pleasure and, at the same time, new questions about legitimacy and about the openness or otherwise of its mode of use within the finished film or programme. Often, such devices are subject to subtle naturalization.

These matters of aesthetic or rhetorical organization frequently play across two related kinds of tension in the documentary account, that between *appearance* and *essence* and that between the *particular* and the *general*. The two together have been ruffling attempts at coherent documentary realism for at least half a century. Both of them stem from the obvious point, touched on earlier, that what the camera is pointed at and, rather differently, what a microphone picks up (later in the book Dai Vaughan uses the term 'pro-filmic' to describe this level of documentary production) is both particular and 'of the surface'. To move smoothly from this kind of 'certified' reality to more general propositions about what is going on often requires crucial articulations to be managed at some distance from what the technology can possible be said to 'capture' and may well require that the audience not be encouraged into too heightened an alertness as to differentiations in the status of what it is hearing and watching. As a number of commentators have observed, an almost indispensible category for bridging the particular/general gap in documentary work is that of the *typical*, a typicality perhaps guaranteed by the authoritative assertions of the narrator/reporter, though this method is less common than it was. It seems likely that the majority of public controversies over television documentary programmes have hinged precisely on the supposed *representativeness* of what has been depicted rather than on the (perhaps also questionable) status of particular images and sounds. As for the attempt to penetrate through 'appearance' or to somehow show the 'inner' via the 'outer' (often viewable as an attempt to build a realism on

propagandist for good citizenship, he was less of a purist on the question of editorial interventions than is sometimes assumed. See, particularly, Hardy, ed., *Grierson on Documentary* Part Three item 4 and Part Four item 3.
[10]An interesting example of a 'prose documentarist' using a visual metaphor to assert this kind of innocence is provided by George Orwell's comment that 'Good prose is like a window pane', George Orwell, 'Why I Write', collected in Sonia Orwell and Ian Angus, eds., *The Collected Essays, Journalism and Letters of George Orwell: Vol. 1* (Harmondsworth, Penguin, 1970).

top of a naturalism), more extensive use of participant speech has undoubtedly contributed a dimension which was lacking in most of the classic films of the 1930s.[11] This is where such an attempt does actually form part of modern documentary objectives; in several recent *vérité*-type projects on British television the search for the essential, along with attempted generality, does not appear to be strongly marked.

But perhaps this is to pass into that degree of detailed analysis which only the various articles themselves have the space to pursue properly. Suffice it to say here that recognition of the internally contradictory nature of documentary accounts as motivated, discursive constructions and, quite often, as pieces of feigning, is only where scholarship, critical analysis and discussion *starts*. I would also suggest that only the most committed of anti-realists could consider the abandonment of documentary to be desirable (however unlikely this is in practice). For the alternatives, sometimes parallelling the setting up of photomontage in opposition to 'actuality' photography,[12] are too-limited in range and in informational and connotational richness to satisfy by themselves the paradoxical but strong and not necessarily at all conservative desire to 'see for ourselves' through images made by other people. What new forms documentary work might take is, of course, an entirely different matter.

The studies which follow have been arranged in a roughly chronological sequence according to the date of the material principally discussed by contributors, though with thematic considerations borne in mind towards the latter half of the volume when questions of date become less relevant.

Historically, the articles examine aspects of documentary from the 1930s to today, taking in not only the lines of development through film into television but also the important but virtually unresearched area of radio documentary and the significant and illuminating cluster of documentary ideas and documentary problems surrounding the venture of Mass Observation.

There are essentially three different kinds of broad approach to be found in these pages and though on occasion all are present within the same article, most pieces show a weighting in one direction or another. First of all, there are historical approaches, which in most cases are concerned, too, with tracing the contexts of documentary-making as an activity of cultural production. Paddy Scannell, in a detailed account which complements

---

[11] A notable exception here is the film *Housing Problems*, produced and directed by Arthur Elton and Edgar Anstey in 1935. This included lengthy sections of people speaking directly to camera about their domestic conditions and was seen to be influential in subsequent television developments. See Elizabeth Sussex, *The Rise and Fall of British Documentary* (Berkeley, University of California Press, 1976) for valuable commentary on this, and on other films of the period, by those involved in the documentary film movement. See also the articles by Scannell and by Bell in the present collection for discussion of the forms of documentary speech prior to the availability of a more lightweight recording technology.

[12] Stuart Hall touches usefully on this issue in his important discussion of documentary photography and photo-journalism, 'The Social Eye of *Picture Post*', *Working papers in Cultural Studies* 2 (1972) pp. 71–120.

very well existing studies of the documentary film movement (some of which I referred to earlier), shows how 'features' and documentary-style programmes formed an important part of radio broadcasting in the 1930s. Central to Scannell's perspective is his analysis of the BBC as an institution in which documentary forms are developed and managed within a set of political determinants as well as in relation to technological possibility and the emerging responses of broadcasting to regional and popular culture. David Chaney and Michael Pickering also concern themselves with the 1930s, though in contrast with a major media enterprise like the BBC, the focus of their study is what they see as the attempt by members of the Mass Observation group to re-think the terms of public communication against existing practice and to bring both a modernist and a fundamentally democratic imagination to bear on the matter of how social accounts are produced, authenticated and circulated. Chaney and Pickering offer both a study of Mass Observation's ideas and a more general argument about the relation between aesthetic and sociological elements in documentary.

Further on in the volume, Elaine Bell picks up on the themes discussed in both these articles in her examination of how the first TV documentarists saw themselves as carrying out documentary's 'specific social job'. What is particularly intriguing in this highly original survey (much of it based on the author's own interviews with ex-BBC staff) is both the account of the handling of questions of artifice and dramatization and, echoing Scannell here, the crucial, institutional classification of the topics and the methods thought appropriate in public communication of this kind.

The second general approach concerns primarily the analysis of specific documentary texts or specific aspects of textual forms or themes, though always with some attention to the political and social factors involved in their construction and consequence. Bjorn Sorenssen, A Norwegian film scholar, looks at what lies behind the widespread attribution of 'poetic' qualities to the wartime films of Humphrey Jennings. By close attention to three texts in relation to contemporary events, Sorenssen attempts to bring out the principles upon which their visionary discourse of nationhood and of commonality in the experience of war is based.

Roger Silverstone follows the notion of a documentary 'poetics' through in a more expanded form in his intensive scrutiny of how science is presented on television. Links with the schematic analyses of Sorenssen are apparent as Silverstone explores the narrative movement and often pleasurable presences of science 'on the screen', comparing its complex mixture of mythic and mimetic elements with the languages of the scientific community itself.

The starting point for Bill Nichols's investigation of documentary language is a reflection on images and words concerning the *Challenger* space-shuttle disaster. Nichols's focus is on certain incongruities in documentary representation of the person, of the body and of death and on the political dimensions of such incongruity. He talks of the 'miniaturization' produced by established representational schemes and uses North

American examples to explore how documentary-makers might respond with more sense of contradiction and paradox to what he terms 'questions of magnitude'.

The third type of approach also raises question of documentary form but places a directly textual analysis secondary to some specific type of extra-textual investigation. In his consideration of *vérité*-influenced programmes on British television, programmes which claim to deliver a purer mediation of what is represented than mainstream practices, Richard Collins makes extensive use of the film-makers' own comments on their procedures and of professional handbooks on documentary method. He connects his discussion of the 'observational' style both with the ideologies which he sees governing news and current affairs output and with earlier debates about realism and naturalism in literary fiction. An article by myself and a colleague, Kay Richardson, attempts to work out from the text in the other direction, raising questions about the nature of the inter-pretative work performed by viewers and looking closely at what sample viewers say about what they see and hear in a particular television programme. This project takes the issue of mediation/transparency so often raised in relation to documentary representation and explores it in relation to documentary reading.

Dai Vaughan, an experienced television documentary editor and also a writer on the history and theory of documentary forms, contributes a dis-cussion which moves across most of the areas I have sketched out above. He provides a series of arguments, reflections and instances which add up to a pointed re-examination of the 'documentary idea' in many of its major aspects and an exploration of its distinctive imaginative appeal.

Finally, I acknowledge that this volume omits several documentary topics which another volume might have included. Such selection largely follows from the decision to stay quite close to the agencies of mass com-munication or (as in the case of Mass Observation) to work which is in direct reaction to them. However, even here it is important to develop more con-nections with the journalistic uses of photography, for instance, and with the history of marginalized film and video production in the 'independ-ent' and more committedly political sectors. Further attention to the 1930s documentary movement and to its most well-known prewar films (e.g. *Nightmail*, *Coalface* and *Housing Problems*) would clearly be valuable too. The overlap with drama is another realm, of great contem-porary relevance, where critical questions need to be followed through.

This book nevertheless seems to me to fill a number of important gaps with work of considerable quality and I am confident that it provides the range of commentary and scholarship necessary to encourage further interest and inquiry as well as to promote the inclusion of documentary work in more courses of study within the fields of communication, media and cultural analysis.

John Corner

1

'The Stuff of Radio': Developments in Radio Features and Documentaries before the War

Paddy Scannell

Introduction

The history of film documentary in Britain is well known. By comparison, that of radio documentary has remained invisible. The reasons for this must include the fact that the film-makers (Grierson and Rotha particularly) were excellent publicists of their own work, establishing a reputation for their productions that has lasted till today. Film, moreover, has established its claims to be regarded as an art form in which author-directors might express their creative vision. And thirdly, the programmes of the film-makers – or at least some of their best examples – have remained in circulation since they were made, and are routinely used today in taught courses on documentary. None of these points apply to radio, but it is the last factor which has been crucial. The development of documentary radio has been forgotten because of what Lance Sieveking referred to as 'the ghastly impermanence of the medium'.[1] The vast bulk of the live output of broadcast radio before the war was lost in the moment of its transmission. There are recordings of some of the best examples of pre-war radio features, but they are hardly ever re-broadcast in full, and are far more inaccessible to the public than pre-war film documentaries.[2]

This article offers a provisional sketch of some of the main developments of the radio feature programme. It would take a substantial monograph fully to deal with the topic, and I have been selective. I offer an account of three lines of growth. There was an initial exploration of the form of radio, giving way to a concern with social documentation, in the London Talks Department in the early 30s. As this impulse was smothered, the major

---

[1]Lance Sieveking, *The Stuff of Radio* (London, Cassell & Co., 1934), p. 15.
[2]I have given full details, as available, about the programmes mentioned to the text. Scripts and production files, where extant, are kept in the BBC Written Archive (WA), Caversham, Reading, which is open to researchers. Recordings extant on tape or disc are kept in the BBC Sound Archive (SA), Broadcasting House, London W 1. Copies of these may be heard in the National Sound Archive, Exhibition Rd, London SW3. Reference numbers for programme recordings are taken from the BBC Sound Archive Catalogue, March 1985.

development of the radio feature was displaced to Manchester, where it flourished in the last few years before the war.

'Documentaries', says Felix Felton, 'are known in the BBC as "Features"',[3] and certainly that was the preferred term in broadcasting before the war. In its development the feature oscillated between the two poles of drama and journalism. Throughout the period it was possible for writer-producers in the BBC to move with ease from one to the other. But gradually the primary value of the radio feature came to be seen as lying in its documentary or factual nature, though the possibility of dramatization was always an option, and emphasis was placed on the full use of the technical resources of radio for the realization of the subject.[4] I have been more concerned with the development of 'actuality' features than with the feature as art or literature. So I have included a discussion of radio talks which, in the early 30s, introduced new methods of social documentation. It was not until 1934 that people were appointed to full-time posts as Features Producers. As a genre, Features remained loosely defined throughout the pre-war period.

The beginnings of the radio feature, 1928–32

In the first few years of broadcasting it had been a continuous scramble simply to fill the hours of transmission with suitable music or voices, and to maintain an uninterrupted flow of scheduled material. But by the late 1920s the form of broadcasting's system of distribution and the content of its programme service had begun to settle. Attention now turned towards a more defined social purpose and towards more considered forms of expression. Radio began to be talked of not only as a new form of communication, but also as a potential art form. It was linked in discussion with film, especially the pioneering work of contemporary Russian film-makers. At the same time, comparisons were made with the theatre of Shakespeare where, in the absence of any realistic visual staging, the combination of the poetry (which conjured the scene in the mind's eye) and the highly flexible open stage, allowed a form of drama which was able with ease to 'cut' from one location or storyline to another. The purely auditory nature of radio seemed to offer similar possibilities. Broadcasting might combine techniques drawn from cinema with a poetic style to build 'sound pictures' that appealed to the listener's inner eye.

The radio feature – the term being borrowed from cinema's feature film – began to be developed in the BBC from about 1928 onwards. Features were special programmes in that they required, it was claimed in *Radio Times*, research and thought as 'original forms of expression, peculiar to radio and not suited to the public stage or concert platform'.[5]

[3]Felix Felton, *The Radio-Play. Its Techniques and Possibilities* (London, Sylvan Press, 1949), p. 99.
[4]John Drakakis, *British Radio Drama* (Cambridge, Cambridge University Press, 1981), p. 8.
[5]'Feature Programmes', *Radio Times*, 31 August 1928, p. 367.

They combined words and music to produce an artistic effect which could not have been produced by either separately. With music, talks or variety programmes it was largely a question of engaging speakers or performers and then rehearsing them in front of the microphone. But the feature programme arranged its material into original forms that exploited the potential of the medium. They were the first kind of programme to be put together and produced by people working in the BBC. In all these ways they were 'the stuff of radio'.

In 1928 Sieveking was hand-picked by Reith to do research into the form of radio. He was given a brief to prepare special programmes as occasional features and to build suitable programmes for broadcasting's special dates in its calendar – Christmas, New Year's Eve and so on. Later in that year the Productions Department in London was reorganized and Val Gielgud was put in charge. A small research group was established within the department whose task was an extension of that given to Sieveking: 'to give any help or suggestion in the presentation of any kind of programme . . . [to] experiment and do specialized research work in regard to the techniques of radio drama'. In sum, its responsibilities were 'research, creation and experiment'.[6] These developments marked the start of a self-conscious intention within the BBC to explore and extend the artistic scope of programme output.

Sieveking was the most grandiose and loquacious exponent of a new art of radio. He was passionately interested in the cinema and the theories of Pudovkin which he tried to transpose to radio production. Techniques of slow motion, close-ups, dissolves, fades, mixes and montage were all combined in the plays and features he wrote for radio in the late 20s and early 30s. The difference between a play and a feature, for Sieveking, was that a feature had a theme but no plot. If it had a plot it was a play. His book on the art of radio should certainly be read as a modernist curio of the period. Innocently self-absorbed, Sieveking saw himself as a pioneer of 'pure radio'. But he declared himself worried by 'the curious habit that exists in England of presuming and asserting that *any* attempts whatsoever at doing anything in a new way proclaims its author as a member of some political party of the Left. Modern painters, sculptors, poets, architects and composers are all supposed by popular opinion to be paid to do what they do by cheque from Moscow. . . . The difficulty is to convince anyone that one is just tremendously interested for its own sake in the thing on which one is working, and that one doesn't relate it to any politics whatsoever'.[7]

The dramatic control panel was the most sophisticated tool for radio production at that time. Sieveking has written a vivid account of his own great moment in radio when he produced his first big feature programme, *Kaleidoscope*, at the control panel.[8] For the new kind of large-scale feature

[6]R19/352/1 WA.
[7]Sieveking, *Stuff of Radio*, p. 31.
[8]*Op. Cit.*, pp. 16–24. The date of the broadcast was 4 September 1928, London.

production one studio was not enough to accomodate all the various components – actors, musicians, choruses and sound effects – that made up the whole. Each element was placed in a separate studio and all were linked to the dramatic control panel at which the producer sat like a musical maestro (or so Sieveking saw himself) orchestrating the whole performance.

There are no recordings of Sieveking's work and I have found no production files or scripts of his programmes in the BBC Written Archive. So an impression of his work must be gleaned from the examples of his plays and features that he chose to put in his book. Without knowing what they sounded like it is hard to be entirely fair. From the printed evidence it must be said that the experimental techniques swamp the substance of the narratives whose content seems banal or pretentious. *Kaleidoscope* was conceived as a 'rhythm representing the life of man from the cradle to the grave' and the struggle of Good and Evil for his soul. Both these agencies were represented by music: Beethoven for Good, Jazz for Evil. Evil is inclined to whisper seductive Romantic verse into the hero's ear, while Good breathes more sober stuff recalling Duty. A farrago of short impressionistic scenes swirl in and out, sketching in fragments in the life of a modern (middle-class English) man.[9]

The vogue for such baroque performances was quite short lived. By the late 30s they were more a matter of parody than an accepted method of production.[10] The problem they posed was their suitability in a medium that addressed itself not to the avant garde public but a much wider audience with simpler tastes. A *Radio Times* article pinpointed the dilemma, remarking that radio producers were trying on the one hand to create a distinctive type of broadcast drama, and on the other to bring theatre within the reach of everyone. These were irreconcileable aims. Val Gielgud was strongly opposed to Sieveking's approach.[11] He had a low opinion of the merits of the dramatic control panel and later returned to single-studio production for radio drama. There were others in the BBC who felt that Sieveking's work should be considered as backstage 'laboratory' experiments which ought not to be conducted in public. Sieveking spluttered against these prosaic attitudes but on the whole his work, after the initially dazzling effect of all the fireworks, had little significant content and was probably more bewildering to listeners than anything else. 'Recalled one's impression of gas in the dentist's chair' was one response to *Kaleidoscope*. By the mid 30s the kind of radio production espoused by Sieveking was a spent rocket, and so was its exponent.

Yet it would be misleading to suggest that these techniques were no more than a flash in the pan. When harnessed to suitable subjects they created new ways of dealing with news, history and politics. Sieveking

[9]*Op. Cit.*, pp. 383–4
[10]Cf. *Multiple Studio Blues*, Regional Programme, 24 November 1938, LP23219, SA.
[11]Cf. Val Gielgud, *Years in a Mirror* (London, The Bodley Head, 1965), p. 52.

described himself as a Christian and a loyal subject of the king. 'All the politics I have can be summed up in a few words: if the excellent civil service could be left to administer the wide liberties of the British constitution, we might be rid of these jigging politicians for ever.'[12] By contrast his close colleague and fellow member of the Research Unit, A.E. Harding, was well known in the BBC for his left-wing views. While sharing Sieveking's modernist tastes, Harding's work was quite different from Sieveking's allegorical whimsies. It included special features for the major feast days in the BBC calendar and a varied mix of literary productions including a memorable feature on the sixteenth-century French poet, François Villon, written in collaboration with Ezra Pound.[13]

Harding's more historical and political productions included *The Republic of Austria, Crisis in Spain* and *New Year Over Europe*.[14] *The Republic of Austria* was a history of that country from the eighteenth century to the present. It was billed in *Radio Times* as a 'Poster in Sound', and the programme blurb gave a plan of the narrative, translations of German words and phrases used in the programme, and an acknowledgment that 'for many of the ideas the author is deeply indebted to the works of T.S. Eliot, Valéry, D.H. Lawrence and G.K. Chesterton'.

Crisis in Spain was a brilliant programme that broke new ground in many ways.[15] *Radio Times* claimed it as the first British example of the reporting in radio form of contemporary events. The Talks Department had arranged a studio discussion of the recent Spanish crisis (the abdication of the king, the establishment of a republic), but proposed to precede it with a dramatic feature to provide colour and a factual chronological background to the debate. The narrative, it was claimed, had no other aim than to record what actually happened during the momentous weeks of March and April. There was no single narrator to control and guide the narrative. Events spoke themselves via 'caption voices' in French, Spanish, German, English and American as events in Spain were relayed round the world by international press agencies, radio and news reporters. Music, with strong royalist or republican associations, was used to build momentum into the sequence of events. Impressionistic montage was used to generate the sense of an irresistible march of events towards the proclamation of the republic. By foregrounding the role of the modern media, the narrative achieved a complex cross-cutting between events taking place in Spain and their simultaneous retransmission round the world. The significance of the Spanish crisis was extended beyond its own frontiers by the formal devices of the narrative itself.

[12]Sieveking, *Stuff of Radio*, p. 32.
[13]*The Testament of François Villon*, National Programme, 26 October 1931.
[14]Respectively, 21 November 1929, 11 June 1931, 31 December 1932 on the National Programme.
[15]Script on film, WA. A Staff Training School recording of the complete programme, produced by Harding, was made in 1938. T28022, SA. It was produced originally by Sieveking.

New Year Over Europe on the last day of 1932 was Harding's final fling in London.[16] The tradition of a special feature on that evening had been established in the late 20s. It was usually a bland medley of events from the year that was passing, but Harding's programme sounded a more ominous and overtly political note whose underlying topic was peace or war in Europe. The 60-minute programme toured various European countries and capitals showing how the old year was being ushered out and the new year ushered in. The original script appears to have been modified for transmission with several more contentious references pencilled out. Thus Italy, though described as a Fascist state, had details of the size of its armed forces removed. One statement that did remain in the script was an assertion that Poland still delivered one third of its national income to the Ministry of War. This aroused the ire of the Polish Ambassador in London who protested to the BBC and managed to stir up a political storm in a tea-cup on the matter. There were questions in the House of Commons, letters to *The Times*, and the upshot of it all, if Bridson's account is to be believed, was that Harding was summoned before Reith and banished to Manchester as Programme Director, North Region. 'You're a very dangerous man, Harding. I think you'd be better up North where you can't do so much damage', so Reith is supposed to have said.[17]

In an effort to pinpoint the artistic mood of the late 20s Orwell recalled the *Punch* joke of around 1928 in which an intolerable youth is pictured informing his aunt that he intends to write. 'And what are you going to write about, dear?' his aunt enquires. 'My dear aunt', says the youth crushingly, 'one doesn't write *about* anything. One just *writes!*' A response which neatly captures Sieveking's attitude as well as a more general mood. A rueful sense of modern life as lacking in fine ideals treads softly through Sieveking's writings (*Intimate Snapshots* is exemplary)[18] and Tyrone Guthrie's *The Squirrel's Cage*[19] which is usually hailed as one of the first real radio plays. A successful, and much repeated, adaptation of Karel Capek's futuristic fantasy, *R U R* , explored the horrors of a machine civilization.[20] The taste for allegorical fantasy was well represented by Charles Croker's *Speed*, a parable of gods and mortals, in which the gods above looked down on the speed-crazy frenzy of modern mortals on earth below.[21] The gods spoke in blank verse, the mortals in colloquial prose, and *Radio Times* asked listeners to be in their 'listening chairs' by 9.35 prompt and ready to pay as much attention as they would in the theatre.

This 'twilight of the gods' mood was abruptly shattered by the economic crisis of 1929 whose political and social consequences defined the next

---

[16]Script in R19/825/1, WA.
[17]D.G. Bridson (*Prospero and Ariel*, London, Victor Gollancz, 1971), p. 22.
[18]22 November 1929, London.
[19]3 June 1929, London.
[20]22 September 1930, National Programme.
[21]2 April 1928, London.

decade. In the face of the march of events in the 30s it was increasingly difficult to maintain a purely aesthetic stance towards art. Sieveking's protest, in 1934, that he was just tremendously interested, for its own sake, in what he was doing, was a plaintive cry against the prevailing winds. The motives for writing had changed. It was not so much a matter of choice as 'the forcible intrusion of social issues'.[22] There was a conscious sense of a break with the past under the clamour of the times, which disrupted the privacy of the individual and the closed little enclave of art and literature. Poverty, unemployment and the looming threat of another war drove art into politics. Under pressure, the intellectuals could not shut their ears to the noise of contemporary history. It would no longer do, just to write. One must write about something: with a purpose, to a purpose.

Talks and social documentation, 1929–1935

This general social pressure was registered, within the BBC, most acutely in the Talks Department. The department, established in 1927, had become a crucially sensitive area of programming when the ban on controversy was lifted early in 1928. One of its main tasks now became the delicate business of finding new methods for the balanced presentation of contentious social and political issues. It is not surprising that its first ventures were cautious and tentative. Gradualism was the watchword. For the most part Talks preferred to graze in safer pastures, 'to interpret the vast field of interests and knowledge which is happily beyond the frontiers of acute current partisanship'.[23]

By 1931 Britain was in the the throes of economic and political crisis, both a result of the catastrophic world-wide slump in trade. As the effects of the recession bit deeper, Talks took the plunge . Major series on housing, unemployment, industrial relations and 'the condition of England' addressed themselves to the urgent problems of the day. Under the direction of Hilda Matheson (1927–32) and Charles Siepmann (1932–5) the members of the department shared a common commitment to radio as a new social form of communication, and a common interest in developing new and effective means of communicating via the spoken word. These talks introduced direct methods of social reportage: eye-witness, first-hand accounts by BBC staff 'observers' of slum conditions in Glasgow, Tyneside and the East End; the unemployed themselves at the microphone to tell what it was like living on the dole. Through such programmes radio began to enter into the very fabric of political life, becoming material evidence – appropriated as ammunition in sharply contrasting ways by government, parties and audiences – for debate and controversy.

---

[22]*Cambridge Left*, Summer 1933. Quoted in Samuel Hynes (*The Auden Generation*, London, Faber & Faber 1976) p. 100.
[23]*BBC Handbook*, 1929 p. 41.

I have described in detail elsewhere the controversy to which these interventions in public life gave rise.[24] Here, I wish briefly to consider some of
their stylistic characteristics, particularly the ways in which the relations
between institution, audience and subject matter are organized in the talks
themselves. Consider how Howard Marshall begins his very first report on
contemporary slum conditions:

> When we travel to strange places I suppose most of us try to picture what
> we are going to see. I know I did when I was rattling up through the
> night to Newcastle, and I know how utterly my imagination failed me.
> Perhaps the gaps between fact and imagination were caused largely by
> contrast; it is odd to breakfast comfortably, as I did, in a Newcastle
> hotel, and then immediately afterwards to cross the great suspension
> bridge over the Tyne into the dreary Gateshead streets. We are apt to
> think of the slums as localized areas – a few alleys here; a bunch of
> houses in a condemned area there – but it isn't like that in the towns
> and boroughs which lie strung along the Tyne. If you look through the
> carriage window of the little train which chugs from Newcastle, through
> Gateshead and Jarrow, to South Shields, you see a continuous belt of
> roofs below you; roofs which cover, not always adequately, hundreds
> upon hundreds of families suffering from unemployment and poverty
> and hunger and ill-health.
>   It was this little train which carried me one night to High Shields
> Station, where I got out and made my way toward George Street,
> Holbourne and Rackondyke Lane. An unpleasant night, rather: a
> piercing wind whistled round the corners, which may have explained
> why the streets were quiet, peculiarly quiet with so many people only
> the thickness of a wall away. And perhaps because a day in Gateshead
> had made me impressionable, I felt, as I turned up my coat collar, that
> there was a strange quality about the stillness, a kind of dumb expec-
> tancy, so that it was almost startling in Cornwallis Square to hear a
> woman shout, 'looking for anyone mister?'
>   Cornwallis Square – it sounds well enough doesn't it? Plane trees,
> Georgian houses, expensive cars, orderliness, dignity – that is the sort
> of picture the name evokes. But Cornwallis Square hardly lives up to its
> name. You approach it, stumbling along a pitch dark passage which
> leads off a dingy alley, and you emerge into a muddy courtyard, perhaps
> 15 yards across. This is the square; round it, just discernable in the flare
> of a flickering gas light, squat a dozen misshapen houses, with a kind of
> verandah on wooden posts giving access to the top rooms, and making
> the whole place look like a collection of mud huts in an African swamp.
> I went into every room in those houses, and in practically every one of
> them lives a family. And I didn't go because I wanted to – to see one
> was quite enough – but because family after family begged me to come

[24]Paddy Scannell, 'Broadcasting and the Politics of Unemployment 1930–1935', *Media
Culture & Society*, vol. 2 (1980) no. 1.

and see their surroundings. The front room was typical of the rest. It was roughly 15 feet by 12, and in it a man and a woman and nine children were gathered. They had another box of a room which was just large enough to hold a bed, and this was their home. The walls were so damp that the paper peeled off them and the ceiling was cracked and crumbling. They had to go to a tap outside for water; there was no sink. They had to share four water closets in the courtyard with other tenants of the square. They were overrun by cockroaches – blacklocks, they called them – swarms of cockroaches which poured out from the cracks and crannies in the walls and terrified the children at night, making proper sleep impossible.[25]

The title of this programme series was *Other People's Houses*, and it is the *otherness* of the subject that is most strikingly underlined by the manner in which it is presented. It is not merely a feature of the descriptive language – the strangeness of the slums, their likeness to darkest Africa (a commonplace image from the nineteenth century for the unknown continent within). It is more pervasively an effect of the relationship between speaker and listener that is organized by appeals to assumed common social attitudes and stocks of knowledge. Thus the space between the imaginary evocation of Cornwallis Square and its reality discloses not only an implied world in common between speaker and listener but also its distance from the slums of Tyneside and the people who live there.

The use of the personal mode is interesting in a number of respects. From the start the Talks Department had been sensitive to the importance of finding forms of talk appropriate to the circumstances of listeners. Listening was recognized as situated in households, in family contexts, in moments of relaxation and leisure. Hence personal, intimate and informal modes of address seemed appropriate to forms of talk seeking to establish an acceptable relationship between institution and audience.[26] More particularly this style of talk was deliberately adopted for dealing with what was then a quite new kind of topic – social issues of general public concern – in order to cut through the established discursive models for handling such issues.

At first, topics such as housing or unemployment had been discussed in individual studio talks or debated in symposia by experts, authorities and politicians. Thus a series on unemployment, early in 1931, included Maynard Keynes, Seebohm Rowntree and Herbert Morrison (then Minister of Transport) with Stanley Baldwin (as leader of the Conservative Party) to wind the whole thing up. Then came six 'lectures' given by Sir William Beveridge which diagnosed 'the disease of unemployment', traced its

[25]*The Listener*, 18 January 1933, pp. 73–4. All the talks in this series, in *SOS*, and *Time to Spare* were published in *The Listener*.
[26]Cf. D. Cardiff, 'The serious and the popular: aspects of the evolution of style in the radio talk, 1928–1939', *Media Culture & Society*, vol. 2 (1980) no. 1.

origins back to before the Great War, considered whether labour or credit were the culprit, dealt with the problem of 'social malingering' and finally estimated the cost of the cure. On reflection, Beveridge wished he had been able to make his talks a little more human.[27]

Other People's Houses ran in tandem with another 12-part series on unemployment called *SOS*. Hilda Matheson regarded them both as a radical break with the established literary, rhetorical and formal methods of illustrating and explaining social issues: 'in both instances the speakers were not official experts using official language, still less politicians; but broadcasters capable of surveying the field as a whole and of presenting it in this new way to the widest possible audience.'[28] Through such novel forms of presentation the radio talk was becoming *relevant*, as a correspondent in *Radio Times* put it, expressing his delight that the BBC had left behind its milksop policy of not touching on controversial issues. And a *Radio Times* leading article hailed the two programmes as 'placing the serious talk in the category of "things to be heard"'.[29] No talks series, it was claimed, had ever aroused such general interest, or had dealt with matters of such urgent human concern. The article concluded with a prophecy that in this live yet dispassionate reporting of facts, no less than in the elaboration of theories, lay the future of the broadcast word. A consciousness of the problems of official forms of talk has long been present in broadcasting. Indeed the impulse behind the search for new forms of social documentation can most simply be understood as a continuing commitment to overcoming the dehumanizing effects of institutional discourse.

One simple but effective method of presentation was to invite the people themselves to come to the microphone to describe their experiences and feelings in their own words. The first programme to apply this method was *Time to Spare*. Felix Greene, the producer of the series, had toured the country, meeting the unemployed in their homes and clubs and selected a dozen whom he took as representative and typical to describe their experiences. Some found it difficult to write their story down though they could tell it well. When Greene tried to transcribe their words he found they spoke less freely. So he invited them to Broadcasting House, took them into a studio and got them talking. Meanwhile, unknown to them, their words were transcribed by secretaries in another room listening to them over a loudspeaker. There was no censorship, Greene claimed. The BBC deleted or altered nothing that the speaker wished to say.[30] Their 15-minute talks (each followed by a shorter postscript by a suitably official person – a doctor, a parson, a politician – to point the moral of their tale) were all reprinted in *The Listener*. They express quite different attitudes and experiences and the example I have taken should not be regarded as

[27]Asa Briggs, (*The History of Broadcasting in the United Kingdom*, Oxford, Oxford University Press, 1965), vol 2, p. 41.
[28]Hilda Matheson, *Broadcasting* (London, Thornton Butterworth, 1933) p. 97.
[29]*Radio Times*, 3 February 1933.
[30]*Radio Times*, 25 May 1934.

representative of the series. It illustrates, I think, some interesting and problematic aspects of this new kind of radio talk. The speaker is John Evans, an out-of-work miner from the Rhondda, and the extract gives the beginning and end of his talk:

> People often ask us, who are out of work, how we manage. Well, the answer is easy. We manage by doing without. You have probably heard how we have to scrape together a few bones and cabbage leaves and odds and ends, and so on, to make a dinner, but I wonder whether you know the effect a sordid struggle of this kind has on people's minds, apart from the effect on their bodies. It is not a question of 'the unemployed struggling to make both ends meet', but of men and women struggling to live. Please do not think of us as 'the unemployed', but as individuals like yourselves. We have the same ambition to get on in the world: we have just the same feelings as you have.
>
> Why should this sordid struggle for mere existence take place? My wife and I have often gone out on Saturday night without a single penny in our pockets. We walk along the streets and see plenty of everything in the shop-windows, so can you blame us for getting bitter? This goes on, not for a short time, but day after day, month after month, and as far as I can see it is going on for the rest of my life. I sometimes feel like throwing a brick through a window . . .
>
> As I've said, I've been out of work for eight years, and I've only managed to get eleven days work in all that time. I am 42 years old with no hope of work in the future. Work used to shape the whole of my life and now I've got to face the fact that this won't be so any more. Somehow or other I've got to live my life independent of the industrial machine. It takes a lot of doing because for years we've been told over and over again that work was the only really necessary virtue. I've tried to make use of my 'time to spare' by reading and so on, but don't for a moment look on unemployment as a heaven-sent opportunity for ramming education down the throat of many who may not want it. There are other things which they may need much more desperately. I know how difficult it is to be keen on one's education when one's mind is constantly worried and preoccupied by the facts of food and mere existence. The question that's in my mind is whether people in comfortable circumstances are really concerned with the troubles and trials of those who are out of work. Have *you* done anything toward solving the unemployment problem? What are you going to do about it? Do you think that because some of you have sent us clothes you no longer need, the problem no longer exists? I wonder what is going to happen! There's a quotation I often think of, 'Poverty is that state in which a man is perpetually anxious for the future of himself and his dependents, unable to pursue life on the standard to which he was brought up, tempted both to subservience and sour revolt and tending inexorably toward despair.'
>
> That expresses much better than I can what unemployment makes

me feel. One moment I could almost lick a man's boots for a favour: another time I could bash him in the face.[31]

The extent to which John Evans speaks here in his own voice is a difficult question. Obviously the production of talk of this kind is for him (as distinct from, say, Howard Marshall) a very rare, if not unique, act and one with which he is not fully at ease. We might reasonably feel the claim he makes that the quotation he often thinks of as expressing his feelings much better than he could, is immediately belied by the unadorned expression of his feelings in his own words in his final sentence. And we might feel that the difference here is one between institutional and individual forms of talk which pose questions about their authenticity, sincerity and truth. It can be seen that Evans speaks at times as a representative (para 1) and at times as a person (para 2). As a representative he speaks on behalf of others like him (the unemployed) to a generalized other unlike him (those in comfortable circumstances). As a person he speaks individually, directly to an absent particularized listener. Moving back and forth between these two positions Evans expresses a fierce resentment of his situation and a hostility towards the middle-class listening public. At the same time he must appeal for their understanding and help. These irreconcileable tensions give the talk its discomforting force and energy.

By 1934 'actuality', and how to achieve it, had become a new topic for discussion amongst broadcasters. Harding predicted that the next development in radio would be the introduction of recording techniques. Actuality recordings would be taken on location and then edited, back in the studio, into 'a pattern of significant sound'. In the mid 30s sound recording (on disc or the Blattnerphone) was possible only in the London studios and was used exclusively for 'bottling' examples of significant broadcast material. There were no facilities for location sound recording – indeed the first documentary film to use location sound was *Housing Problems* (1936). But in the summer of 1934 Lawrence Gilliam hired a recording van from a film company to make the first radio feature using actuality sound recordings taken on location.[32]

'*Opping 'Oliday* was broadcast on 15 September 1934 on London Regional. It offered a 'sound picture' of East Enders harvesting the hops in the Kent fields.[33] The programme was broadcast live from the studio with a narrator, the recorded 'microphone snapshots', two short talks giving personal sidelights on hop picking, and finally an outside broadcast linkup for a singsong from a Kent pub where the pickers were celebrating the end of their 'oliday. This was the first broadcast programme to realize that populist impulse at the heart of documentary which allows people to speak for themselves. No longer are they merely described by another in a studio

---

[31]*The Listener*, 5 April 1934, pp. 700–1.
[32]Felton, *The Radio-Play*, p. 99.
[33]Script on film, WA. All the recorded actuality inserts, but not the programme as a whole, are on MT451 SA.

talk, or else read a scripted talk from the studio in which they express the viewpoint of 'the ordinary person'. Now they speak from their own everyday environment, and produce impromptu talk, via an interviewer, for the microphone. Broadcasting has gone out into everyday life to capture 'the essence' of that reality as lived by those who speak of it in order to re-present this experience to listeners.

The nature of that representation needs to be considered with some care. What Stuart Hall has called 'the conditions of recognition' are framed in a preliminary way in broadcasting by the timing, placing and titles of programmes.[34] Note first the knowing cockney idiom of the title which situates the programme as an exercise in folk culture. Pat Forrest, who worked on the programme with Gilliam, described its aim as giving listeners 'an 'opping 'oliday without the work'. It is thumbmarked as a lighthearted look at an aspect of the lives of cockney folk.

Such conditions of recognition have to be worked into the manner and tone of the discourse itself. Here's how the narrator sets the opening scene at London Bridge where the people have assembled overnight to wait for an early morning special train to take them down to Kent:

> It was 2.30 in the morning. People were lying huddled in gutters, and near the walls which bear poster pictures of expensive continental resorts. But they're not going to Monte Carlo. The crowd consists mainly of women and children of all ages, but more men this year. We all know the reason for that. I wish you could have seen the children – poor little things, some of them huddled up in perambulators. There was a bright moon which, together with the dusty station lights, showed how pathetic a thing like this can be.

Here the language of address – particularly the use of I, you and we – establishes a common way of looking at the programme's subject matter, a similar set of social and cultural dispositions. You and I, institution and audience, know how pathetic the sight of poverty can be. We all know (don't we?) why there are more men here this year. We hardly need mention unemployment. . . . This knowing collusion embraces the speaker and the listener but excludes the subject of the programme. The hop pickers are not included in the audience. The programme is *about* them but not *for* them. They have been taken up as an interesting topic, and made to reappear for another audience, another class, and in another context.

The early 30s were a 'moment' of experiment and innovation in the London Talks Department. The form and content of programmes had not yet been systematized, and neither had their producers. But the broadcasters' new-found commitment to engaging with the major issues of the day gave rise to all sorts of protests from a largely right-wing press, from

---

[34]Stuart Hall, 'Television and Culture', *Sight and Sound*, Summer, 1976.

both ends of the political spectrum and at times from the general public. Howard Marshall was denounced by one angry listener as 'either the world's biggest liar or else as trying to play the funny man'. As the pressures on the department increased it had an increasingly troubled history. Hilda Matheson had resigned in 1932 in an atmosphere of intrigue and bitterness, and Reith soon became suspicious of her successor, Charles Siepmann. Matters came to a head in 1935 when what looks very like a purge was imposed on Talks. All its leading lights were 'promoted' to posts that took them a very long way from Broadcasting House. Hilda Matheson described it as 'a dispersal and a disintegration unparalleled in any other department'.[35]

At the same time, an internal division of labour was coming into being which separated programme making from policy making. New production departments were created: Variety in 1933, Drama and News in 1934. Lawrence Gilliam was transferred from *Radio Times* to Gielgud's Drama Department with a brief to make 'special programmes'. He became Assistant Features Director in early 1934. As departmental boundaries became more rigid the shared commitment to the social role of radio and to programme innovation was dissipated. The dismantling of Talks marked the arrival of corporate control within the BBC. In the Autumn of 1935 Hilda Matheson saw signs already of 'a widespread arrested development' in the Talks Department. For the next few years its members, deeply demoralized and lacking any decisive leadership, contented themselves with safer, less contentious topics. As the European crisis grew ever more grave in the second half of the 30s the most striking thing about the work of talks and features in London was an *absence*: the lack of any programmes dealing with the major political issues of the time.[36] Caution had become inbred in Broadcasting House. In the late 30s most of the interesting developments in programme making took place not in London but in Manchester, North Region.

North Region features, 1935-1939

Harding's 'expulsion' to North Region was London's loss and Manchester's gain. As soon as he arrived there he set about recruiting a group of highly talented people – journalists, actors and writers – to programme making, encouraging them to find new ways of expressing the character of Northern England and its people.[37] Under Harding's influence North Region's programmes began to realize the task delegated to the regions – of reflecting the life and variety of the area they served – by establishing a relationship with the audience that was radically

[35]Hilda Matheson, 'The Record of the BBC', *Political Quarterly*, vol. 6 (1935), no. 4, pp. 506–18.
[36]Cf. Paddy Scannell, 'The BBC and Foreign Affairs 1935–1939', *Media Culture & Society*, vol. 6 (1984) no. 1.
[37]Briggs, *Broadcasting in the United Kingdom*, vol. 2, p. 330.

different to that between the National Programme in London and its nationwide audience.

The original model for Harding's ideas as to what feature programmes from the regions should aspire to was a programme made in 1930 called *The Western Land*. This was a scripted feature about life and work in Cornwall as told by a farmer, a fisherman, a tin-miner and a flower grower. It was broadcast on 29 October from St Hilary's, Cornwall, and relayed to London by landline. To listeners at that time it sounded just like four people conversing at ease among themselves with sounds from the village and the countryside heard in the background. Harding thought it was one of the most remarkable programmes ever broadcast, and he deeply regretted that there was such little chance of this kind of programme ever becoming a regular feature of the National Programme.[38] He regarded the BBC as the one national organization in a position systematically to collect and present the great wealth of material all over Britain, of which *The Western Land* formed a part. His first effort in this direction was the feature series *Harry Hopeful* which began on North Region in 1935.[39]

For this project Harding enlisted the services of an aspiring young Manchester poet and writer, D.G. Bridson. There were no mobile recording facilities in Manchester at this time. What Harding wanted to create in the studio were sound pictures of people and places as if they had been shot on location. Bridson conceived of an imaginary central character, Harry Hopeful, an out of work glass-blower's assistant on the tramp in search of work, meeting and talking to real people in the real places he visited. Bridson was fortunate in finding a 'natural' for the part – Frank Nicolls, a clock mender from Irlam who was already a regular performer in Manchester's *Children's Hour*. The locations chosen included well known beauty spots – the Dales, the North Yorkshire moors, the Peak District. Together Bridson and Nicolls went to these places and talked to the local people whom they had invited to take part in the programmes. As Nicolls talked to them (he had that rare ability to put people at their ease and draw them out in conversation) Bridson made detailed notes of what they said. Later he worked this material into a script, a copy of which was sent to each participant. A few weeks later he and Nicolls returned with portable wireless equipment and a radio engineer. The microphone was then set up in the homes of the participants and they each rehearsed their part with Nicolls while Bridson listened on headphones in the car outside. Thus the speakers were accustomed to the microphone in familiar surroundings and adjustments could be made, if necessary, to make the script sound more natural. Later the full cast was assembled in Manchester's main

---

[38]Harding to Gielgud, 3 November 1930, R19/352/1.
[39]There were two series of this programme. The account that follows is compiled from Bridson, *Prospero and Ariel* , pp. 53–6, and N2/50, WA. There are several scripts in WA, and two complete recordings: 'Saltersgate to Staithes, or Harry Hopeful's Day in Cleveland', 22 October 1935, LP771f1-3 SA, and 'Cressbrook to Ashbourne, or Harry Hopeful's Day in the Dales', 13 April 1936, T1048 SA.

studio. After one complete run-through came the live broadcast itself, per-formed before an invited audience which included the families and friends of the participants.

The series was very well received within the BBC. In London it was seen as one of the very first programmes from the regions to raise the quality of material above the level of anecdotal talks or dialect plays. It was proof of a new-found cultural vitality and resourcefulness in the provinces. For Bridson, as for Harding, the series fulfilled two deeply held beliefs; that broadcasting should reflect the lives and opinions of ordinary people and, more particularly, that it should project the real character of North Region. The success of the programme established Bridson's reputation as a new and original radio talent and helped clinch for him the post of Features Programme Assistant (NR) in 1936.

Bridson was to have a long and very distinguished career in the BBC as a writer and producer for radio, and his work in Manchester before the war reflected his wide and varied interests. He wrote and produced verse dramas, literary and poetic features, anniversary programmes and histo-rical features. Many of these are described in his own excellent biography. But central to his work was a concern to put over a new image of the North. In this respect *Harry Hopeful* and the four programmes he made about the region's major industries in the next few years may be seen as the clearest expressions of this intention.

His first big industrial feature, *Steel*, was made shortly after Manchester had acquired its own Mobile Recording Unit.[40] Now that he could use actuality inserts Bridson had in mind a really ambitious programme for radio along the lines of the recent documentary film, *Coalface*. He planned to surpass the film which had, in his view, mishandled some very interesting possibilities in choral speech and singing. *Steel* would combine poetic narrative, music and choral verse with recorded actuality 'sound shots' from a steel foundry. The whole thing, he wrote in a memorandum, 'should build up not so much a mere recorded actuality programme as an aesthetically significant and emotionally stirring programme on lines and on a scale previously untouched by the Corporation'. He commissioned an original orchestral score from the Birmingham composer, Desmond McMahon – the first time this had been done for a radio feature. Sound recordings were made at the East Hecla factory of Hadfields Ltd (other big steel companies were piqued that they had not been chosen) and Sheffield was agog at the thought of a big radio programme about the industry which made their city famous.

McMahon's symphonic suite was an integral part of the programme. It was played as an overture and then skilfully married into the poetic text that Bridson had written using chanted verse and sung choruses. The feature was presented as a symphony in four movements: *allegretto*,

[40]23 February 1937. This account is compiled from N2/124, WA. Complete recording, T28010 SA.

andante, allegro scherzo and *allegro finale*. The first movement begins by invoking the elemental qualities of the land and the men of the North country. A poetic *mise en scene* moves from the moors and granite out-crops circling Sheffield to daybreak in the town itself as the men make their way from various districts to the factory gates to clock on for the morning shift. A chanted chorus invoking the might and power of 'industry's resounding roar' is overtaken by the music which brings the movement to a climactic end. The second and third movements recreate the industrial processes which transform the scrap and pig iron into milled steel. We hear nothing from the men who work in the factory. Music and verse choruses, intermingled with recorded sound, conjure up instead a heroic vision of the abstract power and energy of modern industry as the mainstay of an emerging new age and a new social order. The final movement begins with a quiet invocation by the poet of what the region means to him which is overtaken by a finale that surges to a closing crescendo invoking a vision of a new destiny and a limitless future.

The programme was again very well received within the BBC, but local reaction was mixed. The Mayor of Sheffield offered his thanks on behalf of the people of the city and praised it as a magnificent idea excellently carried out. The Deputy Chairman of Hadfields offered his congratulations with only one reservation: 'it was perhaps a little too much of a fantasy, but that [response] is only to be expected from a hard-headed lot of people who spend most of their lives in the manufacture and manipulation of steel.' The *Daily Independent* was more blunt. 'Sheffield Laughed when BBC Went Poetic Over Steel' ran the headline, and the article went on to complain that all this poetry and word-spinning made the programme lack conviction. Bridson took the point. While he continued to write and produce features that combined verse and music these methods were now confined to literary and historical subjects. For his three subsequent industrial features – *Cotton, Wool* and *Coal* – he returned to the methods of *Harry Hopeful*, recruiting the young Joan Littlewood, fresh from RADA, as the presenter.

The last of the three, *Coal*, was particularly tricky.[41] To begin with there was a great deal of difficulty in finding a suitable pit on which to base the programme. Bridson wanted to get the North East accent as a change from those of Yorkshire and Lancashire heard in the previous two programmes. He also wanted to tap the very rich vein of Tyneside colliery songs. Beyond that he wanted a mine where the conditions weren't too good (otherwise the miners wouldn't believe it), and where the management would cooperate in a programme that boosted British coal at the same time as enlisting sympathy for the miners. The task of finding a suitable location was passed to Roger Wilson, the region's Publicity Officer. He eventually came up with Messrs Straker and Lowe, owners of Brancepath Colliery,

[41] 17 November 1938. This account compiled from N2/16, WA. The disc recordings contain extracts, not the complete programme. LP31338f1, SA.

Wilmington, County Durham. In a note to Bridson, Wilson assured him that Wilmington was a small town and that the pit was mechanized so there was plenty of unemployment which he could work into the picture. Moreover Brancepath had its own brass band, one of the best in the area.

Though a pit had been settled on, the difficulties were by no means over. It soon transpired that the wage rates in the mine were slightly above average for the area, a fact which mystified the union people since the arrangement had been reached 'somewhat independently' of them. Wilson was very keen to make friends with the unions in order, as he put it, to 'secure our rear', and he felt it essential that the Durham Miners Association should be consulted. On the other hand he did not want them brought in too early since they might cramp the whole programme. He recommended seeing their representatives officially when the script was well under way and 'we know the ground we propose to stick to'.

While all this was going on Bridson requisitioned London to authorize the purchase of two sets of overalls and two pairs of gumboots for himself and Joan Littlewood. Thus prepared they set off for Wilmington.

> A month's work went into making the programme during which time Joan and I familiarized ourselves with every aspect of the miner's life. We went on shift with the men by night and morning; we helped with the hewing, loading and putting; we got the dirt engrained in our scalps and every pore of our bodies. Joan lived with a miner's family – the son had been killed in the pit – while I put up in no greater comfort at the local miner's pub. By the time *Coal* came on the air, there wasn't a miner at the pit who didn't know us and treat us as one of themselves.[42]

As the programme took shape Bridson wanted to make sure that both the owners and the unions felt they had been fairly represented. He sent a draft script for comment to Captain Howe, the manager of Brancepath, with a cover note adding that 'we always find it best to prepare a script from the men's angle first and then have it vetted by the managers'. At the same time he contacted the President and Secretary of the Durham Miners Association. The script was returned by management with minimal emendations and as the day of performance drew near Wilson primed the local press and wrote to Wilmington's MP asking him to listen and inviting his comments on the programme.

Coal was performed on 17 November 1938 and evoked an immediate and sympathetic response from all over the country, particularly for one of the participants, a hewer who had been out of work for so long that his body had gone soft. He was unable to return to work at the coalface when a job did eventually come up. Money poured in to the Newcastle office, especially from listeners in the home counties, and Bridson arranged for it to be distributed among the miners in such a way that it did not come to

[42]Bridson, *Prospero and Ariel*, p. 69.

the attention of the Means Test men. The remainder was distributed among the families of men on short time to buy Christmas presents for the children.

In his own account of these industrial features, written many years after they were made, Bridson suggests that in intention and in effect they were simple and transparent. They were something new at that time and they proved that everyone had something to say and a point of view that deserved a hearing. For Bridson, the techniques he used served only, as in *Harry Hopeful*, to let people speak for themselves within the framework of a live studio broadcast. The production file of *Coal*, however, reveals the undisclosed strategies that organized the ground eventually occupied by the programme as broadcast. These hidden expediencies were not apparent in the seemingly artless presentation of the performance itself.

Meanwhile other techniques of social documentation were being developed in Manchester which relied on the use of recorded actuality material for their effect. The pioneer of this kind of programme was Olive Shapley, who joined the staff in Manchester in late 1934 to work, at first, on *Children's Hour*. In her first few years there she, like everyone else, gained a thorough grounding in all aspects of radio work. She helped in the studio production of some of Bridson's programmes. She breathed new life into *Children's Hour*. She produced some of the radio plays written for the region. There was greater scope for individual initiative, more flexibility between different areas of production, more cooperation between programme makers in Manchester at that time than in London.

In 1937 the Manchester studios were refitted with the latest equipment, including the new and improved Dramatic Control Panel already in use in London. Shapley was immediately fascinated by its possibilities when combined with the Mobile Recording Unit, and began to concentrate her work on making programmes in which recorded actuality was mixed, through the panel, with studio presentations and commentary. The recording van was 27 feet long and weighed, when fully loaded up, more than seven tons.[43] Its maximum speed was 20 miles an hour. Inside were two turntables, each operated by a technician. The recording time of each disc was a maximum of four minutes. As one disc came to an end, recording was continued on the other turntable – thus securing uninterrupted continuity of a sort. The new studio equipment could accomodate up to six discs at a time, with remote control to lower the pick-up head onto the precise groove at which to begin the required recorded insert.

Two recording vans had originally been commissioned by London to collect topical items for inclusion in the news bulletins. But they were unsuited for this and were passed over to the regions. Wales, Scotland and West Region however had many hilly and narrow roads which the vans could not negotiate. So by the time one of them arrived in Manchester

[43]Technical details from E. Pawley, (*BBC Engineering, 1922–1972*, London, BBC Publications, 1972), pp. 189–90.

there was some uncertainty as to whether they had any useful purpose at all. Bridson had used it for *Steel* but only for background effects. It was Olive Shapley who first took the van all over the region to record people talking in their homes, at work and on the streets. Single-handed, she brought to maturity the use of recorded actuality as the basis of the radio feature in those last few years before the war.

Her programmes broke new grounds for radio both in technique and in their subject matter. There were programmes about homeless people, about shopping, about the barge people who worked the canals, about long distance lorry drivers, about an all-night transport cafe. There was *Broadcasting With the Lid Off*, a trip behind the scenes to show a day in the life of the Manchester office.[44] When London got wind of this there was much indignation at the indecency of baring the BBC bosom to the microphone. Head Office wanted to cancel it, but it was too late to withdraw it from the schedules. Opinion amongst the Manchester staff about the merits of the programme varied greatly but there was a general view that it had been worth doing. A report on it to Basil Nicolls (Controller of Programmes, London) assured him that by a different method it would have been possible to present the BBC as a more efficient and glamorous institution but it was felt such fantasies should be discouraged. Nicolls accepted the report with the comment that there was no objection to the BBC unbending, *occasionally*.

The structure of Shapley's early programmes was very straightforward, consisting of a narrative commentary to introduce and link the recorded material which formed the substance of the programme. This is how Wilfred Pickles introduced *Pounds, Shillings and Pence. A Study in Shopping*:

> Good evening everybody. Before we get going in this shopping programme there are one or two things I want to tell you about it. Now it's what I'd call a 'homely' programme. No flourish of trumpets about it, you know, but the sort of programme you'll recognize yourselves in maybe. The records you're going to hear were made at a little town called Sowerby Bridge. Sowerby Brigg, I call it, coming from that part of the country myself.[45]

And here is how Olive Shapley herself introduced *Canal Journey*:

> On this occasion I went after the human story – as the newspapers say – and tried to get the canal people I met to tell in their own words something of what their life is like. In spite of all jokes to the contrary they are not a very voluble race and some of them found it hard to believe that anyone could find the details of their ordinary life interesting and, when they had been reassured on this point, it wasn't very easy

[44] 12 January 1939. Details from N2/11, WA.
[45] 30 April 1938. NR Scripts, WA.

for them to put their ideas into words. All the records you'll hear were made without script or rehearsal.[46]

The mode of address of these two programmes should be compared with that of *'Opping 'Oliday* and the London talks on housing and unemployment. It can readily be seen, I think, that the language here works in a quite different way. It is more informal, relaxed and intimate. It sets up a more equal relationship between the speaker, the subject of the programme and the audience. Such reportage, combined with her sympathetic skill as an interviewer (a quite new technique which she had to discover for herself), led one contemporary critic to describe Shapley's programmes as 'little masterpieces of understanding and authenticity'.

Shapley developed her skills quickly and by 1939 was making programmes on a more ambitious scale. *They Speak for Themselves* was billed in *Radio Times* as a radio enquiry into Mass Observation – 'that new idea with which we have had to reckon so surprisingly in the last year'.[47] This hour-long programme combined all the technical resources of radio available at that time; studio presentation and discussion, combined with recorded actuality overlaid with musical links and dramatized reconstructions of recent events. A month later came one of Shapley's last programmes before the war, and perhaps her masterpiece.

There is a strong likeness between the unemphatic reportage of Olive Shapley – her 'feel' for her subjects – and Elizabeth Gaskell's novels of Manchester life in the 1840s. *The Classic Soil* returned to the Manchester of those years for an hour-long programme comparing working-class life then with circumstances 100 years later.[48] The authority used as the basis for the comparison was not, however, Mrs Gaskell but that other famous observer and analyst of Manchester in the 1840s, Frederick Engels. Extracts from *The Condition of the Working Class in England* were read in the studio by a German resident in Manchester who was born in Engels's home town. The passages described the appalling housing conditions, the wretched clothes and the miserable diet of that new-formed proletariat who inhabited that 'classic soil upon which the industrial revolution grew to full estate'. These acounts formed the basis for a comparison with the housing, diet and clothing of working people in Manchester and Salford in 1939. The programme was conceived and written by Joan Littlewood and produced by Olive Shapley, who made all the many recordings used to build up a richly textured account of contemporary working-class life and experience.

The programme covered all levels of working-class experience from the relatively well-to-do, through those who just managed to make ends meet, to those below the poverty line for whom mere existence was an

[46]25 August 1939. NR Scripts, WA.
[47]1 June 1939. NR Scripts, WA. Complete recording, T28038 SA.
[48]6 July 1939. NR Scripts, WA. Complete recording, LP25677 SA.

unrelenting struggle. It is full of subtle contrasts and shadings that are funny and desolating in turn. Men and women, young and old, all give their testimony. There are no cutaways to officialdom, to the voices of authority. It was, said Shapley, recalling it 40 years after it was made, a 'shameful programme' because it was so onesided. Manchester Corporation and Head Office both took exception to its lack of balance. For though the programme showed that things had improved for some – there's a housewife who describes the joys of her new council flat and the wonders of her new electric carpet cleaner – the overwhelming impression is one of resilience in the face of enduring poverty. The last words of the programme belong to a young girl who works in one of the cotton mills. Her words sum up the experience, the circumstances and the expectations of a class and of a generation:

> I work in the cotton mill in the card room. I've had to work hard ever since I left school, and me mother and father before me. That's all there is for me – work, eat and sleep. What else is there? If you don't work you don't eat. I know when I was out of work for two years I walked the shoes off me feet, and if I hadn't found work when I did (*pause*) I'd've done away with meself. I'm thankful enough to be working now. Although it's hard I never grumble. All I ask is steady work to keep meself in bread and butter. I don't want money and plenty of luxuries. All I want is a comfortable living. But what's the good of looking into the future? I've enough to do to worry about tomorrow.

The features written and produced by Bridson and Shapley in the second half of the 30s had no equivalents elsewhere in the BBC. They were acknowledged in London to be the leading programme makers in their field. Their work, however, must be seen as part of a wider pattern of developments in the general programme output of North Region in those years. The distinctive brand of regionalism produced by Manchester was one which foregrounded ordinary working people both within the programmes and as a major part of the audience for whom those programmes were made. This double focus on the everyday lives and tastes of the majority was in sharp contrast with the National Programme throughout the 30s. In the National Programme working people appeared in programmes either as 'victims' (as occasionally uncomfortable reminders of how the other half lived), or as stereotyped representatives of 'the man in the street'. When the man in the street made his appearance – as he sometimes did in London's talks or features – he was handled with an uneasy facetiousness that served to underline the difference between 'them' and 'us'. Working people were only marginally present in London's output and only marginally recognized as members of the 'great audience' for the National Programme. In Manchester they were acknowledged as the majority audience for the regional service and were catered for accordingly.

By the late 30s the regional offices had won considerable control over all day to day decisions about their programming policies and schedules. The greater flexibility and freedom enjoyed by their programme makers created a climate which encouraged innovation. It is not that there was no talent in London. Lawrence Gilliam, for one, chafed under the restrictions of the dead hand of policy control in Broadcasting House. Early in 1939 he floated the idea of a topical series on the lines of the American *March of Time* films. He recognized that for policy reasons all the major political events of the time would be out of court, but still felt this left a vast field of non-controversial issues which could be worked up into a regular feature series. 'If we can prove to the authorities that we can tap a new source of topical features, without running them into a lot of trouble, we can go a long way to filling one of the Corporation's biggest gaps – that is, topicality.'[49] A them/us mentality, with producers trying to steer their way round the authorities by tailoring their ideas to what 'they' might accept, had become a reflex way of thinking in London. Programmes like *They Speak for Themselves* or *The Classic Soil* were major features on contemporary matters of general interest and concern that were beyond the scope of London at that time.

The stuff of radio

Before the war the development of the radio feature was uneven and chequered. It never amounted to more than a tiny fraction of the total output in London or the regions, and its importance lies less in its bulk than in the ways it registered the search for effective forms in radio. A concern with the formal properties of radio was natural enough in a new medium of social communication, but the inescapable dilemmas of avant-garde practices, when applied to a medium of mass communication, soon presented themselves. *Crisis in Spain* and *Steel* were both highly effective in their own terms, but bewildering and perhaps offensive for listeners. The 'difficulty' of early features had some similarities with the response of audiences to the musical avant-garde. But 'difficult' music could be better defended on the grounds that it was, in any case, the most formal of all the arts, and that the cultural mission of broadcasting included the responsibility of exposing the public to the first fruits of contemporary composers, native and foreign.

In features (and in drama) the BBC did not succeed in persuading the leading writers of the day, with reputations established in another medium, to apply their talents to radio. It is true there was a trickle of feature programmes by the leading literati of the day – Pound and Auden made very occasional contributions – but in general they ignored radio.[50] For one thing the financial returns were meagre in the extreme. It might be an incidental confirmation that one had arrived to be asked to do the odd

[49]Gilliam to All Regional Directors, 1 March 1939. R19/352/1 WA.
[50]Auden wrote *Hadrian's Wall*, produced by John Pudney, 25 November 1937. See NR Scripts and N2/47 WA.

radio talk, but literary reputations were still to be won through established forms and confirmed by the usual agencies of legitimation.

From the mid 30s there was a perceptible tendency for those recruited to features work in the BBC to have a literary pedigree (Geoffrey Bridson, Rayner Heppenstall and John Pudney for example), but it was World War II that enabled the BBC to 'capture' writers with established reputations. Louis MacNeice, who joined the BBC in 1941 and remained with Features until shortly before his death in 1963, confessed that before the war he had thought of radio as 'a degrading medium, both vulgar and bureaucratic, and not even financially rewarding'.[51] He added that he might well have been a snob at the time. Perhaps, but a further factor was that 'ghastly impermanence of the medium' that Sieveking had referred to. A thing of beauty might well be a joy for ever in the shape of an urn or poem, but a radio feature was written on the wind. It is not mechanical reproduction as such that destroys the aura of the aspiring art object in broadcasting, but the ceaseless ebb and flow of a varied output. Broadcasting has no sense of occasion, of a time and place set apart from the routines of day-to-day life, which affirms the difference of the work of art. The demands of continuous production, the constant need to feed the voracious appetite of the microphone, and the pressures on producers from a bureaucratic hierarchy are all inimical to the service of the Muses. In the several books by or about individuals who have worked in radio features there is a palpable sense of the gradual erosion of creative flair under the cumulative burden of such pressures.[52]

The final haven of the literary feature was to be the Third Programme. It had no secure foundation before the war. But nor did the other lines of development traced above – forms of social documentation, actuality programmes about work and the lives of ordinary people. We can now see the methods of *Other People's Houses* and *Time to Spare* as the forerunners of basic techniques in news, current affairs and documentary programmes. But at that time there was no News Department and no news reporters. A News Department was set up in 1934 and had a staff of nearly 40 by 1939. Even so the techniques of news presentation and reporting that we now take for granted were not established until the late 50s. The news interview was unknown on radio before the war. The new techniques of reportage developed by Talks in the early 30s existed in a vacuum. When the political pressures on the department increased, their response was to draw in their horns and refrain from such kinds of programme. There was no continuity in the social documentation of public matters of general concern on the National Programme in the 1930s. The *routine* treatment of such issues by broadcasting is a phenomenon of the 60s and after.

Similar points must be made about the populist feature programmes

[51]Barbara Coulton, *Louis MacNeice in the BBC* (London, Faber & Faber, 1980), p. 44.
[52]Coulton, *op. cit.*; Bridson, *Prospero and Ariel*; Rayner Heppenstall, *Portrait of the Artist as a Professional Man* (London, Peter Owen, 1967).

developed in Manchester between 1935 and 1939. When war broke out the regional service was suspended, and at the end of the war it was restored in a much diluted form. The kind of rapport that North Region was beginning to establish with its audience – a friendly and informal relationship as exemplified by the *Harry Hopeful* series – was appropriated for instrumental purposes in the course of the Second World War. *Harry Hopeful* became *Billy Welcome* played by Wilfred Pickles in a series of industrial features scripted and produced by Bridson and broadcast live from the factories.[53] They were designed to maintain the morale of the workforce and to demonstrate the importance of the industrial front to the rest of the nation. 'Rank propaganda disguised as entertainment' was how Pickles later described them. Nevertheless Pickles took over their format for his own show, *Have a Go!*, the most popular programme on radio for most of the 50s. The work of Olive Shapley had no direct successors. The use of recorded actuality as the basis of factual radio programmes was not irreversibly established until the mid 50s, when the portable magnetic tape recorder became a basic tool of the radio broadcaster.

But in spite of their restricted impact at the time these programmes were of great importance in the development of broadcasting. Most generally they helped to broaden the social base of broadcasting, making it more fully representative of the society it served. It is easy to make the point about the ways in which some of the early talks on housing and unemployment underlined social divisions, and we have long since become familiar with such forms of personal testimony. The location shots of slum dwellers in the film *Housing Problems* and Orwell's accounts in *The Road to Wigan Pier* are received and distant images of the working class as victims. In their own time they spoke only to small and self-selecting audiences. But the contexts in which *Other People's Houses* and *Time to Spare* both operated gave the programmes an inescapable radical edge and a hard political thrust. There had not been heard before on radio such a spelling out of the facts of making do on the dole or of living in a rat-infested slum. Nor had working people been heard to tell of the conditions they endured and their feelings about them. Access to the microphone for such speakers was a significant extension of broadcasting's social range. Radio addressed not the particular publics of the daily newspapers, not the specialized readership of the Left Book Club, not the tiny audiences for the film documentaries, but a new kind of general public, society at large. As such, these interventions – coming as they did, not after, but at the height of the crisis – had an immediacy and widespread impact, sharpened by the fact that the BBC had not yet learnt to time its programmes with discretion. The programmes on housing and unemployment coincided with new moves by the government to deal with the issues they confronted.

[53]David Cardiff and Paddy Scannell, ' ''Good Luck War Workers!'' Class, Politics and Entertainment in Wartime Radio', in T. Bennett, C. Mercer and J. Woollacott, eds., *Popular Culture and Social Relations* (Milton Keynes, Open University Press, 1986).

The most remarkable thing about the *Harry Hopeful* series was the sound of a live audience laughing, applauding and joining in the programme. It was unlike anything heard on radio at that time, and it showed that broadcasting could create its own forms of public and participatory pleasures from the stuff of ordinary life and experience. The most popular shows on radio and television – from *Have a Go!* to *That's Life* and *Eastenders* – are the heirs to this discovery. At its best North Region regularly succeeded in making enjoyable, unpretentious programmes for its largely working-class audience. The voices of Wilfred Pickles, Frank Nicolls and others who performed regularly in plays and features, spoke to and for the listeners in the North and did much to compensate for the official voices of the BBC's staff announcers. Whenever Manchester made programmes about local places and people it was a matter of pride for those who lived there and headline news in the local newspapers. When Olive Shapley took Mrs Emmerson from Cragshead, a large mining village near Durham, to a Normandy mining village for a week as part of the preparation for *Miner's Wives*,[54] it was a nine-days wonder in the Newcastle press. Her discreet, sympathetic and finely observed programmes avoided any prescriptive official definition of their subject matter. A note in *Radio Times* on *Homeless People* promised that 'no BBC voice will intrude at all'.[55] That democratic impulse at the heart of documentary, to let people speak for themselves, to show the ordinary lives and pleasures of ordinary people, was well served by the pioneering efforts of programme makers in Manchester in that brief golden moment before the outbreak of war.

[54]29 March 1939. NR Scripts, WA.
[55]*Radio Times*, 26 August 1938. Broadcast September 6 1938. NR Scripts, WA.

Note

Mass Observation was a research movement founded in 1937 by three men – Charles Madge, Humphrey Jennings and Tom Harrisson – with the aim of conducting 'an anthropology-at-home': a study of the British people, their social life and popular culture. It was a form of social investigation which took place outside the boundaries of academic sociology, and which recruited a body of voluntary observers from the public at large who reported generally on everyday life as well as responding to specific topics. While its activities during World War Two are certainly of great interest, its most radical and potentially far-reaching ideas and intentions were in our view germinated during its pre-war phase, and particularly in association with Madge and Jennings. It is on this phase that we intend to concentrate in this chapter.

We have already written in a general way on the early work of Mass Observation. See D. Chaney and M. Pickering, 'Democracy and Communication: Mass Observation 1937–1943', *Journal of Communication* 36.1 (1986). The aim of this piece is twofold. Firstly, we develop a more analytical discussion of the project in relation to the role of the author and the generic features of documentarism as a whole. In the second part of the chapter we concentrate on Madge's role during the early years of the movement in order to present a rather different view than that advocated by, and associated with, Tom Harrisson, for it is Harrisson's that has so far largely prevailed.

The Mass Observation archive is now kept at the University of Sussex, where its valuable resources are becoming increasingly used by sociologists of culture and social historians. The most significant publications of Mass Observation up to World War Two are *Mass Observation* (London, Frederick Muller, 1937), *May the Twelfth* (London, Lindsay Drummond, 1938), and *Britain* (Harmondsworth, Penguin, 1939), though it also worth mentioning *The Pub and the People* (London, Gollancz, 1943, repub. Welwyn Garden City, Seven Dials, 1971) as the only publication to come out of the 'Worktown' research in Lancashire. For a recent anthology of Mass Observation writings, see Angus Calder and Dorothy Sheridan, eds., *Speak for Yourself* (London, Cape, 1984, republished in paperback, Oxford, OUP, 1985).

2

Authorship in Documentary: Sociology as an Art form in Mass Observation

David Chaney and Michael Pickering

Jennings was arguing with me about the basic problem that, in his view, the film director . . . has to solve. 'It's the whole question' he said, somewhat cryptically, 'of imagination in an industrial society'[1]

I

Documentary accounts provide a quite distinctive type of picture of the world. Their legitimacy derives from a fidelity to actually existing situations and circumstances which they represent. Their predominant sense must be of the 'real world', the material and social world in which people live and not one which has only an imagined reality. Milton's hell or Morris's utopia are impossible subjects for the documentary genre, while their cultural application or ideological use are not. The essential requirement of documentary is that what is signified has to be accepted as realistic, but it is precisely because this quality is so highly relative that it needs to be understood as rhetorical.

Our usual expectation of documentary is that a degree of certainty and truth can be assumed where this would not be granted – or rather, taken-for-granted – if we were considering metaphysical speculations, political beliefs or personal testimonies. We wish to turn this expectation on its head by suggesting that the most useful way of attempting to understand the sort of picture of the world a documentary provides is by asking how it is constructed as an acccount, rather than whether or not it is accurate. In suggesting this, we are pointing to the aesthetic conventions and devices employed by the documentarist in producing an account primarily legitimated by its reporting of facts. If, as Moretti has forcefully argued, rhetorical analysis is dependent on sociological description and explanation, then it has also to be said that a reflexive methodology of social research equally entails some kind of rhetorical analysis.[2] Acknowledging

---

[1] George Pitman, 'Men in Our Time', *Our Time* (July 1944), pp. 12–13.
[2] Franco Moretti, *Signs Taken for Wonders* (London, Verso 1983), chapter 1.

29

this in relation to the genre of documentary calls into question our conventional understanding of distinctions between fact and fiction. We need therefore to focus upon the rhetoric of documentary, the ways in which facts are given meaning and significance.

What is central to the structure of this rhetoric is a characteristic use of an instance as emblematic of a general case. This is more than a stylistic feature; it may indeed be held to constitute the core of documentary method, as Garfinkel, in adopting the concept of documentary method from Mannheim, has made clear: 'The method consists of treating an actual appearance as "the document of", as "pointing to", as "standing on behalf of" a presupposed underlying pattern.'[3] Within this method the researcher works in a dialectical manner between the determinate instance and its underlying pattern so that each can be held to illuminate their mutual relevance. The contrast between literal description and documentary method should not be taken to imply that the latter is a flawed version of the former. What a surveillance camera conveys is literal, but redundant as cultural expression. Its social instrumental function in detecting (or deterring) crime and the invasion of property is devoid of any effort at interpretation of the everyday world. Any form of documentary accounting involves by contrast a process of 'fact production'. This is always a process with a purpose. The task of historicizing through biography, for instance, 'consists of using the documentary method to select and order past occurrences so as to furnish the present state of affairs its relevant past and prospects.'[4]

Dorothy Smith has made a distinction in relation to documentary form between what actually happened and 'what actually happened' where the latter consists of an account that purports to be isomorphic with the former.[5] The existence of phenomenal reality is not being questioned here. Attention is being directed to the procedures through which such reality is made available to members of a society: 'The organization which actuality acquires in the accomplishment of a fact is . . . constructed in the context of *telling*. The organization that is created aims at this telling and aims there at the purposes for which it will be told.'[6] Accounts are occasioned enterprises. They have been accomplished as part of a purposeful programme that may not be immediately apparent in the account itself. The records of an organization such as a hospital, for example, ostensibly serve as resources for the treatment of the individuals they document, but they also serve, at the same time, as ways of legitimating the remedial practices of that organization. In looking at the making of accounts, we can see that the orderliness of experience which is displayed is accomplished by the ability to describe it in ways that are comprehensible to others, and this

[3] Harold Garfinkel, *Studies in Ethnomethodology* (New Jersey, Prentice-Hall, 1967), p. 78.
[4] Garfinkel, *op. cit.* p. 95.
[5] Dorothy Smith, 'The Social Construction of Documentary Reality', *Sociological Inquiry* Vol. 44, No. 4 (1974), pp 257–68.
[6] Smith, *op. cit.* p. 258.

ability implies a shared, like-minded community of others. But we can go further and say that the factuality of the social world is not only displayed by accounting schemes, but tends as well to become reified in that the taken-for-granted nature of everyday accounts generates a necessity to use conventional formulations. This process of reification is particularly suitable and helpful for those organizations, such as hospitals, prisons and the police, where the terms of the documentary record come to provide a level of 'organized consciousness' that acts as a central mode of social control.

Any document is therefore necessarily political. Documentation is inescapably an expression of the social relationships of its production and reception. This involves questions about those who are institutionally empowered to describe aspects of the 'real world', and about the potential consequences of the descriptive categories and conventions employed. The 'knowledge' of the everyday world which organizational documents possess and mobilize is 'thus ideological in the sense that [its] social organization preserves conceptions and means of description which represent the world as it is for those who rule it, rather than as it is for those who are ruled.'[7] This point is central for our understanding of the rhetoric of documentary, for the 'how' of documentary construction is inseparable from the 'why' of its accounting, and the rhetoric of neutrality generates the paradox of the impossibility of neutrality.

An emphasis upon purpose enables us in principle to distinguish organizational documents from the documentary investigations of historians and other social scientists. These are a type of study in which a record is exegetically compiled from contemporary and/or appropriate documents. In some cases, of course, this record is compiled without considering the political implications of document construction; such 'documentary histories' then remain prisoners of the reifications inherent in their primary sources, or else mystify the social relations inherent in documentary construction and assimilation. In the documentary arts there is usually a clear intent to subvert the constraints or corrode the accretions of conventional understanding. This more subversive alternative can only be realized by allowing the account, the performance, a different status in relation to its topic. This involves a more self-conscious version of the process of accounting. In self-consciously reporting the everyday world the documentarist assumes not only that his or her account will be of interest to a general audience, but also that the world of normal experience can be seen in new ways so that it is de-familiarized. In this respect a documentary is a project imbued with modern presuppositions that the social order is a contingent, practical accomplishment.

So one cannot class a documentary report as successful because of the quality of its facts. Rather success is achieved through the quality of the sense it creates of what authorizes the selected facts as appropriate to the reality represented. That which makes a documentary is not provided

[7]Smith, *op. cit.* p. 267.

by characteristics of the topic but by the type of telling, the narrative, through which the topic is articulated. In the case of documentary as that term was conventionally used in the 1930s, narratives were authorized by trading on notions of social relevance. In this conception the documentarist has to preserve a precarious position from which she/he can report on happenings and situate these events so that their social implications can begin to be assessed.

Following H. Gustav Klaus, we can identify five basic components of the documentary impetus of that period: (1) an emphasis on ordinary rather than extraordinary people and situations, the condition of 'the masses' in an insistently anti-exotic here-and-now; (2) a concern with social conditions, environments and problems, treated in the main apolitically, detailing the symptoms rather than the causes of social evils in the rationalist expectation that increased empirical knowledge would automatically generate strategies of reform; (3) a focus upon the factual, bred of a general feeling that social reportage was the most appropriate form of representation for the age; (4) an anti-individualist stress upon cooperative teamwork conducted in the field; (5) a populist orientation towards what we might call a sociology-from-below, based upon the enabling conditions of the historical conjuncture of the later 1930s and 40s. (These can, of course, only be regarded as general tendencies rather than hard-and-fast terms; the list should also not be assumed to be comprehensive.)[8]

Isolating these categories in this way enables us to recognize, in a very general manner, some aspects of documentary representation which characterize it as an intrinsically modern project. It has been objected that accounts of cultural forms in which a strong connection between epoch and form is made both involve neglecting the creativity of individual authors and overemphasizing effectiveness as a criterion of worth. Both charges are relevant to the historical reputation of Mass Observation. On the one hand the explicit attempt to let the people speak for themselves involved subverting the authority of the intelligentsia and was consistent with a crisis of confidence within intellectual fractions.[9] On the other hand the eclecticism of topics surveyed, and the unsystematic reporting procedures used, have led Mass Observation studies to be patronizingly praised as naive sociology.[10] In this paper we shall argue that the cultural context of Mass Observation should not be used as an explanation of its inadequacies but the reverse. It was because Mass Observation took up the radical premises of documentary initiatives more thoroughly than many other groups in the 1930s that their early projects were more challenging than either 'poetic idiosyncrasy' or 'unsystematic sociology' would suggest. It was precisely

[8]H. Gustav Klaus, *The Literature of Labour* (Brighton, Harvester, 1985), pp. 130–6.
[9]Cf. M. Green, *Children of the Sun: A Narrative of 'Decadence' in England after 1918* (London, Constable, 1977).
[10]E.g. Angus Calder, 'Mass Observation 1937–1949', in Martin Bulmer, ed., *Essays on the History of British Sociological Research* (Cambridge and London, Cambridge University Press, 1985), pp. 121–36.

because Mass Observation posed such radical questions about representing everyday life that their archives cannot now be pillaged indiscriminately by social historians looking for nuggets of information.[11] We have to think through the relationships between observer and observed and the construction of accounts to understand the politics of social knowledge.

A concern with the means of accomplishment, symptomatic of a reflexive social consciousness, is not of course peculiar to the documentary enterprise. Indeed, in recent years it has become a central motif in certain types of methodological practice within the social sciences.[12] The intellectual antecedents of authorial self-consciousness can be straightforwardly traced back to the innovations in social and cultural ideas, roughly around the beginning of this century, commonly referred to by the term modernism. We have already stressed the modernity of the documentary initiative, but now to make a connection between the commitment to social realism enshrined in documentary principles and the frequently wilful retreats from reality characteristic of modernist experiments will seem paradoxical. The contradiction is puzzling only if modernism is treated as having involved an excessive concern with escaping social constraints, with non-representational content, with a self-regarding authorial individualism, and an ahistorical emphasis on the growth of personal consciousness or vision. Within the multiplicity of groups, manifestos and styles that constitute the range of modernist ideas in different cultural forms these elements can be found, but more importantly they represent different modes of response to a commonly felt necessity to address a distinctive crisis, an overwhelming novelty in social circumstances that recast every aspect of the business of telling: 'Modernism . . . contains a highly authentic response, one which turns on the assumption that the registering of modern consciousness or experience was not a problem in representation but a profound cultural and aesthetic crux . . . a problem in the making of structures, the employment of language, the uniting of form, finally in the social meaning of the artist himself.'[13]

Modernism at its inception was regarded as a comprehensive breach with the past, and with traditional aesthetics and thought. It canvassed for a perpetual process of change, and argued for newness as an essential feature of a distinctively modern art. This compulsive sense of the need for change and innovation was itself both a response to an accelerated degree of social change, to the rapidly occurring technological development of the modern age, and an inheritance of the stylistic eclecticism of urban-industrial culture. The gradual replacement of systems of patronage with systems of distribution and reward through a variety of more impersonal market

---

[11]E.g. Penny Summerfield, 'Mass Observation: Social Research or Social Movement?', *Journal of Contemporary History* Vol. 20, No. 3, (1985), pp. 439–52.
[12]E.g. B.A. Babcock, 'Reflexivity: Definitions and Discriminations', *Semiotica* Vol. 30, No. 1/2 (1980), pp. 1–14.
[13]M. Bradbury and J. McFarlane, *Modernism 1890–1930* (Harmondsworth, Penguin, 1976), pp. 28–9).

mechanisms in the great majority of cultural forms, meant that the 'naturalness' of style in previous eras could no longer be regarded as self-evident. Style became seen as an ideological manifestation, not just in retrospective analysis but also in contemporary debate and in the development of criticism. Avant garde-ism, for example, assumes an intimate interdependence between innovation and authenticity that would have been meaningless prior to the establishment of a market-based system of cultural production.

At its most precious, a stress upon artistic autonomy can lead to well-founded charges of aestheticism. But in the same way that decadence is not a necessary consequence of artistic experimentation, so an unselfconscious naturalism is not an inevitable corollary of social realism. Indeed we can go further and say that in documentary practice the tensions between the competing claims of social mission and poetic quality, between a mechanical sense of realism and the role of creativity in representing actuality, and between the appeal to the head as opposed to the heart, should be understood as characteristic of documentary purposes and practice rather than peripheral or aberrant.

For all those attempting to develop forms of representation consistent with the distinctive features of the age, the central problems were seen to stem from the development of the new relations of cultural production noted above, which in turn conditioned the ways the author–audience relationship was conceived by modern artists and theorists. While modernism and realism should not be understood as mutually exclusive alternatives, interpretations of author–audience relationships can be ranked on a continuum which stretches from individualistic aesthetic autonomy at one end to a form of social command at the other. Perhaps unsurprisingly, individualist aestheticism has tended to be associated with more private forms of expression – private at least in their production, and in some ways in their reception and appreciation as well – such as easel painting, sculpture and the novel. Such forms within modernism have often been associated with an assertion of the aesthetic autonomy of the creator or author, an assertion generally made as a reaction to popular cultural tastes and 'mass' democracy. There have, however, been other, more public aspects of modernism which have responded to their audiences and to popular tastes in the light of the idea of social command, and which furthermore have also claimed some collective warrant in interpretation. Paradigmatic instances to which we would point are architecture and town planning as the dramatic organization of social space and interaction, though certain types of cinema could perhaps also be mentioned. Innovation in these cultural forms is not seen as deriving from the tortured psychological turmoil of the isolated genius, but rather from the modern necessity of responding to historical circumstances or 'the spirit of the age'. Hence, for example, the 'widely disseminated argument that modern architecture exercises some special unassailable claim over us since it is not a "style" which we are free to like or dislike as we choose, but is an expression of some unchangeable "need" or requirement inherent in the twentieth century with which we must conform.'[14] In such versions of cultural collectivism it is often suggested (although rarely followed) that anonymity is appropriate for the artist/author, and it is also consistent that factory metaphors stressing organization, mechanization, authoritative rules and irresistible force are frequently associated with a celebration of impersonality.

It should be clear, therefore, that particular strands within modernism were not only consistent with the documentary impulse, but can be seen as well to have generated certain questions within documentary practice which, as we shall make clear, Mass Observation in its initial phase posed very forcibly. Before setting out the details we shall discuss briefly the meanings and implications of the first epithet in its title – that of 'mass' – in order to extend a little further the question of the audience. An ideology of authorship which is committed to some form of social command is inevitably confronted with problems in attempting to respond to the anonymity of a 'mass' audience. The elitist idiosyncracies of an avant garde obviously contradict the conventions and conformity of everyday life. It is therefore to be expected that in any form of representation that is oriented to the social, the nature of the mass audience, indeed the very concept of massness itself, will be of central importance. This can clearly be seen to have been the case internationally in the several facets of the documentary movement where there is an explicitly close connection between anonymity and collectivism as cause and ideal. It was also more specifically present in the ideas and ambitions behind the genesis of Mass Observation. This was a particularly appropriate name for an organization dedicated to tackling 'the technical problem of how to organize and present the reality of this collective social world.'[15] Laing suggests that the term 'mass' had five connotations for Mass Observation: (1) new social conditions; (2) mass as the 'common man'; (3) the mass as observers; (4) collection and organization of material; and (5) mass as public.[16] In the second part of this chapter we will explore in greater detail the dynamic connections between these conditions and conceptions and how they came to generate a particular research practice.

To conclude this first section we will simply note some points about the particular significance of the development of mass communication for the social rhetoric of documentary. The technology of mass communication has not only vastly increased the possible size of audiences for particular performances, and generated new forms of performance, it has also transformed the politics of public life. Individual life-worlds are

---

[14]David Watkins, *Morality and Architecture* (Oxford, Clarendon Press, 1977), p. 9.
[15]Stuart Laing, 'Presenting "Things as They Are": John Sommerfield's *May Day* and Mass Observation', in Frank Gloversmith, ed., *Class, Culture and Social Change* (Brighton, Harvester, 1980), p. 156.
[16]Laing, *op. cit.* p. 155–6.

enormously expanded, while simultaneously being made more complex and ambiguous. The documentary impulse is one form of response to the multiplication of social realities, a response that interrogates what has brought it into being: 'Documentary is a method. It is a method of approach to public information. It is concerned with, and is part of the machinery of mass communication which, of course, includes all the mass media without exception.'[17] There are two main aspects to the grounds of documentary in mass communication. The first is technological: 'documentary does not truly exist without the technology of mass communication';[18] and as facilities for unobtrusive recording have developed documentaries have in one sense become more spectacular – although not necessary more sophisticated as pictures of social reality. The second aspect is concerned with the potentialities for democratization inherent in the massification of communication (recognizing that the growth of an informed citizenry has been profoundly thwarted by its assimilation to the imperatives of the mass market). The development of the mass media has involved, at least tendentially, the substitution of localized identities and attachments by a symbolic construct of a national political community. The need for a project like Mass Observation could not be perceived before this social and ideological transformation of community made possible by the media of mass communication. It is unsurprising therefore, and particularly appropriate as we shall go on to argue, that when reflecting upon their work two years after Mass Observation had been set up, two of the founders should have chosen the radio as a metaphor to characterize what they had created: 'Through Mass Observation you can already listen-in to the movements of popular habit and opinion. The receiving set is there, and every month makes it more effective.'[19]

II

Having sketched out some characteristics of the distinctive work of the documentarist in producing a picture of modern social reality, we shall look in detail at the project of Mass Observation, concentrating in particular on the career and ideas of Charles Madge. The most straightforward view of the focus and aims of Mass Observation has been provided by Marie Jahoda, a largely unsympathetic contemporary sociologist. In reviewing their early work she observed their subject matter to be everyday life, and noted their stress on 'the necessity of knowing everyday life'.[20] Mass Observation was thus a process of documenting everyday social reality, of producing a detailed record of mundane experience.

[17]Basil Wright, *The Long View* (London, Secker & Warburg, 1974), p. 108.
[18]A.W. Bluem, 'The Documentary Idea', in R.M. Barsam, *Nonfiction Film* (New York, Dutton, 1976).
[19]Charles Madge and Tom Harrisson, *Britain* (Harmondsworth, Penguin, 1939), p. 10.
[20]Marie Jahoda, review article on Mass Observation, *Sociological Review* Vol. 30 (1938), p. 209.

Harrisson, retrospectively describing the aims of the founders, has emphasized that, while endorsing the importance of social arithmetic, they also sought knowledge of public opinion and public sentiment through 'a study of diaries and subjective writings, private comment and interviews on general subjects' as these made for 'depth and under-standing, as well as providing the actual intelligible "reading matter" which still remains valid decades later.'[21] The documents to be produced by observation were not therefore literal descriptions, but revelations of underlying themes and forms in ways which display the subversion possible in documentary arts. What was being addressed was the notion of a collective social reality – a world which exists independently of individual will although it is only experienced in personal terms. In attempting to set out the lineaments of everyday reality they were therefore mimicking the project of social praxis in human activity: moving from objectification through internalization to objectification.[22]

The well-known letter to the *New Statesman* announcing the formation of Mass Observation contains the outline of the initial strategy followed during the first year of the project.[23] Research was coordinated at two centres. A group led by Harrisson lived in Bolton and recorded observations of working-class life and culture. Meanwhile, Madge in London organized the collection and collation of observers' reports from all over the country relating to both specified days and specified topics. (Nearly two years later these roles were exchanged for a year so it is not appropriate to claim, as Harrisson later tended to do, that all the more 'anthropological' work was conducted under his aegis). The pamphlet *Mass Observation* was published towards the middle of 1937 over the names of Madge and Harrisson with a cover designed by Humphrey Jennings and a forward written by Julian Huxley. This pamphlet clarified their methodological aims: 'Mass Observation', they wrote, 'intends to make use not only of the trained scientific observer, but of the untrained observer, the man in the street. Ideally, it is the observation of everyone by everyone, including themselves.'[24] They used the metaphor of detection to describe the method although they did not seek a distinctive type of social object, such as the criminal; every member of society was of equal interest, and they did not therefore 'intend to intrude on the private life of any individual, as individual. Collective habits and social behaviour are our field of inquiry, and individuals are only of interest in so far as they are typical of groups.'[25]

The shifting in perspectives between individual experience and collective behaviour is paralleled by a contrast between the 'untrained' and the 'trained scientific observer'. The latter contrast can be read as

---

[21]Tom Harrisson, Introduction to Tom Harrisson and Humphrey Spender, *Britain in the Thirties* (London, Unicorn Press, 1975).

[22]Jean-Paul Sartre, *The Problem of Method* (London, Methuen, 1963), p. 97.

[23]*New Statesman and Nation*, 30 January, 1937.

[24]Charles Madge and Tom Harrison, *Mass Observation* (London, Methuen, 1937), p. 97.

[25]Madge and Harrison, *op. cit.* p. 30.

displaying either intellectual arrogance or naivety. It is, however, more correctly understood in the context of an attempt to extend the role and reinterpret the power of author in social documentation. The interplay of perspectives is not a weakness but something appropriate to 'fact production'. In what was a refreshingly democratic initiative, again connecting up with their aspiration to a non-alienated social praxis: 'The process of observing raises him [the "untrained observer"] from subjectivity to objectivity. What has become unnoticed through familiarity is raised into consciousness again'.[26]

Madge left Mass Observation in 1940, most immediately because he was unhappy about the decision to link the services of the organization to government propaganda during the war. There was, however, a deepening rift between Harrisson and himself over how the organization should develop and the methods to be used. This would probably have led in any case to a split had not the war intervened. (Humphrey Jennings had largely stopped contributing in 1938 after working on and writing up the *May the Twelfth* study). A contrast between Madge as poet turned social reporter and Harrisson as ornithologist turned social scientist is too straightforward, but retrospective accounts have either been written by Harrisson or largely from his viewpoint. We shall, therefore, concentrate more on certain aspects of the biography and interests of Madge in order to correct this imbalance. The virtue of this is that it should enable us to clarify, from a different angle, the relationships sought by Mass Observation between the collective reality of the 'masses' and ways of collecting and collating relevant observations.

Madge went up to Cambridge as an undergraduate to read Part 1 of the Natural Sciences Tripos in 1930. He already had a small reputation as a poet and undoubtedly thought of himself as a poet, although having other interests. Shortly after his second registration began, this time reading English (he had to leave quite early in his first year through illness), he was converted to communism, and not long after that he left the university in romantic circumstances. In London he continued to work at his poetry and became actively involved in various radical and avant garde circles. In 1935, largely through the influence of T.S. Eliot, he was appointed reporter/jobbing sub-editor for the *Daily Mirror*, at the time making a determined bid for mass readership through sensationalist journalism. Instructed to concentrate on Sex, Scandal and Crime, he wryly commented two years later: 'Behind these three grisly abstractions, I glimpsed the afterglow of another trio in whose names much confusion has been wrought: Beauty, Truth and Goodness. Sex, Scandal and Crime are the poetry of modern journalism.'[27] In 1937, as we have noted; he was a

[26]Charles Madge and Humphrey Jennings, 'Poetic Description and Mass Observation', *New Verse* No. 24, Feb–March (1937), p. 3.
[27]Charles Madge, 'Press, Radio and Social Consciousness', in C. Day Lewis, ed., *The Mind in Chains* (London, Mullar 1937), pp. 153–4.

leading figure in the founding of Mass Observation. Through his work with Mass Observation Madge became interested in the economic features of working-class budgeting and when he left the organization in 1940 he took a job as economic researcher with the National Institute for Economic and Social Research. After some years in various types of research work (research on trade unions for PEP; editorial work with the Pilot Press; Social Development Officer at Stevenage New Town), he was eventually appointed to one of the first chairs in sociology at a British university (Birmingham) in 1950.

Madge was ambivalently connected with both the Communist Party and, more loosely, with those British intellectuals interested in the neo-modernist movement of surrealism – principally through his friendship with Humphrey Jennings. He was influenced by the surrealists' willingness to experiment with forms of expression and their commitment to sub-verting, even assaulting, relationships between author, material and audience. The surrealist emphasis upon a common vocabulary latent in everyday experience but worthy of extraction as a means of heightening understanding was attractive to Madge – particularly as it legitimated the artistic use of imagery and experiences from the 'vulgar' world of popular culture. Interest in the different forms of fantasy in everyday life was not peculiar to the surrealists but more widely shared amongst avant garde tendencies, although a belief that the self-conscious nihilism of certain modes of performance was sufficiently radical to constitute a response to the demands of social relevance was a more specifically surrealist posture.[28] Although Madge was sympathetic to many strands in surrealism he never-theless kept his distance, in general because he found the style too literary and too intensely artistic. While endorsing the interdependence of poetry and politics, in relation to neither communism nor surrealism did he find a way of crossing 'the partition of verse' between 'good private poetry' and 'good public poetry'.[29] A fascinating example of an experiment working at this boundary, and significantly through utilizing 'found materials' of newspaper text, was a piece written in 1935 – *Bourgeois News*.[30] Madge uses a collage of items from news stories to create a wandering surreal narrative that has a logic of style if not of content. The rhetoric of head-lines, scandals, bizarre juxtapositions of text and image, all seem to constitute a dynamic mythology of popular experience that overlays conventional methods of accounting and reporting.

The extent to which those experimenting with forms of representation can be expected to be fully aware of the social implications of their ideas is debatable. It is fundamental to our approach that experiments are generated by social conditions which make them possible, but the exact

[28]Cf. P.C. Ray, *The Surrealist Movement in England* (London, Cornell University Press, 1971).
[29]Charles Madge, 'Poetry and Politics', *New Verse* No. 3 (1933), p. 1.
[30]Charles Madge, *The Disappearing Castle* (London, Faber, 1937).

form and expression of a particular innovation will derive from specific circumstances and individual characteristics. From articles published in little magazines in the late 1930s by Madge and Jennings it is apparent that they believed that the seemingly simple project of observing everyday life transforms the literary activity of the observer from that of privileged individualism to that of co-author. This is not to claim that they would in any sense have explicitly endorsed Benjamin's dialectical materialist thesis that 'the place of the intellectual in the class struggle can only be determined, or better still chosen, on the basis of his position within the production process.'[31] Their intervention was not politicized in that way but was, instead, more an expression of a culturalist commitment to challenge the ideological divide between 'them' and 'us' and to tap a level of social reality that is best described as implicit in everyday consciousness.

Initially this sense of a layering of reality has to be confronted in ordinary language. The words of mundane experience are not haphazardly chosen but generate particular structures of response and appreciation: 'in actual social usage, all the jungle of words grow up together in Darwinian conflict until they establish their own ecology and functions.'[32] We do not commonly recognize the drama of everyday experience because quite reasonably we concentrate on functional aspects: 'Every report is a landscape with figures: the sharp focus is on the figures, and the landscape retires into varying degrees of subjectivity. In order to get focused into this hinterland, the background of social fantasy, we have been experimenting on what for lack of a better name has been termed the "dominant image of the day".'[33] One experiment which emerged from these ideas took the form of a collective poem written on a collaborative basis by 12 Oxford undergraduates. The method used is not particularly important, what is interesting are the initial assumptions that a shared 'social landscape' might be apprehended by collating the 'predominant images' of individuals. The result should have been a poetic mode of 'daily journalism' capable of recording a continuous stream of events.

Documentary accounts, if they are to be faithful to the complex and diverse experiences of different participants, have therefore to facilitate mutual interaction through communicating a social landscape. Although a term like 'fantasy' was often used to refer to shared structures of feeling this does not mean that there was an implicit retreat from reality, nor that they could only be studied by a method such as free association. Mass Observation forcused on social fantasy as virgin material for scientific interpretation. The term 'science' (understood as equivalent to empiricism) was used rather loosely in Mass Observation publications and manifestos, but it did

[31]Walter Benjamin, *Understanding Brecht* (London, New Left Books, 1973), p. 93.
[32]Charles Madge and Humphrey Jennings, 'They Speak for Themselves: Mass Observation and Social Narrative', *Life and Letters* No. 17 (1937), p. 37.
[33]Charles Madge, Oxford Collective Poem, *New Verse* No. 25 (1937), p. 16.

signal that an important feature of their project was that the mode of documentation they were setting up required intellectual rigour and no concessions to romanticism. The whole project depended upon the subjectivity of individual perceptions being neutralized by the 'objectivity' of editorial compilation and integration. The role of author was therefore a form of science, a mode of production which is consistent with the potential democratization of art in mass communication, and which would produce 'a poetry which is not, as at present, restricted to a handful of esoteric performers. The immediate effect of Mass Observation is to devalue considerably the status of the ''poet''. It makes the term ''poet'' apply, not to his performance, but to his profession like ''footballer'' '.[34]

We have noted that Benjamin's contemporary view of authorship as production rested on more rigorously materialistic grounds than any that would have been endorsed within Mass Observation. There is, however, one common feature of the separate attempts to rethink the notion of authorship. This is the significance of innovations in communication facilities, in particular the popular newspaper. Benjamin argued that progressive writing, which means responding to social command, could not be guaranteed by 'correct' views or subject-matter, but only by rethinking the relations of literary production. The central forum for innovations in mass literature is the newspaper: 'we are in the midst of a vast process in which literary forms are being melted down. . . . The newspaper is the arena of this literary confusion. Its content eludes any form of organization other than that which is imposed upon it by the reader's impatience.'[35] In the capitalist press this 'impatience' is exploited by an unselective assimilation of facts with an equally unselective recruitment of readers' views and sensational interests. Although the potential was possibly idealized and belied in practice, Benjamin detected in the Soviet press an incipient erosion of the distinction between author and public: 'Authority to write is no longer founded in a specialist training but in a polytechnical one, and so becomes a common property.'[36]

Madge took the progressive implications of mass journalism in a different direction, although one connected by a common concern with the documentation of social reality. He saw that the novelty of this form of communication lay in its providing a vantage-point for the collective consciousness (or social fantasy). In an article on newspapers, radio and social consciousness he cited with approval some phrases from A.J. Cummings as appropriate to both the press and the BBC: '[they have] brought a remarkable change in the intellectual life of the people by giving them some common basis of opinion, some data on which to form collective opinions, however false or incomplete such opinions might be.'[37] It is because we

[34]Madge and Jennings, *New Verse* article, *op. cit.*, p. 3.
[35]W. Benjamin, *Brecht*, p. 89.
[36]Benjamin, *Brecht*, p. 90.
[37]Madge in Lewis, ed., *The Mind in Chains* p. 162.

participate, however reluctantly, in the collective consciousness of shared reading and listening – and thus in an inescapable 'community' – that the terms of personal experience are shaped in ways we cannot always appreciate. The subject of ordinary life, in other words, is in many ways structured by the vocabulary of the media of mass communication. We are therefore brought back to the intimate interdependence between media of mass communication and documentary practice we noted in the first part of this paper. The methodology of documentation is dialectically engaged with other forms of mass communication. In order to avoid merely reproducing conventional knowledge, those working in Mass Observation had to be as closely concerned with how knowledge is expressed, that is with the politics of authorship, as with what it is about.

The uses to which the power of the mass media are put are inextricably bound up with the nature of capitalist society. The quasi-intellectuals of these new industries have to attempt to reconcile their audiences' experiences with the ' sordid interests of newspaper-owner or advertiser.'[38] A consequence of these contradictory aims is that the stream of 'news' (and entertainment) acquires a vitality of its own: 'The best sub-editors and layout men are dominated by the mass-wish not only consciously, but unconsciously as well', so that: 'The newspaper and hoarding serve as vehicles for the expression of unconscious fears and wishes of the mass.'[39] It is because we are so ensnared in a world of news that we take it for granted and willingly suspend our disbelief: 'If we treat news in the same way as watching films or reading fiction, it means that we regard it not as objective fact, but as poetic fact. It also means that when we stop reading it, the news ceases to have the same hard, inescapable force that the objective fact has; it becomes a poetic memory, affecting our feelings and not our actions. Factually we become anaesthetized. . . .'[40] This poetic quality to the news can mean that it becomes a mode of collective art transcending the conventions of traditional forms; it can, of course, also mean, as Madge was clearly aware, that we do not recognize a subtle mode of indoctrination and willingly collude in our own subjugation.

We have argued that in attempting to put into practice the documentary idea of letting people speak for themselves and create documentary records of their own experience, Mass Observation was faced with the problem of the type or form of the reality it was trying to address. On the surface this appears as a tension, itself characteristic of modernist aesthetics, between the rhetorical associations of poetry and science. The decision to put the organization at the service of the government in reporting civilian morale may have only catalysed more personal tensions, but it did effectively mean that a form of science as author-ized observation became institutionalized and was no longer contentious. If the alternative is characterized as 'poetic

[38]Lewis, ed. *op. cit.* p. 162.
[39]Lewis, ed., *op. cit.* p. 151.
[40]Lewis, ed., *op. cit.* p. 151.

observation' with an implication of non-scientific fantasy, this is misleading both in terms of individual beliefs and in terms of the nature of
shared social beliefs. Both Madge and Harrisson increasingly adopted a
language of conventional science to describe their own work. Madge agreed
with Harrisson's account that 'fundamentally the trend has been towards
more firmly based, scientific and statistical work [for Mass Observation]
because in *practice* this has turned out to be the best way of tackling
difficult human problems of our own civilization.'[41] He feels now (in
personal conversation) that if anything he was more rigorous than
Harrisson and less inclined to extravagant extrapolation; indeed he
described their work 20 years later as a commitment to 'the need for more,
many more facts of almost any kind, about average human behaviour and
beliefs', so that some 'sort of net' could be 'spread to catch that fleeting,
glinting apparition, the essence of the time'.[42]

The more fundamental difference between Harrisson and Madge was
not based on a conception of science as facts but on their understanding of
the relationship between facts and social reality. Harrisson's observations
were omnivorous but uncritical. He has been quoted as advising that the
'anthropologist who wants to go deep should try and spend long periods
not so much listening to (let alone questioning in) words, but watching
and recording exactly what he *sees.*'[43] Trevelyan, a friend of Harrisson's, in
describing his association with the Bolton study has remarked that 'Tom
was passionately interested in people as they *are* and only remotely
concerned in changing their lives.'[44] Harrisson's remarks from 1940 quoted
above come from a series of memoranda he and Madge exchanged at the
time of the latter's resignation. In his reply Madge perceptively noted that
Harrisson tended to take problems for granted and as well as asking people
about their reactions to problems, Harrisson also asked how they had made
up their minds. Madge argued that these processes may not be open to
introspection, and suggested that the more successful Mass Observation
projects had been carried out on the transformation of views, on how
attitudes become institutionalized: 'what have the successful panel
subjects in common? . . . they all deal with social prejudice-attitudes at
the stage before they have crystallised into definite organized institutions
. . . *we are describing the mechanism by which institutions arise.*'[45]
Madge's alternative did not commit him to a different set of empirical

[41]Tom Harrisson, 'The Conception of Mass Observation' (1940, Mass Observation Archive),
p. 6.
[42]Tom Harrisson, *Britain Revisited* (London, Gollancz, 1961), pp. 277–80.
[43]A. Corlett, 'Mirror for the Masses' (Newcastle, Newcastle upon Tyne Polytechnic, 1983),
p. 5.
[44]Julian Trevelyan, *Indigo Days* (London, MacGibbon & Kee, 1957), p. 86.
[45]Charles Madge, 'The Mass Observation Panel and its Function' (1940, Mass Observation
Archive), p. 5. Cf. Harrisson's less sophisticated conception of Mass Observation as 'trying to
write [today's] history in the present', ('Mass Observation and the W.E.A.', *Highway* (Dec.
1937), p. 47.

practices to Harrisson and there is no reason to believe they seriously differed over the legitimacy of social arithmetic. His approach was different, however, in that it was an extension of his concern with the landscape of social imagination that grounds patterns of behaviour. His eye was for the processes of interaction and the rhythms of discourse through which attitudes become stabilized as appropriate for different contexts and roles.

Mass Observation did not suffer, as Martin Bulmer has alleged, 'from the instigators' conception of what they were doing as a form of art.'[46] On the contrary, this aspect of their approach enhanced the nature and quality of their project. We have argued that the documentary impulse in the 1930s was an expression of a commitment to recognize the implications of social responsibility. Ideas of artistic abstraction from the everyday world were suspended in favour of intervention in that world. This manifested a general attitude of subversion in which new forms of knowledge were to be generated to be placed at the disposal of new masters: 'It was a shift summarized in Myfanwy Piper's remark: "We are more serious now, not really playboys but agents".'[47] We have tried to show that rethinking the social command of the audience meant a reconsideration of the autonomy of authorship. In its initial years Mass Observation attempted to develop a literary apparatus that could have met Benjamin's prescription that it 'will be the better, the more consumers it brings in contact with the production process – in short, the more readers or spectators it turns into collaborators.'[48] It is to the enduring loss of social science and documentary practice that we have not been able to build upon their initiative.

[46]Bulmer, *British Sociological Research*, p. 11.
[47]David Mellor, 'Mass Observation: The Intellectual Climate', *Camerawork* No. 11 (1978), p. 5.
[48]Benjamin, *Brecht*, p. 98.

Note

Humphrey Jennings became involved in the British documentary movement in 1933, when he joined the GPO film team as an art director for Cavalcanti's film *Pett and Pott*. With his diversified background as a literary scholar, painter and poet and through his associations with British surrealism and Mass Observation he soon emerged as an outstanding, albeit controversial figure in the documentary movement.

His wartime documentaries have since come to be regarded as a high point of the movement. Through a series of films for the Crown Film Unit (as the GPO Film Unit was renamed after 1940) his films came to be regarded as the invocation of British wartime spirit. The most important titles include *London Can Take It* (1940 co-dir. with Harry Watt), *Words for Battle* (1941), *Listen to Britain* (1942) (co-dir. with Stewart McAllister), *Fires Were Started* (1943), *The Silent Village* (1943) and *Diary for Timothy* (1944–45).

After the war, Jennings made three documentaries, *The Cumberland Story* (1947), *Dim Little Island* (1949) and *Family Portrait* (1950) where he tries, not entirely successfully, to present his cross-cultural image of 'British qualities' in a post-war setting. In 1950 he died in a climbing accident, while working on location in Greece.

Literature on Jennings was for many years scarce, but 1982 saw the publication of two useful volumes on Jennings. The anthology *Humphrey Jennings: Film-Maker, Painter, Poet* edited by Mary-Lou Jennings (London, BFI, 1982) contains a biographical sketch with interesting selections of Jennings's poems and drawings, as well as Lindsay Anderson's 1954 article on Jennings for *Sight and Sound*. For a more detailed biography, A.W. Hodgkinson and R.R. Sheratsky *Humphrey Jennings – More Than a Maker of Films* (Hanover, Univ. of New England Press, 1982) presents some interesting analysis of the work of Jennings. For a more compact analysis, Jim Hillier's chapter on Jennings in Alan Lovell and Jim Hillier *Studies in Documentary* (London, Secker & Warburg, 1972) is highly recommended. In 1985, Jennings's giant project of portraying the Industrial Revolution in Britain through a *montage* of contemporary documents was finally published. *Pandaemonium*, edited by Charles Madge and Mary-Lou Jennings from Jennings's papers (London, Andre Deutsch, 1985) undoubtedly will be helpful in gaining insight into Jennings's scope as a multi-media artist.

The English language editions of Jurij Lotman's work referred to in the text are *Analysis of the Poetic Text* (Ann Arbor, Ardis, 1976) and *The Structure of the Artistic Text* (Ann Arbor, Univ. of Michigan Press, 1977).

Editor's Note – The films discussed in this article are obtainable for 16 mm screening. The British Film Institute can give further information concerning availability and costs.

3

The Documentary Aesthetics of Humphrey Jennings

Bjorn Sorenssen

'The only real poet the British cinema has yet produced'.

The assertion that Humphrey Jennings (1907–1950) is one of the leading figures in the history of the British documentary movement remains unchallenged. As the director of films like *London Can Take It* (1940), *Words for Battle* (1941), *Listen to Britain* (1942), *Fires Were Started* (1943) and *A Diary for Timothy* (1944–45) he has become firmly established as the figurehead of the British documentary movement during the war years, the period generally regarded to be the apex of that movement. This recognition is largely a result of a reappraisal of Jennings as a filmmaker, beginning with Lindsay Anderson's article in *Sight and Sound* April/June 1954. In this connection, Jennings was used as an example of the documentary style advocated by a new generation of British documentarists, the young filmmakers associated with the short-lived enterprise of 'Free Cinema'.

The word most frequently used to describe Humphrey Jennings's film style is 'poetic', and Jennings seems to be regarded as the 'poet' of the British documentary movement by most writers on documentary. Even John Grierson, the father of the movement, who definitely did not have a very high opinion of Jennings as a filmmaker, grudgingly acknowledges this: 'Jennings was a minor poet. I don't think he was a great poet. He was a minor poet.[1] Lindsay Anderson in his article 'Only Connect. Some Aspects of the Work if Humphrey Jennings' in the Spring 1954 issue of *Sight and Sound* had no reservations on this point: 'In fact it might reasonably be contended that Humphrey Jennings is the only real poet the British cinema has yet produced.'

The epithet 'poet' is, of course, very much in evidence in any description of Jennings, especially if the biographical details of his life are taken into

---

[1] In interview with Elizabeth Sussex; Elizabeth Sussex, *The Rise and Fall of British Documentary* (Berkeley, University of California Press, 1975), p. 110.

account. His background as a Cambridge scholar doing postgraduate work on the poetry of Thomas Gray, in addition to his close association with literary scholars such as I.A. Richards and William Empson, clearly suggests a natural source for any poetical connotations in the Jennings *œuvre*.

Furthermore, Jennings was an accomplished poet himself, although no published volume of his poetry appeared in his lifetime.(A year after his death a volume, *Poems*, was published in New York.) Against this backgound it is easy to understand why words like 'poetic' and 'poet' spring to the mind of those trying to describe the Jennings style.

However, the main reason for the epithet used to describe Jennings as a filmmaker lies in the quality of his films, and again there seems to be common consent that the most fitting description is 'poetic', an observation the casual viewer of a Jennings film will undoubtedly subscribe to. In Jack C. Ellis's *A History of Film*, the author elaborates somewhat on the description of Jennings as a 'poet': '. . . . Jennings adds the touch of a poet – a visual–aural poet who can capture the precise image for a feeling-state that yet has symbolic reverberations of English tradition and wartime urgencies.'[2]

It is interesting to note that, despite the consensus that seems to exist among film critics and film historians about Jennings's 'poetic' qualities, there have been very few attempts at a closer definition of how this concept manifests itself in his films. The aim of this article is to focus on the question that naturally arises in this connection: What do we mean when using the word 'poetic' about a cinematic work? And this question leads to another: is it possible to talk about a specific 'poetic film language'? In my attempt to answer these questions, I have found it useful to draw attention to the theoretical studies of the Soviet semiotician Jurij Lotman and his work on the structural analysis of what is referred to as 'the Artistic Text'. My article does not attempt to introduce a new terminology in this field, neither does it intend to use the Lotman framework for anything other than as a point of reference for a further discussion. Hence, the discussion of the three Jennings films in question should not be regarded as the basis for a complete theory, but can be looked upon as an attempt to elucidate some of the structural traits inherent in the films of Humphrey Jennings, traits that are usually ascribed to the 'poetic' nature of his work.

Jurij Lotman and language as a 'secondary modelling system'

The second of the questions mentioned above deals with the concept 'poetic language', and before going further it will be necessary to discuss the use of 'language' in this context, since a vaguely or loosely defined use of this word can quickly lead to misunderstandings.

For film theoreticians the word 'language' has represented a very

[2]Jack C. Ellis, *A History of Film* (Englewood Cliffs, Prentice Hall, 1979), p. 229.

tempting, albeit problematic linguistic analogy for the cinematographic medium. As early as 1915, Vachel Lindsay pointed to similarities between Egyptian hieroglyphs and what he perceived as the 'language of the moving pictures'; a decade later Sergei Eisenstein made a similar observation with regard to the Chinese pictographical alphabet. Later theoreticians frequently alluded to the linguistic qualities of the cinema, often referring to general conventions in filmic narration as a 'grammar of film', 'a syntax', etc.

The linguistic approach to film theory made a significant stride forward with the introduction of semiotic (or semiologic) theory based on the linguistic and philosophical principles introduced by Ferdinand de Saussure and Charles Edward Peirce and represented by theoreticians such as Christian Metz, Roland Barthes and Umberto Eco. Christian Metz's article *'Le cinema: langue ou langage?'* in *Communications* No. 4 (1964) heralded the period of semiotic film theory, a period that yielded a thorough and substantial theoretical discussion on the cinema seen in the light of linguistic and semiotic theory, but one which also tended to create its own rather rigid terminology.

One unfortunate side-effect of this development has been a tendency that has left the original quest into the relationship between film and linguistic theory overshadowed by a forbidding multitude of terminological and taxonomical systems. This problem immediately confronts us when we try to answer our relatively simple question of why one, more or all of Humphrey Jennings's films can be described as 'poetic'. Neither Metz's nor Eco's, nor any of the many other detailed explanations of codes existing in the world of film semiotics can provide the answer, for the simple reason that the question points specifically to *one* of the many possible relationships between film and linguistics whereas the systems in question profess to be all-embracing in this respect.

Because of this tendency towards rigid formalization inherent in the tradition of French film semiotics, it is perhaps necessary to chose another departure point for a closer examination of the concept of 'poetic film language'. Such a point can be found in the works of the Soviet semiotician Jurij Lotman, the most prominent representative of the so-called 'Tartu School' of literary theory in the Soviet Union.

Lotman is generally regarded as representing a continuation of the Russian formalist tradition of the 1920s as well as being influenced by Roman Jakobson and the Prague linguistic school of the 1930s. Lotman's main theoretical contributions can be found in *The Structure of the Artistic Text* (1970) and *Analysis of the Poetic Text* (1972).[3] He has also published a volume of writings on the semiotics of film, *Semiotics of Cinema* (1973).[4] However, it is interesting to note the paradox that, in this

---

[3]Jurij Lotman, *The Structure of the Artistic Text* (Ann Arbor, University of Michigan Press, 1977) and *Analysis of the Poetic Text* (Ann Arbor, Ardis, 1976).

[4]Jurij Lotman, *Semiotics of Cinema* (tr. M. Suino, Ann Arbor, University of Michigan Press, 1976).

context, his works on the artistic text and the poetic text seem to be more relevant than his writings about film.

As any attempt at giving a full description of Lotman's work in a few paragraphs would appear futile, we shall be content with a short presentation of his use of the concepts 'language' and 'code' in order to find a starting point for the discussion of three of Jennings's wartime documentaries.

'Every system whose end is to establish communication between two or more individuals may be defined as language'.[5] With this statement Lotman presents a rather wide definition of language which he immediately proceeds to specify by pointing out that the concept encompasses three categories: *natural languages* (e.g. Russian, French, English), *artificial languages* (the metalanguage of scientific descriptions) and *secondary languages* or *secondary modelling systems*. In this third category belong the 'artistic' languages of literature, visual art, music, etc. The importance of Lotman's use of this definition of language is that it indicates an infinite number of 'languages' that can easily be related to each other.

More important still, it permits the construction of a hierarchical system illustrating the relationship between such 'languages'. In this case the relevant 'languages' are 'literature' with its interdependent sub-categories 'poetry' and 'prose' and 'film' with the interdependent sub-categories 'fiction film' and 'documentary'. These sub-categories may be described as 'languages' belonging to the third category, that of 'secondary modelling systems', and may in turn contain other sub-categories of this kind (e.g. the various genres of fiction film or the *'cinema vérité'* concept of documentary).

Lotman handles the problematic concept of 'code' in an equally open manner when he uses it in connection with the many secondary modelling systems that constitute what he refers to as 'artistic language'. In natural languages, code is usually discussed and described in its synchronic aspect, with Lotman the concept also applies to the diachronic aspect of secondary modelling systems, often describing several synchronic cross-sections. A result of this is that it is possible to envision a virtually infinite number of codes pertaining to a work of art. However, he makes an important distinction between two types of relationship between sender and receiver in the communication of texts in the artistic language. The first type corresponds to the accepted use of codes in connection with natural languages and occurs where sender and receiver use a common code. The second type is characteristic of artistic language and implies a situation where the receiver deciphers by using a code different in kind from that of the sender. According to Lotman, this complex relationship involves the problem of correlating the artistic code of the author with the analytical code of the reader.

[5]Lotman, *Artistic Text*, p. 9.

Secondary modelling systems are manifested in texts. As for the concept of 'text', Lotman, as in his discussion of language and code, again tends to a wider definition, allowing, for instance, a group of homogeneous texts to be viewed as one text.

In the case of Humphrey Jennings this means that one can choose to view his entire filmic output as one text, with the analysis of the texts within that text (i.e. the individual films) contributing to the metalanguage utilized to analyse the larger textual entity.

Before applying some of Lotman's principles to a study of the 'poetic' quality of the Jennings films in question, one of Lotman's general statements on the nature of poetry should be taken into account. With reference to information theory, he asserts that one of the main characteristics of poetry is its paradoxical ability to convey an increased amount of information compared with non-poetical verbal texts. The paradox is that, in imposing the restrictions of poetic language on a verbal text (rhyme, metre, etc.), one finds that the number of meaningful elements in it acquires the capacity to grow.

Words for Battle – the verbal connection

Words for Battle was made in 1941. During eight minutes it presents seven texts read by Laurence Olivier, each text 'illustrated' by film segments. The texts are, in their order of appearance, excerpts from Camden's *Description of Britain*, Milton's *Areopagitica*, Blake's 'Jerusalem', Browning's 'Home Thoughts From the Sea', Kipling's 'The Beginnings', Churchill's famous speech of 4 June 1940 ('we shall fight on the beaches . . .') and finally Lincoln's Gettysburg Address. Three of the texts are excerpts from poems, the other four may be termed 'belletristic prose'. The poetic connotations in this film are quite obvious as it is fully possible to regard the film as a visual paraphrase of the texts. The editing takes great care in juxtaposing images to correspond with the text down to single-word level. This is done to such an extent that when a deviation from this principle occurs, it appears as a puzzling and irritating flaw. In the initial excerpt from Camden the principle is followed closely: the words '. . . The earth fertile with all kind of grain . . .' are juxtaposed with a long shot of a landscape of wheat fields; '. . . Abundant with pasture . . .' is illustrated with a long shot of landscape with cattle in the foreground. During this sequence a convention is so convincingly established that when the words '. . . beautified with many populous cities, fair boroughs, good towns and well-built villages' are read while the image of a landscape with a copse of trees (introduced to the words '. . . plentifully wooded . . .') lingers on the screen for a short time, it conveys the same feeling as encountering a halting rhyme in an otherwise well-crafted poem.

To further illustrate how this concept of editing corresponds with the accepted rules of verbal poetry, we can even present a case of what appears to be 'alliteration'.

In the Milton sequence, where the author's words 'Methinks I see a mighty and puissant nation rousing herself after sleep' are placed over an aerial view of an industrial landscape, the images take on the character of metaphor with the juxtaposition of the words 'Methinks I see her as an eagle mewing her mighty youth . . .' against shots of a Hurricane fighter and RAF pilots. The metaphoric treatment continues after a short transition ('While the whole noise of timorous and flocking birds' / aerial photo of moving evening clouds) with a direct reference to the Germans in which '. . . with those also that love the twilight' is placed directly over a sequence that starts with a shot of the German flag with the swastika, to be followed by shots taken from *Triumph of the Will* and German newsreels portraying the Nazi leaders. In a pan shot showing an assortment of prominent Nazis, we find this unique attempt at alliteration in film. At the end of the panning movement, we (and certainly the British audience at the time) immediately recognize the face of Joseph Goebbels, a fact that is underlined by an editing trick which makes the moment the pan reaches Goebbels' face coincide with the word '*gabble*' in Milton's '. . . and in their envious gabble . . .'

This technique of 'mickey-mouse-editing' to make images correspond at word level, is, interestingly enough, a technique taken up by some of the directors of today's music videos.

The technique is used consistently in the film, whether the texts are in rhymed verse, as in the Blake, Browning and Kipling sequences, or in prose. In the Blake sequence, built over two stanzas of the 'Jerusalem' poem from 'Milton', Jennings lets a steaming locomotive move across the screen in a low-angle shot to the words: 'Bring me my chariot of fire'. If the preceding sequence was metaphorical, the Blake sequence is predominantly metonymical, transferring Blake's hope of building

Jerusalem
In England's green and pleasant land

to the post-war British generation by letting the images convey the happiness of children evacuated to the countryside.

The introduction to Browning's poem underlines the dependence on the literary text: the opening shot is simply a close-up of the first lines of the poem, and this dependency is characteristic of the sequence as well as of the film as a whole. The images function either as visual paraphrase of the text or as a metaphor, as in the case of these lines from 'Home thoughts, from the Sea'

Sunset ran, one glorious blood-red, reeking into Cadiz Bay;

(Long shot, evening backlight, of convoy in the Mediterranean – from Jennings's 1939 film *SS Ionian*)

Bluish 'mid the burning water, full in face Trafalgar lay;

(Dissolve to transitional shot of ensign being raised, cut to medium shot of statue of Nelson on the words 'full in face Trafalgar lay')

In the dimmest North-east distance dawn'd Gibraltar grand and gray;

(Dissolve to pan shot of the Gibraltar harbour, cut to shot of Rock of Gibraltar.)

In the sequence with Kipling's 'The Beginings', the author's recurring line 'When the English began to hate' is enhanced with different images from the aftermath of German air raids on London.

The final sequences, with Churchill's and Lincoln's speeches, follow the set pattern, again with interesting attempts at attaining visual and aural coincidence down to single-word level. A low-angle shot of a soldier with a Sten gun looking out to sea is chosen to illustrate the words '. . . We shall defend our island, whatever the cost . . .' and Lincoln's words on government of the people by the people and for the people are actualized by placing them together with shots of the Lincoln statue in Parliament Square (in fact the only original footage shot for this film), drawing attention to the houses of Parliament as a background.

In *Words for Battle* we encounter a relatively simple and easily identifiable relation to verbal poetic language. If we want to use the concept 'poetic film language' here, we can relate it to the accepted form of verbal poetry. However, in order to proceed to a more general discussion, it is necessary at this point to sort out some of the theoretical concepts in question.

To illustrate the concept of 'languages' in connection with the relationship between film and literature, we can start with the following model:

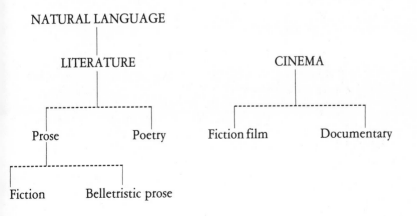

In this model a difference between literature and cinema as secondary languages becomes clearly visible. While literature as a secondary modelling system is directly related to a natural, or primary, language, no similar relationship can be said to exist in cinema. At the same time it is an undeniable fact that cinema language usually does enter into a relationship with natural language, as is the case with dialogue in fiction film and commentary in documentary, although there is no organic connection like the connection literature / natural language.

Another aspect of the model is that it proves to be unsatisfactory for comparative purposes when it comes to describe cinema and literature as secondary languages according to their sub-categories. Whereas 'prose' and 'poetry' may be described as respectively 'prose language' and 'poetic language', we find no such parallel in the two sub-categories of cinematic language.

If we proceed to make a further breakdown of potential sub-categories according to editing principles in film languages however, we arrive at a possible comparative level:

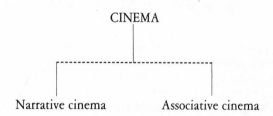

CINEMA

Narrative cinema   Associative cinema

These sub-categories can be applied to fiction film as well as documentary, their position in the hierarchy of filmic secondary languages depending on the context. If we relate this to the literary languages of prose and poetry, we find a systematic similarity that allows us to set up a general relationship:

PROSE FICTION / NARRATIVE CINEMA
POETRY / ASSOCIATIVE CINEMA.

With the first pair of categories, we find that they share a predominantly *syntagmatic* orientation, while the second pair can be described as predominantly *paradigmatic*.

Throughout *Words for Battle* the associative and paradigmatic quality of the film is obvious. The editing draws heavily on extra-textual codes in order to establish its discourse. In addition to this, there is also the connection to primary language through the paradigmatically oriented language of poetry.

The 'poetic language' to be discerned in this film relies heavily on the established conventions of the secondary modelling system of 'literary poetic language', or poetry. In this respect the relationship can be described as a hierarchical one, where the literary language is the predominant factor and the cinematic language is defined to a large extent with reference to the literary model.

This obvious attempt at transferring the concept 'poetry' from the realm of literature over into the filmic was immediately recognized, and apparently also immediately disliked.

Words for Battle was summarily and rather testily reviewed in the May 1941 issue of the *Documentary Newsletter*. The anonymous reviewer did not appear to think very highly of the literary texts Jennings had chosen to work with, and found the use of Handel's 'Water Music' for the ending ludicrous:

> *Words for Battle* is an illustrated lanternslide lecture, with Olivier's curate-like voice reverently intoning various extracts from poetry, verse and topical political speeches. That tough old republican revolutionary, Milton, rubs shoulders with minor Browning . . . and lesser Kipling. Winston Churchill with his 'fight on the beaches' is elbowed out of the final pay-off by Lincoln in Gettysburg war-aims vein. . . .

The next mention of the film that we find in the *Documentary Newsletter* is even more critical. In an otherwise very positive review of *Fires Were Started* as the 'Film of the Month' in DNL 4/1943 some 'bad faults' are pointed out:

> But Jennings must be held entirely to blame for the three or four occasions when, with somebody playing the piano or reading or reciting poetry (in his worst *Words for Battle* manner) he goes all arty for a moment. . . .

Although the overall evaluation of Jennings as a filmmaker has changed over the years, this attitude is echoed in Dai Vaughan's book on Stewart McAllister, *Portrait of an Invisible Man*:

> *Words for Battle* is generally considered the first of the canonical Jennings movies; but I must confess I have never much liked it. It is not the patriotism itself which worries me, but rather the feeling that it goes out of its way to choose its texts from the repertoire of the popular classics: a whiff of the Palgraves. . . . *Words for Battle* is a film which works better in the head than on the screen.[6]

Vaughan's objections to the film seem mainly to be based on the fact that the choice of texts leaves very little scope for visual manœuvre and that the film therefore becomes a prisoner of the strict verbal impositions of the chosen texts. I find it hard to share these objections since Jennings's

[6]Dai Vaughan, *Portrait of an Invisible Man* (London, British Film Institute, 1983), p. 74.

defined purpose with the film was to let the verbal text take prominence, subordinating the cinematic treatment to the established code of verbal poetic language. By doing this he actually succeeds in enhancing the imagery in some of the texts (e.g. the Browning sequence), while in other cases the visual commentary on the texts represents a reinterpretation based on a transference over time. In *Words for Battle*, poetic film language can be seen as an *extension* of poetic verbal language.

Listen to Britain – the language of non-verbal poetry

The final sequence in *Words for Battle* is markedly different from the rest of the film. As Lincoln's words on democratic leadership fade out, or rather, are drowned by the sound of military vehicles passing his statue in Parliament Square, a transition is made and the last 30 seconds of the film clearly move into another idiom.

The natural sounds represented by the clatter of tanks through London streets dissolve into the final movement of one of Handel's 'Water Music' suites (the film is introduced by the overture). Jim Hillier, in his excellent study of Jennings in *Studies in Documentary*, describes this last sequence:

> The film becomes wordless, and the final images follow the faces of ordinary men and women, in and out of uniform, while the music and noise reach their climax. The values and the greatness implicit in the quotations is transferred to the ordinary people who represent continuity with the past and are both the source and embodiment of its values. The effect is irresistible.[7]

This sequence of *Words for Battle* heralds the cinematic principle that Jennings's next film, *Listen to Britain*, co-directed with Stewart McAllister, is based on. Doing away completely with commentary, the film seems to place itself diametrically opposite its predecessor.

And yet the two films have one general principle in common – the presentation of material in one medium and the elaboration of it in another. In *Words for Battle* the material is presented in the form of poetry or belletristic prose and then treated in images made to relate to the verbal message; in *Listen to Britain* the starting point is non-verbal sound consisting of realistic sound-effects and music. The musical pieces presented do in some cases contain words, as in the text of the songs heard in some of the sequences, but the words here are clearly subordinated to the music.

While Jennings's first attempt at expanding the documentary form was met with mixed emotions, *Listen to Britain* was immediately recognized as the remarkable work of art it is, and today it is generally regarded as Jennings's finest achievement. This praise has often come at the expense of

---

[7] Jim Hillier, 'Humphrey Jennings' in Alan Lovell and Jim Hillier, *Studies in Documentary* (London, Secker & Warburg, 1972), p. 85.

co-director and editor Stewart McAllister; it is to be hoped that Dai Vaughan's book on McAllister will correct this injustice.

So unusual was this Jennings/McAllister experiment with documentary form in 1942 that when the film was made ready for release, it was decided to furnish it (apparently with an American audience in mind) with an explanatory 'foreword' by Leonard Brockington that looks and feels like a clumsy intrusion on the film's style. Through a rather misguided sense of respect for the original, Brockington's introductory address is still retained in circulation prints of the film today.

The formal quality characteristic of *Listen to Britain* is to a large extent to be attributed to the way the film is edited, but it is also interesting to draw some attention to the dramatic structure of the film. Like the 'City Symphonies' of Ruttmann and Cavalcanti, it is organized around a 24-hour time cycle, a fact that is not immediately conspicuous, mainly because its chosen cycle departs from the morning-to-night pattern set by this type of pre-Griersonian documentary and instead offers an afternoon-to-next-afternoon structure. This makes the development of the film less predictable, something that again helps the viewer to focus on its many interesting transitions.

And it is mainly through these transitions that the film has made its name in film history. Its trademarks, according to most textbooks, are the sound overlaps and the instances where sound precedes the image, thus making sound the determining factor in the relationship between sound and image.

When trying to specify the way Jennings and McAllister's film language in *Listen to Britain* is 'poetic', it seems necessary to operate with another kind of definition of this concept than that applied to *Words for Battle*, where the model of verbal poetry is so deceptively close at hand. In using a word like 'poetic', we have already borrowed a concept that by definition belongs to the language of literature, and this loan, when transferred to the language of cinema, must therefore hint at a structural similarity.

Which leads us back to the pair of correlations mentioned above:

PROSE FICTION/NARRATIVE CINEMA
POETRY/ASSOCIATIVE CINEMA

There can hardly be any objection to describing the editing principles of *Listen to Britain* as 'associative', the absence of narrative editing being one of the foremost characteristics of the film. So, based on general structural principles, the term 'poetic' may be applied to this category of film language. In the case of *Listen to Britain* we shall pursue this principle from a general down to a more detailed level.

The juxtaposition of images and sounds follows a complicated pattern in this film, where one of the characteristic transitional agents is to let sound predetermine the context in which to place the image. This is often done by playing with the conventions accepted by the viewer, as in the scene from the Blackpool ballroom.

Here dance music is faded in on a scene from the beach – so far there is nothing in the scenery to suggest the source of the music, at this point it might as well be another example of the nondescript background music so often used in 'wordless' documentaries. As the music increases in volume, there is a medium close-up of servicemen in helmets, overlooking the ocean; from this shot there is a cut to a poster announcing 'Members of HM Forces in Uniform 1/2 Price' and an increase in the music level before we cut to a long shot inside a ballroom, when the music goes up to full volume and turns out to be from the orchestra in the ballroom.

After an establishing shot from the dance floor, a cut is made to what at first sight appears to be traditional 'cutaways', medium shots of young people enjoying themselves at a table. But these cutaways take on a life of their own when realistic sound is introduced over the music, conveying snatches of their conversation. After this there is a cut to a wide-angle shot of the dancing floor; this shot is the longest in the sequence and allows a large number of pairs to pass into and out of the frame seen from a camera viewpoint that permits the viewer to see the persons on the floor as individuals. During this shot the orchestra breaks into 'Roll Out the Barrel' and we hear and see the dancers 'joining' with the orchestra by singing the words.

After this shot, the transition is again made to the two servicemen in helmets down by the beach, and the sound of the orchestra is faded down to the same level as it had been in the previous identical shot. After a short while the image then fades out, as if to underline the character of a self-contained story in this sequence.

If we look closer at this sequence, we find some interesting and maybe unsuspected similarities with the technique utilized in *Words for Battle*. Instead of having a piece of verbal text as departure point and reference for the images and their transition, we find in this sequence that a piece of ballroom music has the same function. The sequence starts with a music fade-in and ends with a music fade-out and the music is heard during the entire sequence. In this respect it can be compared to the function of the literary texts of *Words for Battle*. In other words, we also find here the principle of taking an established 'text', in this case a manifestation of the vast and complicated secondary language of music, reinterpreting it in cinematic terms, and imposing a new meaning on it by the juxtapositioning of images.

The structure of the sequece, with its initial and final shots of servicemen on duty watching over the ocean at night, makes it clear that this is more than just a statement of 'in spite of all difficulties – life goes on'. When we return to the two soldiers on the beach, with the music sounding vaguely in the background, we have become more acutely aware of their function as sentinels on guard against the dangers represented somewhere out there on the ocean. The contrast between the ballroom music and the sombre mood of the nighttime seashore, a contrast which in the beginning seemed puzzling, has taken on a significant quality.

And here we have arrived at one of Lotman's central theses on poetry as an artistic language: the special ability of poetry to contain and convey an amount of information that seems to be disproportionately at odds with the formal limitations it constrains itself to accept. Lotman makes this statement on the nature of poetry:

> 1 Any element on the *parole* level can be elevated to the rank of meaningful elements.
> 2 Any formal element appearing in the language may in poetry acquire a semantic character thereby obtaining supplementary meanings.
>
> Thus, certain supplementary restrictions imposed on the text compel us to perceive it as poetry. As soon as one assigns a given text to the category of poetry, the number of meaningful elements in it acquires the capacity to grow.[8]

And it is exactly this 'growth of meaningful elements' that the elaborate manipulation of music, sounds and images by Jennings and McAllister manages to attain in *Listen to Britain*. The structural elements of the Blackpool dance hall sequence is repeated throughout the film, in each case opening up interpretations that reach far beyond the immediate meaning brought about by the sounds and images presented.

If we can draw a parallel with the 'poetic film' devices in *Words for Battle* on this general structural level, there are also some interesting parallels to be drawn in the way filmic language relates to the other, predominant, secondary language. In *Words for Battle* this was verbal poetry, in *Listen to Britain* it is music, and here we find an adaptation of the filmic language to the conventions of the predominant musical language not unlike the cited attempts at finding filmic parallels to poetic conventions, as with the example of 'alliteration' in the Milton sequence in *Words for Battle*.

In *Listen to Britain* the most prevalent element of this kind is editing according to the rhythm of music, already then known as 'mickey-mouse-editing' after the technique had been introduced in Disney's 'Silly Symphonies' cartoons. Musical rhythm has always been an ideal in film editing, with a tradition going back to the silent films. A similar effect is also attained by synchronizing images and music with the same inherent quality, as in the introduction to the 'Calling All Workers' sequence, where the shots of traffic match the urgency conveyed by the music. In the same sequence Jennings and McAllister synchronize the rhythm of the machines with the song 'Yes My Darling Daughter' while the female workers in the factory join the refrain and synchronize *their* movements with the rhythm of the song.

[8]Lotman, *Poetic Text*, p. 33.

These techniques were, however, hardly new to film audiences at the time, although the persistent use of this kind of editing made the film stand apart. The film does present an innovation in this field, where the musical concept of *harmony* is brought over into the filmic idiom. After the sequence where the comedians Flanagan and Allen entertain in a factory canteen at lunchtime, a transition is made to the National Gallery and a lunchtime performance of a Mozart piano concerto by Myra Hess with the Queen present.

The transition is effected by joining two identical chords, a final chord from Flanagan and Allen and one of the opening chords of Mozart's G-major concerto KV 453 and cutting on this chord. The effect is stunning. Through this ingenious trick the directors join high and low culture aurally and visually, an intersection is created in which all of the themes pertinent to the film meet and we seem to experience a moment of what can almost be characterized as 'information overflow'.

If concentration of information is a hallmark of poetic language, this transition can undoubtedly be characterized as 'poetic'.

Diary for Timothy – a synthesis and the problem of the 'poetic image'

In the preceding pages I have tried to show that *Words for Battle* and *Listen to Britain* share some important structural characteristics. Yet it is quite obvious that these two films also represent two extremes when it comes to the question of the relationship with verbal language, the 'poetry' in *Words for Battle* being completely bound to verbal discourse through its juxtaposition of images and texts in poetic and belletristic language, while the most conspicuous formal trait of *Listen to Britain* is the complete absence of such a relationship.

These separate characteristics come together in Jennings's final war film, *Diary for Timothy*, made during the last year of the war and dealing with this period.

It differs from the two earlier films mainly in its extremely complex narrative structure, which is a far cry from the simple associative devices employed by Jenning and McAllister in the earlier films. *Diary for Timothy* presents four parallel stories involving a farmer, a railway engineer, a hospitalized RAF pilot and a Welsh miner, and to bind these stories together there is the baby Timothy, born on 3 September 1944. This complex narrative necessitates yet another element, in the shape of a commentary written by E.M. Forster and read by Michael Redgrave.

The commentary is couched in the rhetorically rich, lofty prose of the kind I have referred to earlier as 'belletristic' and its main function is to make the various shifts between the parallel stories intelligible.

In spite of this very marked difference, we find many of the elements of the two other films present in *Diary for Timothy*. Jennings utilizes the *Words for Battle* technique of visually paraphrasing verbal text on several occasions and in doing this adds a *seventh*, associative, level to the six narrative levels already mentioned. When the commentary runs: 'For five years, Tim, we have had the blackout, but this evening for the first time we have only to dim the streets . . .' the images accompanying the words do not belong to any of the five established narratives, but are stock shots showing men outside St Paul's with dark lanterns and lamp-lighters lighting a street lamp.

In another instance he plays with images at word level during a sequence which illustrates the effect of V 2 rockets on the war-weary British by inter-cutting between John Gielgud as Hamlet in the graveyard scene and workers in a canteen, discussing the V 2. In a medium shot one of the workers uses a salt cellar and a mustard pot to illustrate the danger: 'Well, if this is the launching site, and that's the objective . . . it travels at 3000 miles an hour. How long does it take to reach the objective?' At this question, Jennings cuts to the theatre performance and Hamlet's answer: 'Nay, I know not' as he stands with Yorick's skull in his hand. This interplay is enlarged as Hamlet's monologue on Yorick is intercut with a V 2 explosion sending the workers in the canteen for cover under the table.

As for 'musical effects' in the style of *Listen to Britain*, we find several sequences utilizing these. In one instance Chopin's 'Polonaise Militaire' is used as the aural background for a montage signifying the optimism which the many victory communiques of the new year (1945) evoked. Unlike *Listen to Britain* this film also contains original music (written by Richard Addinsell) with an easily recognizable theme presented at the beginning. In a sequence near the end, where we watch the young RAF pilot doing leg exercises in the hospital, we find that music and movement have been synchronized to the theme music.

Both forms come together in the most evocative sequence of the film, relating to the debacle at Arnhem in 1944. In this sequence Myra Hess again is chosen to represent the ideals of music, with a National Gallery performance of Beethoven's 'Appassionata' sonata.

The sequence is introduced by a bugle call and a shot of the newspaper headline 'ARNHEM'. The soundtrack now occupies the centre of interest, presenting a BBC report about the hardships which the British airborne forces underwent during this disastrous operation. Interest is focused on the words with the help of a montage showing wireless receivers and listening people. During the following words in the radio despatch, music is introduced – first at low level, then gradually increasing:

For the last three days they had no water, very little but small-arms ammunition, and rations cut to one-sixth.
Luckily or unluckily it rained, and they caught the water in their capes and drank that. These last items were never mentioned: they were Airborne, weren't they; they were tough and knew it. All right: water and rations didn't matter – give them some Germans to kill, and one chance in ten, and they'd get along somehow.

At 'water and rations' the *pianissimo* bars of the first movement of the 'Appassionata' sonata are faintly heard, and at the end of the sentence there is a cut to a close-up of the hands of Myra Hess playing the first *forte* chords of the movement. The camera then tracks back to a long shot of Dame Myra at the piano. What follows is a sequence of shots very much similar to those of the Mozart concerto in *Listen to Britain*.

But instead of letting the music and images create their own associations, some of the words from the previous sequence are now repeated on the soundtrack over the music: '. . . luckily or unluckily it rained . . .', forcing the attention of the viewer back to the plight of the airborne soldiers. This is emphasized by a cut to shots of rain falling on the surface of a water tank in a city street. While the 'Appassionata' continues in the background of the soundtrack, the commentary uses this shift in images as a transition to a further step in the narrative: 'It's in the middle of October now and the war certainly won't be over by Christmas, and the weather doesn't suit us. . . .'

From there, commentary and images go on, still over the 'Appassionata', to the theme of war damages before returning to Myra Hess, and only during this last meeting with the music does the director fall prey to the temptation of overemphasizing a point. Referring to the music, the commentary runs: 'Did you like the music that lady was playing? Some of us think it is the greatest music in the world, yet it's German music and we're fighting the Germans. There's something we'll have to think over later on . . .' and then the music fades out.

The complexity of this sequence is characteristic of the whole film with its interplay between several levels of meaning in sound and images, and we find the principles of 'poetic film language' demonstrated in *Words for Battle* and *Listen to Britain* clearly present.

In addition to perfecting and integrating the earlier experiments, *Diary for Timothy* points to an additional 'poetic' angle, to be touched on only briefly here: that of the 'poetic image'. In the earlier films the emphasis was placed on the editing process through the juxtaposition of images that to a large extent were chosen from pre-shot material. In *Diary for Timothy* there were more possibilities of premeditated photography, allowing for deliberate formal compositions within the frame. This allows for an extra formal agent – the *mise-en-scene* element, or what Eisenstein more specifically describes as *mise-en-cadre*, 'montage within the frame'.

One such example of 'poetic imagery' in the film can be found in the Christmas sequence, where the pessimism and the autumnal feeling are reinforced by several visual and aural references to the situation. ('Death and darkness, death and fog, death across those few miles of water' / Shots of freezing men, foggy landscape, the engineer on his locomotive driving through wet darkness.) Then, the pervading feeling changes completely on the words: '. . . until out of the fog, dawned loveliness, whiteness, Christmas Day . . .' From a beautifully composed close-up of frost-covered grass, the camera pans slowly over a frosty landscape while a boy's treble voice intones a Christmas carol. The effect is the same as of elaborate montage, the difference is that the montage is done completely *within* the shot.

The interesting problems that arise in connection with the concept 'poetic image' are outside of the chosen scope of the present article, but it is worth drawing attention to a comment by Charles Madge on Jennings's use of the word 'image' because it also in a sense sums up the nature of the 'poetic' film language which distinguishes Jennings's work:

> It is not only verbal, or visual, or emotional, although it is all these. It is not in the elements, but in their coming together at a particular moment, that the magical potency lies.[9]

[9]Charles Madge, 'A Note on Images' in Mary-Lou Jennings, ed., *Humphrey Jennings: Film-maker, Painter, Poet* (London, British Film Institute, 1982), p. 47.

Note

John Grierson first used the word 'documentary' in 1926 to describe Robert Flaherty's film *Moana*. He later defined the term as, 'the creative treatment of actuality'. He made many documentary films sponsored by the Empire Marketing Board and the GPO, his most famous being *Drifters*. Paul Rotha met Grierson at the EMB and worked with him briefly before making his own sponsored documentary films. He moved to head the BBC Television Documentary Department in 1953. The Department broke up in 1955 and Rotha left television. Duncan Ross, the world's first 'Documentary Writer and Script Supervisor', had previously worked with Rotha. Robert Barr, former Fleet Street journalist, produced the first television documentary, *Germany Under Control*, on 16th September 1946, and was for some time Acting Head of the Documentary Unit before Rotha's appointment. Grace Wyndham Goldie was one of the most influential figures in current affairs until her retirement in 1970. She was involved with the television service as a correspondent for *The Listener* since 1936, and became a producer in 1948. Her book, *Facing the Nation: Television and Politics 1936-76* (London, Bodley Head, 1977) is an authoritative guide to the development of factual television.

The BBC Written Archives Centre at Caversham, Reading contains a great number of documents relating to the development of broadcasting, including lists of programmes, scripts, memos, short articles intended for internal circulation, and other contemporary material. It is not possible to view television programmes of this period as they were transmitted 'live', although the BBC has kept a small number of filmed inserts, and the British Film Institute has some complete programmes dating from the mid-1950s.

4

The Origins of British Television Documentary: The BBC 1946–1955

Elaine Bell

In an article on the documentary in television published in *The BBC Quarterly* in 1950, four years after the post-war reopening of the television service, Duncan Ross wrote,

> In 20 years the word 'documentary' has spread all over the world to describe almost all films of social significance. . . . The word has now overflowed its original intention and is often applied to radio programmes, books, articles, and paintings. Indeed, it has been so tortured and transformed even within the limits of cinema that, at times, it must be a wise Grierson who knows his own child. It is, however, perfectly at home in television. Indeed, so many opportunities occur in television for 'the creative interpretation of reality' through the visual image that Flaherty himself has said that the eventual future of documentary lies there.[1]

What forms did 'the creative interpretation of reality' take in television's first formative 10 years, and why? How much was television documentary influenced by the already developed film and radio forms, and how much was innovative? By whom, and for whom, were programmes made and what were they trying to achieve? In order to address these questions, it is first necessary to place documentary output within its institutional context.

The development of television within the BBC

As early as 1934, the Selsdon Committee was formed to consider the development of television. There were certain difficulties in connection with television's introduction; not only were the obvious questions of mode of finance and nature of control to be settled, there were in addition two competing systems, Baird and EMI, whose technical merits needed to

[1]Duncan Ross, 'The Documentary in Television', *The BBC Quarterly*, Vol. V, No. 1, (1950), pp. 19–20.

be tested. Selsdon decided that both systems should be developed until one or other had proved itself satisfactory, that the BBC and the Treasury should share the cost of development out of their respective shares of the licence fee and, in view of the close relationship anticipated between sound and television broadcasting, that the BBC's monopoly should be preserved. The BBC now had a mandate to develop a new form of mass communication. The response of its senior officials could hardly have been more indifferent – television was seen as of very little significance. Although this was later to have unfortunate consequences, Grace Wyndham Goldie recalls that, 'in these first years, though few of them realized it, the handful of men and women working in television programmes were fortunate in that they were almost completely ignored; by the public, by politicians and by the BBC itself. . . . The development of television seemed of negligible importance. So, with few people interested and practically no-one watching, television producers were free during those first years to experiment with programmes and to discover what the possibilities and limitations of the new medium actually were.'[2] These first experiments took place in Alexandra Palace, a huge, shabby and remote Victorian edifice chosen by the BBC mainly for its height above sea level rather than for its proximity to the centre of London, Broadcasting House and BBC administration. The television staff's sense of isolation was compounded by the way in which they were regarded by their colleagues in sound broadcasting – as wasting their time on a passing fad. The BBC's autocratic founder, Lord Reith, does not even mention the inauguration of the world's first television service in November 1936 in his autobiography, although his resignation from the post of Director-General was still two years away.

Although by 1939 there were only 20,000 television sets in private use with an estimated audience of 100,000 people concentrated within a 40-mile radius around London, sales of sets were increasing rapidly, and television did most of what it has continued to do ever since. However, there was a very heavy emphasis on drama, very little current affairs content, and no news. A typical night's viewing might be a play transmitted live, a newsreel, and a Disney cartoon, filling the hours between 8.30 and 10.00 p.m. A high proportion of production staff came from the theatre and film worlds. Goldie notes that at Alexandra Palace those staff moving from sound broadcasting were regarded as inexperienced amateurs who made word-based programmes which did not transfer well to a visual medium. The development of electronic, as opposed to film, cameras made it possible to show events as they happened. Outside Broadcasts (OBs) began to show 'live' sporting events, and even a rare glimpse, if not of a debated political issue, at any rate of a politician, when Chamberlain's return from Munich was broadcast. Politics and current affairs barely

---

[2]Grace Wyndham Goldie, *Facing the Nation: Television and Politics 1936-76*, (London, Bodley Head, 1977), pp. 28, 32.

impinged upon total television output, and insofar as the latter type of programme was virtually a radio talk with illustrations, very little innovation in factual television was achieved.

By 1939 television had established itself as a moderate success. The inefficient Baird system had been dropped in favour of the EMI system, popularity was growing rapidly, and the standard of programmes, 'had gone up at least 100 per cent in quality and entertainment value'.[3] However, its range of transmission was still so restricted that it was a luxury for a minority, and the BBC felt able to close it down on the outbreak of war. And yet the way in which this was done demonstrated, if not disdain, at the very least a lack of appreciation of the television staff. Cecil Madden, who produced the first television programme in August 1936, recalls that when the power was turned off halfway through a Mickey Mouse cartoon, 'Broadcasting House didn't even have the courtesy to tell us that we were being faded out, and we weren't even allowed the time to send an announcer to say goodbye. They simply turned the switches off.'[4]

In 1943 the coalition government set up a committee under Lord Hankey to prepare for the reinstatement and redevelopment of television after the war. The Report received very little attention, not surprisingly since so few people had ever seen a television programme or had any idea of what a television service could provide. The most exciting postwar development was generally felt to be the offering of a greater choice of radio programmes with the ending of a single programme system and its replacement by the Home, Light and Third Programmes. Nevertheless, the television service was resumed in hopeful mood on 7 June 1946, the day before the Victory Parade which all of the few people with a television set would want to watch and which was such a perfect subject for television's Outside Broadcast cameras. The new service immediately faced two interrelated obstacles. The first was the organizational structure of the BBC itself. The second was the continuation of that dismissive attitude of the BBC administration towards television which was so prevalent before the shutdown.

A detailed examination of the structure of the BBC during this period is beyond the scope of this article, and is exhaustively undertaken by Asa Briggs in the fourth volume of his history of the development of broadcasting in the United Kingdom.[5] However, the following feature of the organizational structure of the BBC has relevance for the context within which the Documentary Unit worked. The separation of the functions of the planning and production processes had a long history within the BBC when Reith split matters of Administration from Output. After the war, the terminology changed to Supply (the production process, including the

[3]John Swift, *Adventure in Vision*, (London, Lehmann, 1950), p. 104.
[4]Cecil Madden, Interview with Denis Johnston, BBC Radio 2, (5 October 1982).
[5]Asa Briggs, *Sound and Vision. The History of Broadcasting in the United Kingdom*, (Oxford, OUP, 1979).

various departments providing programmes) and Output (the planning process, including the commissioning and funding of programmes) but with equally unfortunate consequences. In theory, since both sections were of equal rank, 'creative' staff could devote their entire attention to the business of programme-making, freed from the burden of administrative detail. In practice, the tendency becomes one of increasing conservatism and fear of risk-taking on the part of producers and Heads of Department, because since Output controls editorial and funding functions, it no longer exists to serve Supply but to act as a purchaser of the products of competing Supply departments. The producers of programmes become concerned to defend or advance their own department's share of the schedules drawn up by Output, the most obvious way being to repeat the same type of programme which has already proved itself acceptable.

The television service was perhaps slightly less affected than was sound broadcasting, because before the advent of commercial television in 1955 the service had a relatively strong sense of internal solidarity. Internal com-petition between different supply departments was certainly present (there was some rivalry between Drama and Documentary, for example, and the latter was at one time in danger of being annexed by an empire-building Talks Department) but the television service's main battle was with the BBC itself. After 1955, the BBC's television service was of necessity more concerned with the competition from an alternative system of broadcasting than with its own alternative services. However, the bargaining process was essentially the same. Domination by a few of the more powerful depart-ments, and avoidance of experimentation, were only avoided insofar as there was a widespread commitment to an ethos of fair shares and fair play in which small groups like the Documentary Unit, making programmes with no obvious counterpart in other media, were allowed to develop. Television's dominance over radio, as far as BBC administrators were con-cerned, was still a decade away. When it became the acknowledged leader, the divisive consequences of separating management and production became apparent once more.

The second obstacle for the new service was television's lowly placement in the management hierarchy, a situation brought about directly by the Director-General, William Haley. It was not until television achieved full departmental status as a Service under a Controller, late in 1950, that it gained a separate seat on the Board of Manangement. From 1948 until then, the whole of 'Home Output' (the three radio Programmes, Regions, Entertainment and Television) had separate Heads, but a single Director with direct access to Haley. He was Basil Nicolls, a man who had been in the Corporation from the very beginning and 'who knew more about the BBC hierarchy than anyone else and did more than anyone else to perpetuate it.'[6] It must have been evident that the television service was growing rapidly – from 456 to 677 staff in two years, and from 14,560

[6]Briggs, *Sound and Vision*, p. 133.

combined licences for sound and television in 1947 to 45,564 in a single year.[7] Yet Maurice Gorham, Head of the Television Service, still had to refer such minor matters as the appointment of additional cameramen and announcers to Nicolls. While trying to make the newly resumed television service thrive in the face of massive difficulties, Gorham (at least initially) dealt directly with William Haley, the Director-General, or his deputy. Haley's backward-looking reorganization effectively demoted television, and prompted Gorham's resignation.

The failure of the BBC to give more autonomy to its television service, a situation heavily criticized by the 1951 Beveridge Report, was to be a stimulus to the introduction of commercial television. Meanwhile it was left to two highly influential staff replacements, Norman Collins as Head of the Television Service and Cecil McGivern as Television Programme Director, to defend television's interests – a move Goldie likened to that of appointing a couple of generals to crush a rebellion, only to find that they promptly joined the rebels.[8] McGivern's appointment was a particularly fortunate one for the television service as a whole and the Documentary Unit in particular. Documentary was his particular interest, and he had been a highly acclaimed radio Features producer. Norman Swallow was not the only member of the Unit to feel that:

> I think the Documentary Unit survived and flourished because of Cecil McGivern. Being a radio Features, i.e. documentary man, he therefore supported those of us who were making documentaries, and I would say historically that he was the right man in the right place at the right time. . . . The fact is that the situation in which we are working now is a situation which he primarily developed, and if British television is the best in the world, or the least worst, or whatever people say, I think it's largely due to him.[9]

McGivern remained at the BBC during this period; Norman Collins's stay was briefer. He resigned when Haley appointed George Barnes, ex-Controller of the Third Programme and ex-Director of the Spoken Word (this pompously titled post involved Barnes in everything relating to politics, current affairs and policy matters as far as television was concerned) to be the new Director of the Television Service. Collins felt, with good reason, that Barnes was a sound broadcaster to the core and a better appointment would have been that of an experienced television enthusiast such as himself. He let it be known on his resignation that the BBC was stifling the development of television, which he foresaw would shortly eclipse sound broadcasting, and that he would be prepared to take a leading role in breaking its monopoly. He promptly did this, and went on

[7]BBC Annual Report (1955–6).
[8]Goldie, *Facing the Nation*, p. 49.
[9]Norman Swallow, from interview with author, (July, 1979).

to become perhaps the single most influential proponent of commerical television. In this extract from a recorded interview, he explicates the BBC's attitude to its television service when he was its Head.

> The BBC had established itself without any question as the major sound broadcasting organization in the world, not by as much as the BBC liked to pretend, because CBS and NBC in the States produced some very remarkable sound broadcasting on their own account, but everything was running very smoothly until this thing called television came along. We were headline news practically every day, and that irritated the old BBC staff. They hated that this newcomer was getting all the publicity, but those in Alexandra Palace were saying, yes, but the BBC is getting all the money. So there was bitter resentment on the financial side. Then the resentment on a slightly deeper level went this way. If a documentary was done on television, it would undoubtedly get a paragraph, possibly half-column, in all the papers, whereas a BBC sound producer who had been over the years producing the same sort of documentary, quite likely far better ones, simply didn't get any memtion in the paper at all, so it wasn't merely a question of injured pride, it was saying well really television now is distorting the serious purpose of the BBC.[10]

This, then, was the institutional context within which Documentary produced its programmes – as a small part of an isolated and under-funded service regarded with at best indifference and at worst suspicion and hostility by the senior members of a broadcasting monopoly firmly rooted in the traditions of sound broadcasting. Yet despite this, it developed a number of new documentary forms which much of today's documentary output unwittingly trades on, and which in 1945 was being described as, 'television's most important contribution to serious entertainment. . . . No doubt about it . . . the documentary must be regarded as television's *only* original feature.'[11]

The beginnings of television documentary

Paul Rotha was appointed Head of Documentaries in 1953, in recognition of the fact that documentary output was sufficiently successful to justify the appointment of someone with an international reputation. It was not a happy time for Rotha or the Documentary Department (as it became on Rotha's appointment). Grierson had already turned the post down because he did not want it on a full-time basis; the staff wanted Robert Barr, the Acting Head, but he refused to accept the post on the grounds that if McGivern had been happy with the way in which the Unit was already

[10]Norman Collins, from interview with author (March, 1980).
[11]Quoted in Arther Swinson, *Writing for Television* (London, Black, 1955), p. 86.

being run he would not have felt it necessary to appoint a Head. Once in post, Rotha was continually frustrated by the endless committee meetings and especially by the restrictions placed on the use of film in making programmes. However, from the point of view of a film historian and critic as well as a film producer of long standing, he saw the potential application of the spirit of documentary to television. He wrote:

> ephemeral as a one-night stand television may be, but to counteract its sudden birth-and-death is its fantastic simultaneous access to a mass audience under conditions wholly different from the movie in the cinema. This is something to reckon with; it is already causing deep thinking on the part of those of us in the creative world who cling to a sense of social responsibility towards those we serve. To those who still believe that documentary has a specific social job to do, this mass access to audiences and quick answer is of paramount importance. It is something new in the documentary experience.[12]

Duncan Ross also attached great importance to the role that television documentary should play in post-war society; he told McGivern that, 'we want Documentary to have more social conscience than any part of the Documentary Movement since the war.'[13]

Those television documentary practitioners like Rotha and Ross who had come from the film world were probably more likely to see television documentary as carrying on the tradition begun by Flaherty and Grierson than those whose background was the theatre (Steve McCormack), journalism (Robert Barr, Norman Swallow), education (Caryl Doncaster) and radio features (Denis Mitchell). However, all Unit members had seen documentary films, were enthusiastic about their integral social conscience, and assumed that television could – or must – perform a similar role, while recognizing that practical limitations demanded the development of new techniques. In order to examine how the members of the Documentary Unit used the unprecedented opportunity provided by this 'fantastic simultaneous access to a mass audience', it is first necessary to examine some of the assumptions underlying what was seen as the legitimate realm of the television documentary.

Paddy Scannell argues that television saw itself in this period as 'projecting and affirming a corporate national life' by conveying a 'panorama of actualities' from the outside world into the home in an unmediated and unproblematic way, while at the same time showing considerable reluctance to engage in controversy, comment and debate. The particular way in which 'the political' and 'the social' were then defined as areas for television to explore, or rather as responsibilities to discharge, had

---

[12]Paul Rotha, *Television and the Future of Documentary*, unpublished internal memo (29 October, 1954).
[13]Ross to McGivern, (17 October, 1951).

consequences central to the way in which the Talks and the Documentary Departments saw their roles, and so for the nature of the programmes they produced:

> Within the Talks Department there developed a new kind of programme (later labelled 'current affairs') to handle political issues. Separate from this was the emergence of new documentary modes to handle social issues. The 'political subject' can be taken in broadcasting to mean 'of or pertaining to the affairs of governments, the major parties, or individual politicians'. Thus a political programme is one that has politicians appearing in it, or that examines political (i.e. party) issues, or the activities of governments. By contrast, the 'social subject' in broadcasting deals with issues of general social concern (housing, unemployment, delinquency, old age, etc.), with the 'problems' of contemporary society. . . . The social precludes the political – i.e. it cannot be subject to political analysis. If it were, it would become a political subject, and its mode of treatment would be quite different, for these are quite separate and distinct territories. To be more exact, the political subject is structured as an accommodation to the concerns of those in political authority; whereas the social subject is structured from *our* point of view (i.e. the audience), and our concerns with current problem areas in our society.[14]

Material from the BBC Written Archives Centre, together with interviews recently carried out with most producers then working in television documentary, bear out this analysis. Most producers, including Norman Swallow, the talented and principled producer of *Special Enquiry* who was regarded as the most overtly left-wing by the other producers in the Unit, did indeed consciously distance themselves from 'the political' to the extent of denying the *general* political implication of their work, while seeking a form of words to express that very point.

Caryl Doncaster observed that, 'we all seemed left-wing at the time, but that was simply because we all believed in the Welfare State, which was the big left issue then.'[15] Support within the Unit for the new interventionism was based far more on humanitarian notions of social justice than on an explicit political allegiance. Steve McCormack, producer of the magazine programmes *About Britain* and *London Town*, recalled,

> we really were interested in London, and how to present the variety, the endless variety, of London to the viewers. We had no political axe to grind. We didn't give a damn about anything. But we were fascinated by what we were doing. . . . John Grierson said to me, 'when we made

---

[14]Paddy Scannell, 'The Social Eye of Television 1946–55', *Media, Culture and Society*, Vol. 1.1 (1979), p. 97.
[15]Caryl Doncaster, from interview with author, (November, 1979).

Drifters, we were really politicians with cameras. We felt extremely left-wing'. But our attitude in BBC television early documentaries was nothing like that at all. You could almost say we were naive.[16]

Swallow was equally forthright about the aims of *Special Enquiry:*

> I said, why don't we do a series of enquiries, which have never been done before, into social problems – social, not political, by the way, always social, never political. . . . I think in human terms, I'm concerned about the problems of human individuals, I go for things I feel strongly about, my heart beats about.[17]

He articulated his position at the time in an extract from an article written in 1952, intended for circulation within the Unit as a personal appraisal of the achievements and short-comings of the first series of *Special Enquiry* (a second series was to follow shortly):

> We wanted to be very non-political. We wanted to break loose from the convention that the truth is somewhere between the Right and the Left, and will in some way mysteriously emerge out of an expression of two utterly contradictory points of view. I believe that truth exists *despite* politicians. Moreover, the routine (and dare I say it without being sacked?) the *BBC* theory that sitting on the fence is in some way a profitable position has never appealed to me. I don't mean that I advocate the embracing of one political party or the other; I mean that the truth can be sought without recourse to political help, and that if it is the truth then (a) it is more inspiring than political debate, and (b) *because* it is the truth, it is unassailable; by definition it cannot be biased one way or the other. To have a violent clash of opinions is dramatic; therefore we had to seek an alternative form of drama if we avoided the obvious one. This alternative form is not hard to seek; it happens the moment a programme stands on its own feet and proclaims a point of view, and takes an ethical stand. 'We believe', etc., ect. Robert Reid began our first programme by saying at once that every human being was entitled to a decent home for himself and his family. He began the second one by saying that every human being was entitled to a job.[18]

It would be difficult to find a better expression of a carefully negotiated personal path through the shifting sands of the truth/politicians and social/political oppositions underlying the early television documentarists' work, at a time when Swallow's truth was out in the world for the taking,

[16]Steve McCormack, from interview with author, (July, 1979).
[17]Norman Swallow, from interview with author, (July, 1979).
[18]Norman Swallow, *Special Enquiry: A Post-Mortem*, unpublished internal memo, (2 March, 1953).

the producer's job being to convey it with as much force and clarity as possible.

The term 'documentary' was used rather flexibly to describe three categories of programme, termed by Arthur Swinson (who wrote documentary scripts and a book on how to write for television, one of the first of its kind), the dramatized documentary, the actuality documentary and the magazine documentary.[19] There were also a number of film studies of modern British artists, notably Graham Sutherland and Henry Moore. The dramatized documentary was a studio-based 'live' production, often with short filmed inserts. It was scripted, and played by professional actors; locations were reproduced in the studio if appropriate, and stories were taken from life with as little modification as possible bearing in mind the technical limitations of the medium. The type of subjects covered by this form of documentary were of general contemporary, but not usually up-to-the-minute, importance. Among topics dealt with in this period were hooliganism, borstal, drugs, working women, children in care, problems of youth, marriage and old age, prostitution, industrial relations and declining industries, while series such as *Made By Hand, I Made News, Pilgrim Street*, about police methods, and the much praised *Course of Justice* which illustrated legal procedure by individual cases, were made. These programmes were popular at once; always written specifically for television and usually by the person who went on to produce them, they provided the major source of new writing for television. Drama output still relied heavily on the adapted stage play and it was difficult to commission new work because most established writers were dissuaded by the ephemeral nature of broadcasts, permanency having more appeal to them at that time than access to a mass audience. Since 'these documentaries about police, welfare workers, neglected children, alcoholics and marriage problems created a school of writers who were beginning to write realistically about society (admittedly from the viewpoint of Us looking at Them) while theatre curtains were still rising on French windows and butlers answering telepones,'[20] it is easy to see why the documentary generated an atmosphere of innovation.

There were several practical difficulties which account for the somewhat strained form of the dramatized documentary. For reasons of cost, the BBC's Film Department would only allow a small (but gradually increasing) proportion of film per programme, and the BBC could not then afford to pay actors the much higher film rates. There were no other facilities for recording so broadcasts were 'live', and since they also had to run for a specific prearranged time, they were scripted and played by actors, The cast were usually 'unknowns', as rates of pay were so low ('we are underpaying artists scandalously now, and I do not want this to be

[19]Arther Swinson, *Writing for Television*, (London, Black, 1955), p. 78.
[20]Peter Black, *The Mirror in the Corner – People's Television*, (London, Hutchinson, 1972), p. 19.

exposed anywhere', wrote Cecil Madden in a general undated memo), and credits were not given, ('I was greatly disappointed to read in the current issue of the *Radio Times* a billing for a documentary programme which included a cast list. For four years or more we have fought to keep our billings free of actors. It has been our argument that this kind of billing kills the reality of the programme. Until now all actors and actresses, many of them well known, have agreed to give up *Radio Times* credits in the interests of the programme', wrote Barr to Madden.[21])

Television had reopened for several years before actors became eager to appear on it, and many refused because of the disaster stories in circulation. The tension of facing advancing, cumbersome cameras under the (then) meltingly hot lights made actors forget their lines, and since they could not drift towards the wings to be prompted (as they might on stage) because camera angles were carefully set up in advance, a career could be ruined before it had begun.

The limitations of the camera equipment demanded much ingenuity in the visual scripting of programmes. It was possible to fade from one shot to another and to cut from camera to camera, and zoom lenses which allowed moves from long-shot to close-up were acquired in 1950, but there was a high probability that at least one camera would break down during transmission, so converting a carefully choreographed four-camera sequence into a series of frenzied improvisations. Gradually, as producers mastered camera techniques, writers learned how to write scripts for the camera, and viewing figures, actors' fees and technical equipment improved, programmes gained a slightly more polished appearance. Yet nobody could see a 'live' scripted programme, particularly a dramatized documentary which depended so heavily on creating the illusion of realism in one of the most contrived situations possible, as a comfortable thing to be involved with.

'Documentary gets its dramatic effects out of truth, out of the audience accepting it as being true',[22] wrote Barr to McGivern. Despite the extraordinary artifice involved in making television documentaries, the audience seemed prepared to accept dramatized documentaries on their own terms. Robert Silvey, Head of Audience Research, commented to Barr, who was anxious that when the dramatized documentary *Missing From Home* was repeated (it was usual for plays to be repeated twice in one week with the cast running through the play for a second time, but not so for documentaries), the audience's illusions could be shattered, 'All the evidence suggests that viewers are perfectly well aware that a documentary such as this is not the same thing as an OB, yet at the same time this realization does not seem in any way to impair their capacity to be gripped by a programme.'[22] However, the *Sunday Times* television critic, Maurice Wiggin, disliked the dramatized documentary because, 'The whole point

[21]Barr to Madden, (4 February, 1952).
[22]Silvey to Barr, (26 January, 1954).

of documentary is that it is literally true. . . . If it is not literally true, it is not documentary but something else – a kind of play-writing. . . . We have had too much fact-based fiction cooked up in the studio and played by professional actors.'[23] Later in the same article, Wiggin comments, 'Not long ago the cameras went to a London hospital at night; we saw the real thing, directly. It was more impressive than any documentary done in the studio.' Yet, as Swinson observed, this programme was not an Outside Broadcast in which the cameras are set up to observe life as it comes, as at a football match; it was a 'built OB,' a totally scripted and rehearsed programme in which the people concerned were speaking lines learned by heart and performing movements worked out by the producer. The performers were playing the roles they played in life, in the setting in which they actually worked, but nevertheless were acting a scripted programme. Wiggin, 'was deceived as to the true nature of the programme. He did not, as he imagined, see "the real thing" at all; what he saw was a reality created by artifice.'[24]

The success of a documentary programme – how far the audience was likely to accept it as 'being true' – depended more on the skill with which a programme used contrivances to conceal its necessarily contrived nature than on the development of techniques enabling the camera to relay more and better pictures from more varied locations. Rotha, Swallow, and especially Barr, interpret the essential nature of documentary in different ways but agree that details of technique, or indeed fastidiously purist criteria of any sort, have little to do with making documentaries. Rotha takes the subject of the programme as foremost:

> You say to yourself, this is a very important subject, I want to show it to as many people as possible, now do I use a pure documentary technique, no actors, no nothing except the real people, or maybe I've got a subject which calls for the use of actors. I don't think documentary should be tied down. Realism in subject, yes, but not necessarily the things you use in it.[25]

Swallow's primary concern is to reach an audience successfully:

> I believe you can communicate *anything*. I think you should communicate whatever you're communicating to as many people as possible, I don't mean this in a kind of snobbish or superior way. I would like those people watching that set to understand what I was saying to them. . . . I think you can actually maintain your standards and still communicate to millions of people, if you do it the right way.'[26]

[23]Quoted in Swinson, *Writing for Television*, pp. 81–2.
[24]Swinson, *Writing for Television*, p. 82.
[25]Paul Rotha, from interview with author, (August, 1979).
[26]Norman Swallow, from interview with author, (July, 1979).

For Barr:

> a Talks, Documentary or Drama offering may be on any subject under
> the sun; they are not to be defined by subject-matter, but by form and
> intention. Of these, intention is the most important.[27]

This is the opening sentence of a long memo intended for internal circulation in which Barr sets out to define what a television documentary is. His
intention was not to propose his own thoughts as definitive, but to forestall
the takeover of the Unit by Talks, whose Head, Mary Adams, wished to
take advantage of the fact that McGivern was having trouble finding a
Head of Documentaries by suggesting the amalgamation of the two.
Barr wished to affirm documentary as separate, and in doing so provides
almost a manifesto for television documentary practice at that time.
He wrote:

> Talks present personal opinion; documentary presents a report.
> Documentary takes into account many opinions; its nature is to select,
> edit, synthesize and present its own conclusion. Documentary is con-
> cerned with action; its form is the dramatization of facts, reconstruction
> of events, and it uses any dramatic device to make its point. It will use
> (and devise) any technique that will give force and clarity to the
> information it seeks to convey. Its intention is to make people feel as
> well as think. Its appeal is to the emotions and it talks in terms of human
> conduct. The court (in Duncan Ross's *Juvenile Court*) we saw was never
> held, but it was true. It was created by accurate observation, sympathy,
> understanding and good reporting. It was, perhaps, a better example of
> this process of law than any individual session of the court could have
> been. That is the justification of the documentary form.

Although 'accurate observation, sympathy, understanding and good
reporting' are applicable to the remaining two types of documentary
developed in this period, the actuality and magazine documentaries were
more akin to journalism than to drama. Similar in style – both used
'actualities' as opposed to actors, both used regular presenters to provide
commentary and interviews and both used a format of switching from
studio to film and back in a technically complex way – their aims and
presentation differed markedly.

Special Enquiry dealt with serious subjects in a serious manner. It
examined national problems such as racial discrimination (a pioneering
programme), illiteracy and slums and, less frequently, such international
problems as refugees, malaria and soil erosion. Norman Swallow described
the series as:

[27]Barr to McGivern, (3 August, 1951).

programmes which have taken issues of general importance and treated them as journalistic reports. In fact our brief for the series was to forge for ourselves some form of television journalism – the equivalent, for example, of the illustrated article of the *Picture Post* type. Our orders are to be tough and incisive, and not to pull any punches.[28]

Stuart Hall describes *Picture Post's* new way of seeing in photo-journalism as, 'the democratization of the subject'.[29] People were photographed, not self-consciously prepared for the camera, but intently absorbed by what they were doing; what was new here, at least in journalistic terms, was a view of the common-place as endlessly important. *Special Enquiry* was unable to perform the same function with a television camera because equipment was then so immobile. What it did take from *Picture Post* was the 'genuinely populist and democratic impulse which crystallized the deeply felt movement towards social democracy of the war years'[30] as its own stance on the social issues it covered, and, like *Picture Post*, it pinpointed exploitation, misery and social abuse, but always in a language which defined these as 'problems' to be tackled and remedied with energy and goodwill; it was instinctively *reformist*.[31] In this respect, as in many others, it has much in common with subsequent current affairs output.

Special Enquiry was the first programme explicitly to speak from the point of view of the audience; Swallow was determined to change the situation in which:

television programmes until [Robert Reid] were always introduced by people with the right kind of accent, and if you're doing a series of the *Special Enquiry* kind, it seemed to be a very good idea that the man who introduced it should speak like the audience speaks, and should be very tough, which of course we wanted emotionally, not politically, perhaps, but emotionally. . . . We should in fact try very hard – this is the main principle, of course – to be doing the programme from the point of view of the audience, not from the top down, but from the bottom up. We were not the Establishment. We were not the BBC telling the people what they should think.[32]

The magazine documentary had a far less serious intention; it was, 'interested in the sights and sounds of life, in curious places and interesting people; it explores widely rather than probes deeply. It is not insensitive to trends, either political or sociological, but records rather than questions

[28]Norman Swallow, unaddressed memo, (27 February, 1952).
[29]Stuart Hall, 'The Social Eye of *Picture Post*', *Working Papers in Cultural Studies*, No. 2 (1972), p. 83.
[30]Scannell, *Media, Culture and Society*, p. 103.
[31]Hall, *Cultural Studies*, p. 109.
[32]Norman Swallow, from interview with author, (July, 1979).

them.'[33] This form was represented by *London Town* and *About Britain*, long-running series devised by Steve McCormack, who produced them, and Richard Dimbleby, their commentator. Almost always among the most popular programmes broadcast, they resembled highly skilful travelogues with less scenery and more people. Rotha treated them dismissively as far too trivia-minded to bear comparison with *Special Enquiry*, which was precisely the sort of programme McCormack and Dimbleby had set out *not* to make. In these series can be found television's first unscripted interviews. This was rare in television at the time for the same reasons that dramatized documentaries used scripts – programmes were 'live', had to run for a fixed time, and nothing could be left to chance – and even McCormack did not always risk unscripted interviews as a matter of policy, even with so skilled an interviewer as Dimbleby.

Documentary is 'one of the these terms which refer not to an entity which may be definitively described but to an ideal. Documentary, in other words, is the history of our attempts to find meanings for the word "documentary". . . . If documentary were capable of definition, it would not be what it is. We may ask of documentary only what it was and what it shall be: and it is possible that many [programmes] called documentary in their day would not seem documentary if made now.'[34] At the heart of the Documentary Department's output lies the assumption that the society in which we live is ordered not by divine ordinance or human nature but by its members' actions. Thus the basis of social change is our own individual and collective behaviour. While this starting-point could serve political activism equally well, we have seen that the first television documentary programmes were inherently reformist.

The new documentary forms were being developed in a backward-looking broadcasting monopoly so hostile to television that the major battles were fought with the Corporation itself. The BBC's organizational structure relied for a balanced schedule upon the cooperation of 'reasonable' people prepared to exercise a degree of tolerance towards artistic forms new to television. (The Documentary Department was never popular with BBC administration.) Scannell has pointed to the particular process of defining political and social subjects in a mutually exclusive way, whereby 'the political' accommodated the concerns of those in political authority and the 'social subject' dealt with issues of general concern while denying their political implication. And undoubtedly in the aftermath of war there was a strengthened sense, by no means confined to the Documentary Department, that what divided us as a nation was less important than what we shared, and that the documentary had a crucial role to play in creating the informed democracy which could provide a more just and humane society.

[33]Swinson, *Writing for Television*, p. 99.
[34]Dai Vaughan, *Television Documentary Usage*, BFI Television Monograph No. VI, (London, British Film Institute, 1976), pp. 1–2.

All this was shortly to change. The monopoly was broken with the arrival of commercial television in 1955, and with it went the assumed dominance of radio over television. The Documentary Department was dissolved as Rotha left and its staff moved to Talks, Drama or, most commonly, to one of the new commercial companies. The strange hybrid forms of early television documentary began to look unwieldy as soon as lightweight equipment allowed programmes to be recorded free from the confines of the studio. The honeymoon period was over. Television documentary, and documentarists, now comparatively unrestricted by rigid technical and organizational constraints and so compelled to reflect upon their task, were never to regain the unselfconscious energy and faith in the future of these first formative years.

5

The Agonistic Narratives of Television Science

Roger Silverstone

Television documentary science occupies a particularly crucial space in the treacherously boggy ground of contemporary culture; a kind of no-man's land, an Alsace, a Golan, between the competing claims of scientific and everyday understanding. The space is deceptively tranquil. The no-man's land is claimed for Everyman. The elegant and seamless programme texts bear little trace of the scars of mediation and transformation which have marked the progress of their production. Balanced or polemic in turn, one programme after another passes across the screen, modestly secure in its own version of the truth, of reality, of virtue, like Lévi-Straussian myths offering, singly and together, momentary resolutions of the essential and essentially irresolvable human, cultural and social dilemmas of the times.

Television documentary science is not of course unique: science appears in other forms of television – in drama, in news; documentaries deal with subjects other than science. But television documentary science sets the paradigm. It mediates between two dominating discourses: the specialist and the general; the literary and the oral; the arcane and the accessible; the progressive and the stable, the empirical and the phenomenological; the disturbing and the meliorating; between, in short, science and common sense, or what Jean-François Lyotard identifies as the language games of scientific and narrative knowledge.[1]

Television is a kind of language.[2] I would like, in this paper, to explore both theoretically and empirically some of the issues raised for a study of television documentary science by such a perception, particularly in relation to the narrative and rhetorical structures of the language of television. I would also like to attempt to integrate into a still embryonic theoretical perspective of my own the insights to be derived from a recent reading of

[1]Jean-François Lyotard, *The Postmodern Condition: A Report on Knowledge* (Manchester, Manchester University Press, 1985), p. 7.
[2]cf. Roman Jakobson, 'Closing Statement: Linguistics and Poetics', in Thomas A. Sebeok, ed., *Style in Language* (New York and London, John Wiley, 1960) p. 377: 'Poetry is a kind of language'.

Jean-François Lyotard's *The Post-Modern Condition: A Report on Know-ledge*, which deals centrally with the relationship between science and the narratives of everyday life in terms of a general agonistics. In offering a view of culture in such terms, Lyotard is suggesting we see culture as a multiplicity of competing and incommensurable language games, each bidding for legitimation, for power and authority in the affairs of men and women; each bidding for the dominant position as the definer of the nature of reality. Agonistics involves not just competition (which might suggest merely antagonistics), but invention; and it has implications not just for the language games themselves, or for the relations between them, but also for the social bond.[3] Language both implies and requires community. Lyotard is suggesting that members of the human species, particularly in the increasingly fragmented culture of post-modern society, find their identity and their community through their language and the knowledge which that pragmatically expresses.

The starting point of his analysis is his recognition of the manifest failure of non-narrative science to dominate knowledge at the expense of the narrative knowledge of everyday life. Science has needed non-scientific narratives to legitimate itself. These narratives, of the progressive spirit of understanding, and of humanity as the hero of liberty, have failed. Science can no longer sustain its claims to be the sum total of knowledge. Lyotard is at pains to point out the fundamental difference in the character and social implications of the language games of everyday life and science. His attempt to do so provides something of a bridge for my own attempts to link textual analysis to the wider questions of social structure and cultural form.

Television science mediates between the discourse and narratives of science and the discourse and narratives of life. The two do not see eye to eye.

The narratives of life, grounding everyday knowledge in custom and experience, provide those who speak them with the competence they need for existence. Fables, myths, folktales, proverbs, established and recognizable forms, ground that experience, give it expression, reinforce that competence. The narratives of life in all their variety and in their authority, generate knowledge (*'savoir'* as opposed to *'connaissance'* – learning, and scientific knowledge itself): 'a question of competence that goes beyond the simple determination and application of criteria of efficiency (technical qualification), of justice and/or happiness (ethical wisdom), of the beauty of a sound or colour (artistry and visual sensibility) etc.'[4]

Science, quintessentially non-narrative, is of a different order. It is denotative or prescriptive. It does not generate a social bond except indirectly or antagonistically (in the establishment of scientific institutions apart from society). Competence in science is the prerogative of the sender, and is

[3]Lyotard, *The Postmodern Condition*, p. 11.
[4]*op. cit.* p. 18.

required neither of the receiver (who must only be intelligent) nor of the referent. Scientific statements depend on proof and demonstration for acceptance; they are not simply a matter of report. Science is cumulative; it has a past.

Of course, it is possible to quarrel with Lyotard's characterization of science and I will have occasion to shortly, but for the moment let it stand. His point is that both science and narrative knowledge are necessary, that they are interrelated, but that they are incommensurable and unequal; narrative knowledge is more tolerant of science than science is of narrative.

> The scientist questions the validity of narrative statements and concludes that they are never subject to argumentation or proof. He classifies them as belonging to a different mentality: savage, primitive, underdeveloped, backward, alienated, composed of opinions, customs, authority, prejudice, ignorance, ideology. Narratives are fables, myths, legends, fit only for women and children. At best, attempts are made to throw some rays of light into this obscurantism – to civilize, educate, develop.[5]

Television speaks of and for the everyday,[6] and in so doing it must come to terms with the knowledge that unaided will be left beyond the pale: incomprehensible, threatening, promising in turn utopia or armageddon. That the relationship between science and common sense is a complicated one goes without saying. Television's and television documentary's contribution to that relationship is equally complicated; it is both facilitating and hindering. It is the site of a polemic not just between the scientist and his popularizer, but between those on the left and the right who argue for a particular view of science.[7] The work which television science does in the mediation of science is therefore neither simple nor neutral, and the texts which emerge express and anticipate the conflicts that sustain both their production and reception. They are the products of, in the broadest of terms, social and cultural struggle. Each text, in its own way attempts a resolution and, in the forms and structures through which that resolution is attempted, provides a model or an example for the everyday.

There is a methodological point to be made here. It concerns the status of the semiotic of the text, and of the relationship of both text and semiotic to the social world which generates and receives it. It goes without saying that a semiology must also be a sociology.[8] A text is certainly the product of

[5]*op. cit.* p. 27.
[6]Roger Silverstone, *The Message of Television: Myth and Narrative in Contemporary Culture* (London, Heinemann Educational Books, 1981).
[7]Carl Gardner and Robert Young, 'Science on T.V.: A Critique', in Tony Bennett *et al.*, eds., *Popular Television and Film* (London, British Film Institute, 1981), pp. 171–93; Greta Jones, Ian Connell and Jack Meadows, *The Presentation of Science by the Media* (Leicester, Primary Communications Research Centre, 1977).
[8]On this point, see V.N. Volosinov, *Marxism and the Philosophy of Language* (New York, Seminar Press, 1973), p. 23.

social and cultural work. It contains the marks, like those on a flint arrow-head, of its own construction. But it is also, as I have already suggested, a claim for attention, and in claiming attention it will assume and inscribe its audience.

In broad terms an understanding of the work of construction involves a *poetics*:[9] a deconstructive account of the narrative strategies of the text, of its plausibility and its coherence, of its achievements in the generation of meaning, beauty, truth. In equally broad terms, and separated by no unambiguous divide, an understanding of the work of persuasion involves a *rhetoric*: an analysis of strategies which a text adopts to reach its audience. Television's texts are ephemeral. Its audience is distant and anonymous. It must speak, clearly and well. It must make many assumptions about that audience and about that audience's own assumptions about itself. In seeking to be heard, in claiming attention, in attempting to persuade, in defining its own legitimation, it becomes a supremely rhetorical medium.

Rhetoric, both classically, and in its modern guise, is a theory of argumentation:

> Rhetoric grasps language not as a form – it is not concerned with utterances as such – but as action; the linguistic form becomes an ingredient of a global act of communication (of which persuasion is the most characteristic type). Rhetoric deals with the functions of speech, not its structure. Its one constant is the objective it seeks to achieve: to persuade (or in the terminology of a later age, to instruct, to move and to please) . . . Rhetoric studies the means that allow a chosen end to be achieved.[10]

When John Reith defined the aims of the BBC as to 'educate, inform, amuse', he was, consciously or unconsciously, defining its essential rhetorical character. It is, overall, my contention that an adequate semiotic of the television text – that is, its poetics and its rhetoric – is a precondition for any satisfactory understanding of the place of any given text in the ideological coherence (or lack of it) of any given contemporary culture. I am well aware that we are a long way from that point of satisfaction, but at least I can mark out a plausible route towards it.

Let me then, provisionally, mark it out now, and having done so I will conclude the essay with an examination of some aspects of the text of a television science documentary in the light of it.

I suggest that a television text has three major dimensions. Each is of itself complex. All are interrelated. But each is identifiable and heuristically useful. The first is the text's narrative structure. The second is its rhetorical apparatus. The third is its ideological status. The first, very

[9] A notion developed with respect to television in Roger Silverstone, 'The Right to Speak: On a Poetic for Television Documentary', *Media, Culture and Society*, 5 (1983), pp. 137–54.
[10] Tzvetan Todorov, *Theories of the Symbol* (Oxford, Basil Blackwell, 1982), p. 61.

:oughly, concerns the what, the second the how, and the third, conditions
and consequences. The first implies an agonistics of a given 'language'
'(television) in relation to other 'languages' (other media, science, life); the
second implies an agonistics of a given 'language' in relation to itself
rhetoric consists, it has often been argued, in the play of the new and the
familiar, or in the deviation from a linguistic norm); and the third,
ideology, consists in the agonistics of 'language' in relation to the real (not
in parenthesis, though it might be).

Since both narrative and rhetoric are both the measure and the
mechanism of a text's effectiveness, the one attending closely to form, the
other to action, it is impossible to speak of them without simultaneously
speaking of ideology. But at the same time ideology is more than the
product of the text's narrative structure and rhetorical apparatus.

Television, Narrative and Science

We all know that opinions are admitted into the soul through two
entrances, which are its chief power, understanding and will. The more
natural entrance is the understanding for we should never agree to anything but demonstrated truths, but the more usual entrance, although
against nature, is the will; for all men whatsoever are almost always led
into belief not because a thing is proved but because it is pleasing.[11]

In a previous paper[12] I attempted an analysis of television narrative
which had as its core a perception of the basic dichotomy so eloquently described by Pascal. In considering the 'What' of the television documentary
text, I identified its two dimensions in the mythic and the mimetic narrative: in the appeal to emotion and to reason through story and argument
respectively. Television science documentaries were, and are, in the
business of persuasion, and of holding an audience. The particular
character of their texts is an expression of the dynamics of a producer's
capacity for invention – visual, verbal – within the constraints of established practice and an established aesthetic. The completed and final text
is a major element in the constraints on production before a frame has been
shot or a sound recorded.

There are two points worth making here. The first has to do with the
nature of the relationship between the mythic and the mimetic; the second
has to do with their status as categories.

Myth and mimesis in a television science documentary are in constant
tension, and that tension arises out of the particular space which television

[1]Blaise Pascal, *On Geometrical Demonstration* (Great Books of the Western World,
Vol. 33, p. 440), quoted in Chaim Perelman, *The New Rhetoric and the Humanities: Essays
on Rhetoric and its Applications* (Dordrecht, Boston, London, D. Reidel, 1979), p. 28.
[2]Roger Silverstone, 'Narrative Strategies in Television Science – A Case Study', *Media
Culture and Society*, 6 (1984), pp. 377–410.

occupies in our culture, both in relation to other media (books, radio, film, newspapers), and to other forms of knowledge and other languages (science, art, politics). Without resorting to textual analysis Lyotard identifies that space very well both explicitly and implicitly.[13] Television mediates not just between producer and audience, but between different discourses. The mythic and the mimetic are, as it were, the symbolic representations of those discourses within the text. On the one hand Lyotard's narrative, on the other science; on the one hand the oral, on the other the literal; the general and the special and so on. If we are to accept that science and narrative are incommensurable (and we might not), then television's mediation of the one to the other (always in one direction, note) will remain unstable. Television documentary science's particular forms and formats, however secure, therefore – and *Tomorrow's World* and *Horizon* in Britain have maintained a style and a place for themselves on television for many years – are at the same time formidably unstable. Each item, each subject, has to be negotiated anew, and a balance between competing discourses struck.

There is a temptation to see the relationship between discourse, representation, text and appeal as a simple one, thus:

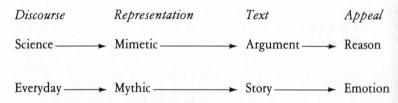

Discourse	*Representation*	*Text*	*Appeal*
Science ⟶	Mimetic ⟶	Argument ⟶	Reason
Everyday ⟶	Mythic ⟶	Story ⟶	Emotion

But things are far from this simple. Firstly, there is no equivalence between everyday knowledge and emotion (everyday knowledge is multidimensional). Secondly science, both in the laboratory and in its own texts, is no paragon of rational virtue.[14] Thirdly, the mythic includes not just the dimension of an heroic narrative, a chronology, on the model of the folktale; but also a logic, a structure, characteristic of Lévi-Strauss's analysis of myth, which attempts to identify a necessary rationality within the mythic system. Fourthly, the mimetic in television documentary is represented not simply or only in argument, but always in the visual representation of the real, and sometimes, by a narrative structure which mimics nature, for example in the passage of the seasons, or which adopts conventions which appear natural, as for example in a journey. Neither of these familiar form

[13]Lyotard, *The Postmodern Condition*, p. 28.
[14]Karin D. Knorr-Cetina, *The Manufacture of Knowledge: An Essay on the Constructivist and Contextual Nature of Science* (Oxford, Pergamon Press, 1981); Bruno Latour and Steve Woolgar, *Laboratory Life. The Social Construction of Scientific Facts* (Beverley Hills, Sage 1979); Paul Feyerabend, *Against Method* (London, New Left Books, 1975).

are arguments in any strict sense of the term, but they are mimetic. Finally, any analysis of argument (as the rhetorical structure of a text) will involve, does involve, its mobilization of, and appeal to, emotion.

The model therefore should look like this:

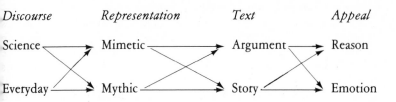

Discourse	Representation	Text	Appeal
Science	Mimetic	Argument	Reason
Everyday	Mythic	Story	Emotion

Instead of a single or unilinear movement between terms, one would need to postulate the magic of the dialectic as the principal movement between and among them.

The forms of television, even those of television documentary, are closer to the forms of everyday life than to those of science. 'Narration is the quintessential form of customary knowledge'[15]

Lyotard's assumption of a correspondence between narrative and everyday life – narrative as the froth on the churning sea of contemporary culture, begs an important question when it comes to television's narratives. For Lyotard narratives are autochthonous, produced and embedded in the culture of the everyday. They have the characteristics of a folklore, and television is both more and less than that. It is less by virtue of the bias in its texts' creation, and in the partiality of their acceptance; it is more, by virtue of the variety of its invention. Television's narratives, however closely locked, above all in their mythic structure, to the folklore of the contemporary world, nevertheless embody only claims for membership to that world, not membership itself. And it is in the persistence and character of those claims: for attention, for legitimation, for an audience, that television displays itself as rhetoric. This is as true for television science documentary as it is for any other of its genres. So what of science?

I have in front of me a scientific paper. It is entitled: 'Weed Control in Dry-Seeded Rice', and it was presented at a Cropping Systems Conference at the International Rice Research Institute, Los Baños, Laguna, Philippines, in March 1980. Its significance is that it was passed by the author to the producer of an *Horizon* science documentary during the course of the research for a film on the social and economic consequences of the introduction of new agricultural technology into the Third World. It was passed to the producer because (I believe) the author thought that it would be helpful in the preparation of the film. It may or it may not have been read. The paper is essentially an assessment of the various ways of

[15]Lyotard, *The Postmodern Condition*, p. 22.

overcoming the intense problems of weed control in dry-seeded rice.

I can in my own paper do little more than identify some of the narrative and rhetorical strategies present in this scientific text, both as a way of indicating differences between science and television (and therefore to some extent reinforcing Lyotard's main argument), but also similarity (and therefore to some extent contradicting him).

The argument in this text is quite clear. It follows the classic form of introduction, division, refutation, confirmation and conclusion: each element in the division is examined, refuted or confirmed in turn, before the final element – herbicides – is defined as the most satisfactory. The case is not strongly put, but qualified throughout.

But the argument has a further dimension – an heroic dimension – and its structure mirrors the mythic structure of much elementary narrative. In such a dimension the author – disembodied to be sure, and quoting himself by surname only in precise equivalence to the many other authors cited – constructs himself as hero. The problem for solution which sets, in its disequilibrium, the narrative in motion, becomes the object of search, and the various helpers are the cited scientists (including himself) called on as significant figures along the way. His enemies are threefold: those sets of experiments with whose results he disagrees (and with which his own research conflicts); common sense (appearing in the guise both of observational reports of indigenous farming practices, and reports of common sense perceptions, which are also, sometimes, called on in support), and the difficulty of the problem itself. The first two in narrative terms constitute the opposers; the last is the villain. The solution, were he to find it, is his princess.

Such strategies as these have many times been noted in scientific texts,[16] and they have been pursued more rigorously than I am able to do here, but I venture to suggest that they are clear enough. They do not, however, exhaust the text; not by any means.

The text contains a number of rhetorical elements which identify it as scientific. First of all it is anonymous: the subject/author is displaced.[17] He appears, as I have noted, only with the same status as the authors quoted.[18] Secondly there is a marked intensity of citation: references which not only provide the critical context for its own argument, but establish the text in an historical progression and give it status.[19]

[16]Charles Bazerman, 'What Written Knowledge Does: Three Examples of Academic Discourse, *Philosophy of the Social Sciences*, 11 (1981) pp. 361–87; Joseph Gusfield, 'The Literary Rhetoric of Science: Comedy and Pathos in Drinking Driver Research', *American Sociological Review*, 41 (1976), pp. 16–34; John Hutchins, 'On the Structure of Scientific Texts', *University of East Anglia Papers in Linguistics*, 5 (1977), pp. 18–39.
[17]Knorr-Cetina, *Manufacture of Knowledge*.
[18]Group μ, *A General Rhetoric* (Baltimore and London, Johns Hopkins University Press 1981), p. 171.
[19]G. Nigel Gilbert, 'Referencing as Persuasion', *Social Studies of Science*, 7 (1977) pp. 113–22.

Thirdly there is its overall mode of address: the text presumes an audience of agricultural scientists. There is no attempt to ground the argument in the personal experience of either author or audience, but only in their experience as scientists who have or can read the same body of research reports that the author has done.

The structure of the argument and the character of the rhetorical apparatus which appears within this text follow and display forms of scientific accounting which involve, above all, the intention to persuade the reader/listener of the plausibility, accuracy and authenticity of what is being proposed.[20] Insofar as these elements appear in a text such as this – albeit in such muted form – they identify a number of formal and structural similarities with the texts of television science.[21] This is not, however, an identity. What is at issue is what Knorr-Cetina calls, in relation to her study of laboratory science, the process of conversion/perversion of science as a social object:

> Why perversion? The transfiguration in a fairy tale of a wizard into a mouse is at the same time a disfiguration of the wizard. The conversion to a new faith, a new language, or a new level of organization is a perversion with respect to the old faith, the original language, or the preceding level of organization. The economy of change is at the same time an economy of conversion and perversion. The products of science are continually transfigured and disfigured as they circulate in transscientific fields. As they move from the scientist's desk to the office of politician, they change into a policy document. As they move to an industrial enterprise, they turn into a tool in the process of industrial production. In the hands of another scientist, they convert into a source of continued thematization or selectivity.[22]

And into the hands of a television science producer? Does science become a fairy tale? And does the scientist become a wizard or a mouse?[23]

The Rhetoric of Television Documentary Science

The history of rhetoric is marked by an oscillation between two poles: the study and practice of the art of speaking well: the study and practice of the art of persuasion. Rhetoric as ornament. Rhetoric as power. Rhetoric shading into and being displaced by aesthetics;[24] rhetoric shading into and being displaced by the study of ideology.

[20]Stephen Yearley, 'Textual Persuasion: The Role of Social Accounting in the Construction of Scientific Arguments', *Philosophy of the Social Sciences*, 11 (1981), pp. 409–35.
[21]Silverstone, 'Narrative Strategies'.
[22]Knorr-Cetina, *Manufacture of Knowledge*, p. 132.
[23]George Basalla, 'Pop Science: The Depiction of Science in Popular Culture', in Gerald Holton and William A. Blanpied, eds., *Science and its Public: The Changing Relationship* (Dordrecht and Boston, D. Reidel, 1976), pp. 261–78.
[24]Todorov, *Symbol*, p. 111.

Efforts at synthesis, even in a revitalized new rhetoric,[25] somehow still maintain the separation. Group μ's rhetoric is principally still an aesthetic; Perelman's is entirely a theory of argumentation, a theory of persuasion. Yet it is impossible completely to separate them, for each is grounded in the basic character of language:

> Rhetoric is rooted in the essential function of language itself, a function that is wholly realistic and is continually born anew, the use of language as a symbolic means of inducing cooperation in beings that by nature respond to symbols.[26]

Rhetoric is language in action, or language oriented to action. Television in our culture does not often engage, of course, in direct efforts at persuasion: the party-political broadcast and advertising are obvious examples of where it does. Elsewhere, and especially in news and documentary, persuasion is directed less towards action than to an acceptance of the message being offered, which may or may not have dynamic consequences.

There is no question that the language of television is rhetorical in both senses of the word, and indeed the particular character of the medium, the ephemerality of its texts and the generality of its audience, together with its essentially figurative character (its images are metaphors of the real), mark it as perhaps the supreme rhetorical medium of our times.[27]

What is the principal claim of television documentary? It is to be seen as successfully presenting the real. In constructing the real in its images and words, in presenting plausible, truthful, verisimilitudinous versions of the world through its symbols, its illustrations, its examples, its models, its narratives, its textuality, it is of its very nature figurative. Early rhetoricians in attempting to define the nature of their object, discriminate between thought and speech, and talk of the latter as a cloak. Recent mythologists and much current media analysis preserve the metaphors, and also the problems, of characterizing texts in terms of constructed deviations, biases, masks, veils.

Roland Barthes[28] identifies the rhetorical structure of the images in terms of the relation between denotation and connotation, but it is possible, while preserving the general principle of that relationship – that is, that a signifier will have two separate and qualitatively different but related signifieds – to take the matter a stage further; and to identify two parallel dimensions to the figuration of the image (and of course also of the words) of television.

---

[25]Group μ, *Rhetoric*; Perelman, *Rhetoric*.

[26]Kenneth Burke, *A Rhetoric of Motives* (New York, George Braziller, 1955), p. 43.

[27]cf. Aristotle, *Rhetoric*, 1, 1357a 1–4, (Great Books of the Western World, Vol. 32. p. 2), quoted in Perelman, *Rhetoric*, p. 12: It belongs to rhetoric 'to deal with such mattters as we deliberate on without arts or systems to guide us, in the bearing of persons who cannot take in at a glance a complicated argument, or follow a long chain of reasoning.'

[28]Roland Barthes, *Image-Music-Text* (London, Fontana/Collins, 1977), pp. 32–51.

Tzvetan Todorov, following Fontainer, distinguishes between a figure and a trope within rhetoric. Their difference is characterized as follows:[29]

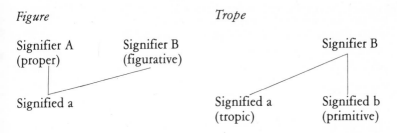

Figure

Trope

A figure is a form with two signifiers and one signified. One signifier is directly representational (proper), the other is at one remove (figurative); for example:

A trope links two signifieds to one signifier, one directly (primitive), one indirectly, perhaps metaphorically; for example:

All of television is figurative in the first sense. Its signifiers – its images above all – replace the products of perception as signifiers of reality (signified a). (This level of figuration is identical to Hjelmslev's 'form of the expression', and therefore is, at its most reductive, coexistent with language itself.)[30] Both television and film have developed their own set of figures – the flash-back, the units of the *grande syntagmatique* as defined by Christian Metz[31] – which define the particular character of the two media. The figures are in turn open to a second articulation, for example in

[29]Todorov, *Symbol*, p. 100.
[30]Louis Hjelmslev, *Prolegomena to a Theory of Language* (Madison, University of Wisconsin Press, 1963), p. 52ff.
[31]Christian Metz, 'Problèmes de Denotation dans le Film de Fiction', in A.J. Greimas, ed., *Signs, Language, Culture* (The Hague, Mouton, 1970), pp. 403–13; Christian Metz, *Film Language* (New York, OUP, 1974), pp. 108–46.

a film such as *Last Year in Marienbad* where that relationship of figured image with reality as its signified is disturbingly refigured.[32] A figure in this sense, and of course it is much more intrusive in the writing of documentary film, is characterized by deviation:

> 'The figures of discourse are the features, the forms or the turns of phrase that are more or less remarkable and more or less privileged in their effect, and through which, in the expression of ideas, thoughts and feelings, discourse deviates more or less from what would have been the simple and common expression.[33]

Film is therefore doubly figurative: firstly in the relationship between its forms and reality, and secondly in the relationship between its forms and themselves. It is also a home for the trope: a signifier with two signifieds. Metaphors and similes are tropes. The synecdoche (where the part stands for the whole) is a prime metaphor of film and television, and centrally embodied in the close-up.[34]

So far I have been addressing only the rhetoric of the look – a shorthand way of identifying the particular character of the medium and its structure. Quite obviously the same distinctions and dimensions apply to the rhetoric of the image (where the content of what is seen is both by definition figurative, and also, often, tropic – for example in the metaphors by which science is represented in the image of the white-coated scientist, of the technology, of the pages of a text-book). And equally they apply to the voice: the spoken word, in commentary and in contribution. Music too has a rhetorical status both in its contribution to the whole, and in its own forms.

To complicate the matter further (we are already dealing with four different dimensions of rhetoric – look, image, voice, music – together with their double valency in figure and trope; that is, potentially at least, eight terms), it is necessary to consider the relationship between them. The work of editing a film[35] consists in the manipulation of voice and image (principally) towards the construction of a plausible, pleasing and persuasive text. In the juxtaposition of image and voice the director is building the major and final dimension of rhetoric into his text, placing side by side, in harmony or disharmony; and placing in sequence, within a structure of expectation and surprise, those elements which already have rhetorical significance. It is in the final acts of assembly that the rhetoric and the poetics of the text coincide.

[32]Noel Burch, *Theory of Film Practice* (London, Secker & Warburg, 1973), pp. 3–16.
[33]Todorov, *Symbol*, p. 99.
[34]Christian Metz, *The Imaginary Signifier* (Bloomington, Indiana University Press, 1982), p. 195.
[35]Roger Silverstone, *Framing Science: The Making of a BBC Documentary* (London, British Film Institute, 1985), Ch. 3.; Dai Vaughan, *Television Documentary Usage*, (London, British Film Institute, 1976).

The discussion of the last few pages, arid though it may appear, is not simply a scholastic exercise. And the rhetorical apparatus of a television documentary text is not simply a matter for analysis – nor simply of concern to aesthetics. It is, in its efficacy, in the work of justification, legitimation and persuasion, of profound sociological significance. There are three aspects to the sociology of the rhetoric of television documentary that I want briefly to consider: first, the nature of rhetorical argument; second, the question of fraud; and third, the relationship between the text and its audience. I can, indeed, only sketch an outline of the relevant questions.

Chaim Perelman in his efforts to define what he calls 'The New Rhetoric', begins by distinguishing argumentation from demonstration.[36] The distinction is textual but also sociological, and it concerns the character of a form of reasoning and persuasion which differs, in its non-formality, from the formal demonstrations of science. The objections that have already been raised against Lyotard's demarcation of science and narrative also, of course, apply here to Perelman: science has its narratives; arguments their demonstrations. Nevertheless the distinction, crucial to his own philosophy, is dramatically useful in marking the difference between science and the rhetoric of television's narratives.

A demonstration – the principal mechanism of scientific discourse – is:

> a calculation made in accordance with rules that have been laid down beforehand. No recourse is allowed to evidence or to any intuition other than that of the senses. The only requirement is the ability to distinguish signs and to perform operations according to rules. A demonstration is regarded as correct or inconvenient according as it conforms or fails to conform to the rules. . . . Once we have accepted the framework of a formal system and know that it is free from ambiguity, then the demonstrations that can be made within it are compelling and impersonal.[37]

That 'once', of course, is crucial, for it rescues science from ontology, and draws it into the realm of the relative and, despite itself, of the rhetorical.

Nevertheless, demonstration and argumentation differ. Argumentation is:

> founded on opinion and concerned with contingent reality. . . . An argumentation is always addressed by a person called the orator – whether by speech or in writing – to an audience of listeners or

---

[36]cf. Perelman, *Rhetoric*, p. 32ff; Perelman's category 'argumentation' includes what I have called both argument and story. It includes elements that I would place both in the mythic and the mimetic. This is to some extent the case because of the nature of his preferred texts (not television and not film) and his principal concerns in philosophy. I will use the word 'argumentation' when referring to his position and concept and argument (as opposed to 'story') when referring to my own.

[37]Perelman, *Rhetoric*, p. 10.

readers. It aims at obtaining or reinforcing the adherence of the
audience to some thesis, assent to which is hoped for.[38]

It presupposes a 'meeting of minds', 'mutual goodwill' between orator
and audience, and a common language.

The transition from science as demonstration to television science as
argumentation/rhetoric may not be quite as dramatic as Perelman and
Lyotard maintain, but it is significant. Perelman's philosophy identifies a
mechanism both for its recognition and its analysis. Lyotard's provides an
indication of its importance.

The perception of television documentary in terms defined now not only
as narrative, but as rhetoric, involves, at best, seeing texts relativistically,
and at worst as fraud. Much recent analysis of the messages of television
involves a demystification, a 'discovery' of bias, a measurement of a text
against the degree zero of the truth. Traditionally rhetoric has also involved
the measurement of a text not just against the degree zero of the truth, but
also against the degree zero of aesthetic neutrality (normality, predicta-
bility, the commonplace). Group μ in their version of the new rhetoric postulate a degree zero text, as a point against which to identify and assess the
presence of rhetorical figures.[39] But if the key to rhetoric is suitability,
appropriateness,[40] rather than the truth, and if the truth depends on
eloquence, then all rhetoric must be seen as fraud.[41]

And finally, what of the audience? Rhetoric requires an audience. It
assumes it and makes assumptions about it:

> The part played by the audience in rhetoric is crucially important,
> because all argumentation, in aiming to persuade, must be adapted to
> the audience, and hence based on beliefs accepted by the audience with
> such conviction that the rest of the discourse can be securely based upon
> it. . . . Indeed, the orator who builds his discourse on premises not
> accepted by the audience commits a classical fallacy in argumenta-
> tion – a *petitio principi*.[42]

I have argued elsewhere for a perception of the television text which
recognizes the levels of plausibility built into its own strategies of
naturalization.[43] The naturalization of a text – the product of both narrative and rhetorical strategies – is the key to its 'truth' and the measure of its
acceptability.

---

[38]Perelman, *op. cit.* p. 11.

[39]Group μ, *Rhetoric*, p. 30ff.

[40]Todorov, *Symbol*, p. 63.

[41]Immanuel Kant, *The Critique of Judgement*, in *The Critique of Pure Reason; The Critique
of Practical Reason and Other Ethical Treatises; the Critique of Judgement*, James Creed
Meredith, trans. (Chicago, Chicago University Press, 1955), 53, p. 535, quoted in Todorov,
Symbol, p. 80.

[42]Perelman, *Rhetoric*, p. 14.

Its acceptance – and, of course, it is not guaranteed, for rhetoric speaks of effort not necessarily of success – depends on the context of performance and on the competence and benevolence of the audience. Television, always operating at a distance from its shadowy audience, must constantly compensate for this inadequacy as a means of communication. Hence it will take few risks. One kind of rhetoric based on one set of assumptions, if passably successful (and however measured) will satisfy more often than not.

The television documentary is centrally concerned with its own legitimacy, which it may assume, but which it must continue to affirm; and with its community, which, too, must be created anew with each transmitted text. A central strategy for the establishing of both is one noted as being crucial, also, for rhetoric. It is the creation of presence. 'Presence' has temporal and spatial dimensions. It is the here and now, and it is the product of the image which is always present, and of the emotions which can only exist in the present.[44]

An Example

I would like, now, to explore two tiny portions of television documentary science as illustration of the arguments offered thus far in the paper (and as comparison to the article on dry-seeded rice, which I have already described).

The two extracts come from the same film, but are from different versions of it. The film, 'A New Green Revolution?' was an *Horizon* production transmitted on 23 January 1984 on BBC2 at 9.25 p.m. It was produced and directed by Martin Freeth.[45]

The film, having been completed and awaiting transmission, was seen in exceptional circumstances by the head of department, who found it dull and required that it be strengthened. The producer/director went away and recut it, adding new shots and sequences, some of which he had shot himself, but most of which came from the film library and other sources. He rewrote the commentary. Much of his attention was directed towards the opening and the closing minutes of the film, particularly the opening, the frame, and it is the two versions of the opening that I want, briefly, to compare.

[43]Silverstone, 'The Right to Speak', p. 146.
[44]Perelman, *Rhetoric*, p. 17.
[45]The case study referred to in the text is: 'A New Green Revolution?', a BBC *Horizon* film transmitted on BBC2 at 9.25 p.m. on 23 January 1984. It was produced and directed by Martin Freeth. A video recording of this film is available, on hire, from the British Film Institute, 127, Charing Cross Road, London WC2.

The production of this film is the subject of my book: *Framing Science: The Making of a BBC Documentary* (London, British Film Institute, 1985).

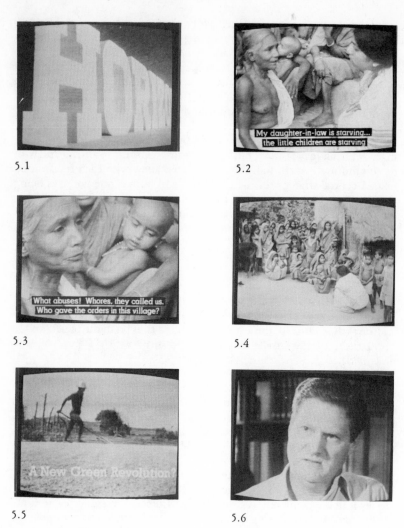

5.1

5.2

My daughter-in-law is starving...
the little children are starving

5.3

What abuses! Whores, they called us.
Who gave the orders in this village?

5.4

5.5

A New Green Revolution?

5.6

The film had passed through many stages during its production. Beginning life as an idea about the threat to the plant genetic resources of the world posed by new agricultural technologies (The Green Revolution) and the involvement of multi-nationals in the world's seed trade, it ended up by being a critical analysis of the role of agricultural science in the Third World, particularly in relation to the plight of the poor and the landless.

5.7

5.8

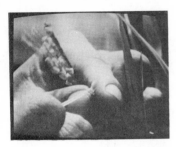

5.9

Much of the work of narrative and rhetorical construction is clearly complete prior to editing: images are shot and questions asked for their answers, and the manner of both to some extent determines the character of the final film. To some extent, but by no means entirely. Most of the work of film-making is done in the cutting room, and the restructuring and rewriting of this film gives some indication of how much can be done, and how much can be changed, as a result of changes in its narrative and its rhetorical structure. The movement which the demand to 'strengthen' the text produced was a movement, I would argue, deeper into the language of television, and further away from the language of science; a move away from the mimetic toward the mythic, and away from argument towards story. In short, it involved a heightening of the rhetorical status of the film and a consolidation of the mythic narrative.

I have already explored the changes between the two versions in broad terms,[46] and to some extent the significance of the transformation does depend on a fuller analysis than I can offer here. However what I have to say can be said by reference to the two pre-title sequences of the two versions (the second of which was the transmitted version), transcripts of both of which now follow:

---

[46]Silverstone, *op. cit.*, pp. 167–77.

Version 1

Image	Sound
HORIZON title	HORIZON title music (Fig. 5.1)
WS group of Bangladeshi women in village	(Talking in Bengali)

Sound

Subtitles

My daughter-in-law is starving; the little children are starving
(Fig. 5.2)

(Zoom in to old lady as she talks) — There's no news of my son . . .
Where is he? What abuses! Whores they called us. Who gave the orders in this village?
(Fig. 5.3)
I won't be able to talk later . . .

(Zoom out as she points) — Why have they done this?
Why have these two children and their mother been hungry for four days?
They broke four pitchers and threw away the rice.

Keith Griffin V/O
Normally the crisis in the Third World, poverty, inequality, hungry, is a silent crisis. Only occasionally does the crisis of the peasantry erupt in the form of violence and civil discord.
It is a huge crisis effecting, shall we say, 40 per cent of the population of the Third World.
(Fig. 5.4)

WS women in village — And this 40 per cent of the population normally suffers in silence.

Philippines landscape Rice in foreground. Man comes in with rake.
(Fade in title)
'A New Green Revolution?'
(Fade out title)

(Fig. 5.5)

Version 2

Image	Sound
HORIZON title	HORIZON title music (Fig. 5.1)

Keith Griffin (Sync.)
(Fig. 5.6)

CU Keith Griffin — The difficulty is that if we persist with our current line, looking for technological solutions to socioeconomic problems, then we will run out of time. These problems of impoverishment, inequality, social tension, of conflict, will explode.

WS group of Bangladeshi women in village — (Talking in Bengali)

Subtitles
My daughter-in-law is starving; the little children are starving.
(Fig. 5.2)

(Zoom in to old lady as she talks) — There's no news of my son . . .
Where is he?
What abuses Whores, they called us.
Who gave the orders in this village?
(Fig. 5.3)
I won't be able to talk later . . .

(Zoom out as she points) — Why have they done this?
Why have these two children and their mother been hungry for four days? They broke four pitchers and threw away the rice.

Keith Griffin (V/O)
Normally the crisis in the Third World, poverty, inequality, hunger, is a silent crisis. Only occasionally does the crisis of the peasantry erupt in the form of violence and civil discord.
(Fig. 5.4)

Narration
Millions of poor people in the Third World may not be silent much longer.
They're caught up in an economic system which is steadily driving them towards red revolution.

Agricultural technology is a crucial part of the economic system.

Knapp (Sync.)
(Fig. 5.7)
WS Normal Borlaug   I have never met a farmer who wasn't
and Ron Knapp near   happier with the new varieties . . .
plots

Borlaug
And the new technology . . .

Narration
(Figs. 5.8 and 5.9)
CU hands   Some scientists believe that by helping
MS man in helmet   people grow more food, they can provide a
sucking pollen from   more peaceful 'Green Revolution' instead.
rice flowers in
greenhouse.

Keith Griffin (V/O)
The scientist has in a sense replaced God.
He can provide the quick fix.

Phillippines landscape.
Rice in Foreground
Man comes in with
rake

Narration
(Fig 5.5)
What can the scientists do?
Are they gods, or are they like the hungry
peasant, pawns in a wider game?

(Fade in title 'A New
Green Revolution?')

(Note that the description of the images and the identification of the speakers is a function of hindsight, and accords with the BBC's own style and practice of producing post-production scripts of completed films.)

The first pre-title sequence runs for two minutes; the second for two minutes 40 seconds including series titles and programme titles in each case. To some extent analysis of these four minutes 40 seconds of television time may seem unnecessary. The transformation from the first to the second version is dramatic and obvious.

The narrative and rhetoric of the film begin with the series titles which both versions share. A camera moves up and across the solid white letters of the word *Horizon*, swiftly, unhesitatingly seeking the edge of the letter 'N' – the literal and metaphorical horizon. The music is a breathless electronic crescendo. All *Horizons* since 1983/84 season have had these titles. I have implied in the rhetoric of my own description of them an interpretation which seems to me to be entirely plausible. Its significance is not just in its persistence at the head of each of the films of *Horizon* whatever their subject or their line, but also in its reinforcement by the confidence of similar titles (and similar content) in other manifestations of television science.

The sequence ends with the same written title superimposed on the same image. The title itself is a rhetorical question. The implication of the figure is that the following text will answer it, but as we shall see the question itself has been framed quite differently in the two versions by virtue of the commentary's words, so that its precise rhetorical significance is different in each case. The image and sound of the man raking rice is in an important sense too, a rhetorical question, for it goes entirely unlabelled, either as to location or purpose. Its unfamiliarity and ambiguity is grounded, of course in familiarity: we can recognize a rake, a dark-skinned barefoot man, seeds lying on the ground, we hear the grating of the wood against a hard surface. But that is all, unless we are priviledged by our own experience or information. In this sense therefore the image reinforces, rhetorically, the question asked by the title, and as such encourages the viewer to stay with the programme-text.

So what of the intervening text? Let me take each extract in turn and deal with it within the broad headings, Narrative – Rhetoric. As far as the narrative is concerned, any comments must depend on an appreciation of what follows the extract; the analysis of narrative is dependent on the coherence of the text; it is essentially syntagmatic. Rhetoric is entirely present, as I have already suggested.

Version 1

The extract consists of the 3 shots: a medium side shot of a group of women, tightening through a zoom to a close-up of one of them talking, bare-breasted and animatedly, to an interlocutor bottom right in the frame, and then a zoom out again; a wide shot of the group as a whole; the title shot which I have already described. Superimposed over the first of these shots is a series of subtitles purporting to translate the words being spoken, and once that is complete, a voice over.

(a) *Narrative*

In formal terms this pre-title sequence consists in establishing the first elements of the frame for the narrative as a whole, both mythic and mimetic. The mythic dominates – there is (by comparison to a scientific paper) no abstract, no statement of objectives, barely an identification of a theoretical or empirical problem which the narrative will address. The mythic frame sets the scene, and does so by placing the viewer in the role of hero (temporarily), for in this first version, there are no narratively defined characters to take on that role. It is the viewer who is despatched, implicitly, on the journey which inaugurates the narrative. The journey is to somewhere strange and unfamiliar. Its initiation is accompanied by a statement of a lack, a problem, an injustice – a disequilibrium. The statement comes from the women, literally in the words as they are translated, but also in the images of concern and distress. The voice-over (whose voice, we will not discover until after the title-shot) specifies the nature of the problem, and casts it, dramatically, in terms of a crisis (a word repeated three times), albeit a muted one (affecting 40 per cent of the rural population of the world who 'normally suffer in silence').

Any evidence of the presence of the mimetic narrative will have to be gleaned from these words, for it is clear in this version (even more in the second) that the narrative of hero and text dominates over whatever might appear mimetically in the form of an argument. However the voice-over words do signal, in their rationality, a case to be made. The problem of the world's poor will be dealt with in the programme in some way or another.

(b) *Rhetoric*

(i) *Look*. The camera and the sound recorder and the whole social and cultural organization of the work of production have intervened between these women and their appearence on the screen. A tiny portion of the continuity (and tragedy) of their lives has been extracted and distilled. In relation to *their* reality, the images are essentially figures; a reality transposed and serving another cause – that of the film. This said, the rhetorical structure of the camera's look is relatively simple: a medium wide zooming to a tighter close-up and back again, a re-establishing wide, and then an image shot from ground level of disembodied feet and a rake.

The close-up of the speaking woman (whose voice we are unlikely to understand, and which in part is muted to allow an English voice to interpose), is a focusing device, individualizing the dismay, personifying the crisis, but yet drastically distanced by the intervening subtitles and voice-over. The presence of the voice, superimposed as it is on the close-up, makes the link between the unfamiliarity of the image and the familiarity of home. Voice and look appear in a dialectic of distance and closeness, in their very form. The strangeness and distance is reinforced by the angle of the title-shot, and the fragmentation of the body which the positioning of the camera produces. This last shot is both figure and trope: figure in its deviation from the expected; trope in so far as it speaks, in its angle and position, of the 'strange'.

(ii) *Image*. The images, of course, are necessarily mimetic, and irrespective of what is being said, or of their own rhetorical status, guarantee the text as a true and faithful account. As I pointed out in my earlier discussion, a vital dimension of the rhetoric of television consists in the interrelationship between its various dimensions. Any analysis of the image, therefore, will overlap with both that of the look and the voice.

There are only two images in this extract (though there are three shots); and these two images reinforce each other in defining a location for the film. The women, as they have gathered in a circle around the camera – still, some holding, some feeding their children – appear like a Greek chorus framing the speaker in foreground. The camera recorded a performance, and the structuring of that performance before the camera (together with the content of what was being said, and the producer's knowledge of the context in which it was being said) granted, even guaranteed, these images a powerful claim for inclusion in the film. Indeed, as images, they were perceived to be of such power that they were chosen not only to introduce but also to close the film. I have already suggested what they stand for, what their figurative sense is; they stand for poverty, for unfamiliarity, for the romance of underdevelopment, for the plight of women the world over, etc., etc. What they stand for (and therefore their rhetorical status) is a function not just of their status as images, but of the relationship in ideology and power between the First and the Third Worlds, between subject and audience.

(iii) *Voice.* Images are, by themselves, ambiguous (a familiar property of the real) – sometimes, of course, as in the case of the title-shot here, deliberately and productively so. The words that we read and hear during these first two minutes run parallel to the images without directly connecting with them. There is a space, a rhetorical space, between image and word, partly as a result of the inevitable space which translation creates, partly as a result of the lack of direct reference by the spoken words to the images themselves. Instead the words are used to establish a context for the film as a whole, and to encourage the viewer to attend. This refusal firmly locks the text into a structure of argumentation. Here is an appeal, both by the woman, as an individual, and by the voice over, as pontiff. The juxtaposition which this represents marks another familiar rhetorical strategy: the generalization from the particular.

The successful achievement of a coherent narrative voice is an ideological achievement of some moment. Whatever the outcome of the efforts of this text, it is quite clear that its voice is going to be critical of established science, and not at all the familiar voice of *Horizon*.

Version 2

This version runs for 40 seconds longer than the first. It begins and ends with the same title sequences. It contains the same shots of the women unchanged and uncut. The words spoken by the women are translated identically. The changes can be simply listed: a new close-up shot of a man speaking to camera; a new voice speaking new words over the images of the women; some cutting of the original voice over. Following the women, there are three new shots (two new images): the first of two men in a field, with backs to camera whose voices we (over)hear; the other a tight close-up followed by a mid-shot of a man in goggles working with a machine on a plant in a greenhouse. There are new commentary words throughout, and a further voice-over contribution which links the first shot of the begoggled man with the title shot of the raking.

(a) *Narrative*

The mythic narrative is dramatically strengthened, by the addition of Griffin as the despatcher at the head of the sequence, and by the presence, albeit unidentified individually, of the scientists as hero (or more precisely as anti-hero) in the shot of the two men in the fields, and in the shot of the man at work. The commentary narration reinforces the message of urgency and threat, and Griffin's final voice-over and the following commentary voice define the whole narrative enterprise as an heroic adventure for exceedingly high stakes.

Any appeal to reason on which the mimetic narrative might depend is swamped now. Only the images preserve the authority of the text as a document(ary).

(b) *Rhetoric*

(i) *Look*. There are four extra shots in the 40 seconds added on. The pace of the introduction is substantially increased; its rhythm itself becomes more urgent. The juxtaposition: women, scientists in long-shot and scientific activity in tight close-up make a link which the text requires but without any clarification of what it is that connects them. Juxtaposition stands, in the structure of the cutting, in place of logic: a visual logic stands for a verbal one.

(ii) *Image*. All the new images, including the opening one of Griffin speaking, are tropes. Each can be seen to represent a generalizable character and institution beyond the text. Each will release a string of connotations which will lock the text as a whole into the wider, ideological context of its reception: the first image of Griffin in close-up is the image of reason, relaxed, in shirt-sleeves, speaking almost directly to camera – the image of anti-establishment seriousness and commitment framed by the books of learning; the three shots of the scientists, the last two of scientific activity, identify and personify science: images of scientists and of scientific activity speaking of *Science*, and once again defining its paradoxical status. These images also define the particular character of the scientific voice on television: the scientist appears; science is anthropomorphized – given human shape. It is the producer/director who now fills the anonymous space; the displaced 'I' of the text.

(iii) *Voice*. The voice increases its dominance in this version, both with the pieces to camera at the beginning and with the new commentary voice, both over the women and over the later shots. In fact this is a different voice from the one which spoke the commentary in the first version (but which had not yet appeared in the extract under examination), changed in order to give the film a more abrasive character, and to increase the production voice's hold on the film as a whole. The words speak of threat as well as crisis; of explosion as well as silence. They contrast the green with the red revolution, implicate agricultural technology as a contributor to the crisis, and cast the scientists as Gods or pawns (wizards or mice). The stakes are savagely raised. The rhetorical questions now appear not just in the title. There can be no doubt that the words frame a narrative, now, of dramatically mythic proportions. Where, and how far, it is sustained; how well the film attempts a resolution of the tensions between the mythic and the mimetic within the narrative as a whole must be questions left for another time.

Conclusion

I have covered a lot of ground; created a Golan of my own. I would like, therefore, now, to draw some of the issues and arguments together as a way of preserving my own claims to be heard, my own claims to be offering a useful way of approaching television documentary.

Underlying a good deal of what I have been saying is a belief that a semiology can also be a sociology; not just that the analysis of texts can provide a starting point for the analysis of their place in culture and society but that their analysis is at the same time *an* analysis of culture and society. Of course it is not possible simply to read off social structure or cultural form from a given text – the more one knows about the context of its production and reception the better. But nevertheless I would maintain that its textual dynamics, in narrative and rhetoric, in form and in content, display the results of a considerable amount of cultural work, and in that display open a route to an analysis of its place within the conflicting ideologies, discourses, language games, of the society as a whole – those discourses which are constitutive, essentially, of the society which contains them. One *can* read society in society's texts.

Hence the stress on narratives as agonistic. They are agonistic in the sense both of opposition and invention. Each text is an expression, a fragment, of a wider, *sui generis*, discourse of its own, as well as a mediator and moderator of other discourses. The television documentary text becomes a fulcrum in our essentially contested and fluid contemporary culture.

These texts are agonistic, therefore, in relation to other texts (i.e. within simple or multiple discourses: television, television-documentary, television science documentary, drama-documentary, etc.) and in relation to other discourses (science, politics, everyday life). And here the crucial significance of the science documentary comes into it. Lyotard may not see how far science and narratives overlap. Indeed his argument rests significantly on the principled *claims* of science to be a discrete activity (albeit requiring legitimation within the narratives it itself so despises). These claims are sustained within rhetorical and narrative forms which can now be recognized. That recognition is itself, of course, subversive.

But the demarcation does exist: an article in a physics text-book, a paper prepared for an international conference, are manifestly and obviously different in claim, character, mode of address and defining context from a television programme which may contain some of the same material or stem, in some way, from the same set of concerns.

The formal structure of some scientific texts, those that are clear about their own heroic status, or operate skilfully the narrative and rhetorical strategies on which popular culture depends, may find the transition to television more easy. The same will be true for the scientist, as individual, as hero. There are many scientists who, under pressure or desire, can turn their science to the forms of another medium. Only their belief that, somehow, the transformation is a neutral one, is a mistake.

Documentary television claims a *prime facie* mimetic status. Such a claim opens its texts to detailed rhetorical and narrative analysis, which despite its formality and apparent narrowmindedness, nevertheless provides a basis for comparison and a basis for assessing the work – fundamentally and always ideological – of which they are the product.

I use the word 'ideological' here in a non-pejorative sense. The implication is not that these texts distort, necessarily. It is that they are the product of a competition between voices, interests, discourses, for legitimation and the right to speak. Television science documentary mediates between science and the everyday. But it must also defend itself against science and the everyday. The political skewing which defines the institutional and cultural environment in which documentary films are produced and received must be recognized, therefore, not in its fixity, but in its achievements and its failures. It is my contention that without detailed textual work, as well as work on production and reception, the measure of those achievements and failures will go unrecorded.

6
Questions of Magnitude

Bill Nichols

> 'There seems to be a major malfunction'
> – NASA's voice-over commentator during
> the explosion of the Challenger space shuttle.
> Cape Kennedy, Florida, 28 January, 1986.

A moment erased from the subsequent narrativization of the Challenger space shuttle disaster on 28 January, 1986 is this initial response by NASA's own voice-of-God narrator. As the enormous, brilliant burst of exploding fuel rips the entire rocket into fiery shards, this narrator can only concede that the malfunction is major. Language as regulation and control, language as anaesthetic for the emotions – a more perfect demonstration of the idiocies of a bureaucratically managed minaturization of human response would be hard to imagine. The words have been lost; not a single report has referred back to them. NASA's own vision has been radically superseded by a national dramaturgy that has sought to render the perfunctory and mechanical as destiny and sacrifice.

That grotesque juxtaposition of event and commentary, evidence and argument, points toward the very disjuncture this article sets out to explore. Those words raise the question of how not only this commentary but also any narrative or expository frame can be of an order of magnitude commensurate with the magnitude of what it describes. Narrative and exposition are always forms of minaturization that seek to encapsulate a 'world' that bears some meaning for us. Documentary presents a world we take to be congruent and coterminous in quality and nature with the one in which we act rather than re-presenting an imaginative transposition of it. What structure might documentaries have that will conjure or restore for the reader those orders of magnitude appropriate to the full dimensionality of the world in which we live?

The question seems particularly fitting for the documentary film form since this form activates conventions that prepare us to expect a privileged status for the indexical link between sign and referent. Our apprehension

107

of this link anchors the image in the specificity of a given moment. Such moments are understood to have been subject to the logic of history rather than the conjurings of narrative. Though every fiction film is a documentary of its actors' performances, and though any documentary may construct images, shots and scenes as thoroughly as the most scripted of fictions, the difference in reception remains profound.[1]

The documentary mode invites a triple reading. One, 'X', is along the signifying plane of narrative emplotment as it moves toward closure and resolution. One, 'Y', is at right-angles to the narrative flow, back toward a known or extra-cinematic referent situated in history. A third, 'Z' axis, as it were, is at right-angles to both of these; this is the dimension of myth, spectacle and captivation with the 'to-be-looked-atness' of the image. The Hollywood cinema of spectacle, the representation of women as the fetishized object of desire and the transcendent image of the star are all important moment along this axis. In fact, each axis, as we shall see, has a different set of implications for the representation of the human body.

Though not unique to documentary this splayed form of engagement operates at a different ratio of the three axes when we take the world referred to by the film to be the commonly known one of historical action. The spatio-temporal universe to which we attend remains the same, but the coordinates at which we intersect it change considerably. The exact nature of these ratios among the indexical, iconic and symbolic signals the effect of a set of conventions that mark off the documentary as a highly distinct genre.

The issue of magnitude raises questions not only of indexical correspondence between a text and the visual world but also of aesthetic and ideological correspondence between a text and the historical world. The magnitudes opened up by a text are not merely a matter of naming something of profound importance but, more tellingly, of situating the reader in a position where these magnitudes receive imaginative, instructive engagement. Questions of magnitude pertain to matters of experiential dimensionality and the strategies by which a given text addresses us rhetorically. The rhetoric of address seeks to enlist our appetite, our desire to know and experience the world, within a form that quells the very desire it also enlists, or that redirects it toward some goal of its own. *Roses in December* (Ana Carringer and Bernard Stone, 1982), for example – a film about the lay nun, Jean Donovan, killed in El Salvador with three other nuns by a government death squad) enlists our desire to understand a barbaric act in order to weave a complex set of homilies on the relation between the individual and the collective, the nature of witness and service, the linkage, at least in Latin America, of religion and

---

[1]See Matthew Bernstein, 'Visual Style and Spatial Articulations in *Berlin, Symphony of a City*' (1927). *The Journal of Film and Video*, 36, no. 4 (Fall 1984) for a careful demonstration of the intensive use of analytic and continuity editing, derived from fiction films, in early documentary.

revolution, and the ethical/political dimensions of death and its commemoration. The goals of commemoration and dedication to the spirit of Jean Donovan, offered through the formal structure of the film as a text and its narrative-like closure – beginning with the unearthing of her body at the unmarked gravesite and ending with the emotionally powerful 'Departure Ceremony' held to mark the departure of new volunteers for Central America – satisfy, at one level, the desire that has been enlisted, even if, at another level, we are led to recognize that the satisfaction of desire requires additional action in the historical world to which the film refers.

Satisfaction presents an elusive figure. Texts often disturb and unsettle in ways that are not put to rest. There are always issues of excess to be addressed, questions of magnitudes that will not fit within a frame, however encompassing, questions which point toward ideology and its relentless work of repression. Some texts may openly incite or encourage responses that are oppositional to the ones promoted by the prevailing ideology. Other texts may prompt such responses indirectly, through their reliance on rhetoric to achieve their objective: to win consent, not compel it. The acceptance, adoption and endorsement of a given set of ideological propositions depends on the formal strategies of rhetoric deployed to prefigure the social field as a discernible and discussable realm.[2] Ideology, in its discursive forms, must rely upon rhetoric because it constructs subjects who subscribe to their own freedom. The consent of such subjects must be won voluntarily, through their own consent, rather than by force. This need to win consent represents the Achilles heel of ideology, its vulnerability and difference from sheer coercive force. Though our freedom may be severely constrained, we are, indeed, free to offer consent or to withold it.

Ideology, as Louis Althusser suggests, depends upon our interpellation within the dominant order of things, our (mis)recognition of our appropriate place. But the moment of interpellation is not only the moment when our identity, place and fate are sealed, it is also a moment of profound jeopardy for the social order. Every interpellation that addresses us and calls for our consent carries with it an implicit moment of negotiation. This rhetorical act inevitably poses the question, 'Don't you agree?'. Seemingly offhand, a mere formality like a casual *'n'est-ce pas?'*, effective rhetoric will sweep right past this moment of potential resistance. Ideology, then, relies on rhetorical form to achieve persuasiveness and carry us past the point when we may reply to its *'n'est-ce pas?'* with hesitance or defiance.

As Frank Lentricchia puts it, 'In the moment of linkage [between form and ideology], form would seize and direct ideological substance, transform it into power over the subject-audience; it would turn our ideology,

---

[2] See Hayden White, *Metahistory: The Historical Imagination in Nineteenth Century Europe* (Baltimore, Johns Hopkins Press, 1973), p. 30.

in both senses [as culture and as lived experience] over to a disciplinary intention. . . . The aesthetic moment of linkage, then, is the manipulative moment at which the subject-audience is submitted to the productive force of ideology.'[3] Rather than the 'manipulative moment' we might call it *the crisis moment* from which consent or contestation emerge.

Whatever we call it, the linkage itself is indispensable. Ideas, concepts and values cannot be simply announced if they are also to be believed. In this, dialectical, sense, the cultural provides the 'base' for those superstructural activities of economic production through which things take on the significance of signs within human communication and exchange. Cultural production invites our consent to an assigned place within the signs and meanings of social space. It renders the flat, objective givenness of the world into a complex realm of inter-subjectivity. The human subject requires introduction to this viscerally engaging realm so that attachments can be made between desire and the world disposed around us. We require an imaginative sense of what it means to belong or participate (what community is like); of what conditional states pertain (what it would be like if . . .); of what subjective states accompany these conditional situations derived from a given set of ideological assumptions, and of the *form* within which these subjective states of being could become incarnate. From such intangibles – the imaginary and symbolic realms within which rhetoric trades – come motivation and purpose, discipline and self-control, belief and advocacy, in short, all those magnitudes of subjectivity that position us in relation to what exists, what's appropriate and what's possible. 'Art [or the crisis moment of linkage between form and ideology] not only imitates life but equally influences it, and it does so by providing, often for the first time, a significant form for those very aspects of subjective human experience it purports only to reflect.'[4]

Questions of magnitude here carry us into the realm of ideology, contradiction, paradox and excess. The utopian longing for community that rhetoric frequently evokes becomes repressed to the level of the subtext and the political unconscious. (In his book of the same name, Fredric Jameson identifies the political unconscious as the repressed site of meditation on the destiny of community, where community proposes an intersubjective realm beyond the monadic regime of desire.) The text becomes the site of contradiction where narrative strategies seek a resolution to those social contradictions they must represent if the text is to exert a hold on us but which they can only register as 'logical scandal':

[3]Frank Lentricchia, *Criticism and Social Change* (Chicago and London, University of Chicago Press, 1983), p. 104.
[4]Giles Gunn, 'The Semiotics of Culture and the Interpretation of Literature: Clifford Geertz and the Moral Imagination', *Studies in the Literary imagination*, 12, no. 1 (Spring 1979), p. 120. See also Fredric Jameson, 'The Symbolic Inference; or Kenneth Burke and Ideological Analysis', *Critical Inquiry*, 4 (Spring 1978), pp. 507–23.

[W]hat can in the former [history] be resolved only through the intervention of praxis here [in the text] comes before the purely contemplative mind as logical scandal or double bind, the unthinkable and the conceptually paradoxical, that which cannot be unknotted by the operation of pure thought, and which must therefore generate a whole more properly narrative apparatus – the text itself – to square its circles and to dispel, through narrative movement, its intolerable closure.[5]

Magnitude in this regard aligns itself with those various strategies by which a text may figure its own awareness of scandal and thereby alert us to the gap between resolution by praxis and by narrative closure. Irony, distantiation, deconstruction, reflexivity, the formalist concept of *ostranie* – such tactics operate to achieve the effect of opening out onto magnitudes not otherwise anticipated. There is not merely the flat announcement of something more that escapes the frame, but the subjective experience of excess, the discovery – usually unanticipated, sudden or dialectical – of a magnitude of existence beyond containment. At this crisis moment, our response to the *'n'est-ce pas?'* of ideological consent hesitates and wavers. We glimpse an alternative domain on the horizon of the existing conditions of existence and in opposition to it. The subjective dimension, given external form by cultural production, here renders the presence of contradiction, paradox and dialectics with experiential force.

Documentary, with the 'stickiness' of those indexical images that refer us back to the historical, makes it particularly hard to let this discovery remain within the province of a formalism, a play within codes, a deconstruction of unity into its disparate parts. 'The documentary effect', as it were, turns us back toward the historical dimension and the challenge of praxis with a forcefulness borne of the text's almost tangible bond to that which it also represents as though for the first time. The very process of minaturization that narrative containment requires proves particularly susceptible to a restoration of scale when the extension of what we see appears to be the world in which we live. Realism, too, has this effect, and when the conventions of documentary and realism combine, the result is a form of instruction and pleasure with considerable significance.

In 'The Voice of Documentary' I argued that many contemporary documentaries which use a string of interviews to reconstruct a suppressed fragment of history lose their own voice in deference to the witnesses recruited by the film.[6] A sense of contradiction or dialectic gets suppressed beneath the unity of collective memory. Some form of distantiation that would foreground the film-maker's own voice seemed necessary if the gap

[5]Fredric Jameson, *The Political Unconscious* (Ithaca, New York, Cornell University Press, 1981), pp. 82–3.
[6]Bill Nichols, 'The Voice of Documentary,' *Film Quarterly*, 36 no. 3 (Spring 1983).

between past and present and between the text and its historical subtext were to impress itself upon the viewer. The most promising form was that of the reflexive documentary begun by Dziga-Vertov and given recent incarnation by David and Judith MacDougall in their ethnographic films (e.g. *Wedding Camels* in the Turkana trilogy). These films stressed the structuring presence of the film-maker at the centre of the events represented and restored a sense of voice to the textual system that was clearly distinct from that of any recruited witnesses or from the imaginary unity of a voice of God commentator.

Instructive though such a reflexive strategy is, it has not been the predominant form adopted by documentaries that have sought to signal those orders of magnitude that turn on excess, contradiction and dialectics. Two other strategies have also emerged. One, which cannot be pursued here in detail, involves a deconstruction of the codes of documentary itself. Such work operates along the margin between documentary and the avant-garde and is well represented by Trinh Minh-ha's *Reassemblage* (1982) and Edin Velez's *Meta Mayan II* (1981).[7] These two films subvert the prevailing codes of ethnography in a far more radical way than the films of the MacDougalls, which continue to operate within the bounds of a realist aesthetic that has gained a self-consciousness about its own conventions, particularly those that efface the presence of the film-maker.

Reassemblage and *Meta Mayan II*, on the other hand, do not make a particular point of the film-maker's presence within a field of social action realistically observed. (In *Reassemblage* the film-maker's presence is sharply felt on the sound track, however – an aural space from which she provides an ironic series of reflexive commentaries as though the image track comprised a set of realist observations in need of qualification rather than a sharp departure from the conventions of realism.) These films trouble the codes of realism themselves, they turn to special effects and expressionistic devices to render the everyday more opaque than transparent, to evoke a poetic texture that harkens back to *The Nuer* and beyond that to the city-symphony films and the work of the dadaists and surrealists. By beginning with the images of another culture, they achieve an effect not unlike that of Bruce Conner or David Rimmer with their manipulations of found footage from our own. These films may tell us little about the ethnographic detail of tribal life in Senegal and northern Guatemala, respectively, but they are clearly not formalist exercises either. They, too, render the codes of realism and the assumptions of science problematic and pose inescapable questions about the voice of documentary as it works to acknowledge excess and confound ideological strategies of containment.

---

[7]Another potent example would appear to be Jean-Pierre Gorin's *Poto and Cabengo*, a film I have not yet seen, but which is described as a highly deconstructive text by Vivian Sobchack, '16 Ways to Pronounce "Potato": Authority and Authorship in *Poto and Cabengo*', *The Journal of Film and Video*, 36, no. 4 (Fall 1984).

The third response also addresses the challenge of how to move beyond the string-of-interviews mode of historical reconstruction. This alternative, no more 'new,' 'novel' or 'pure' than reflexivity or deconstruction, has proven particularly prevalent. I refer to the (only apparently) naive emphasis on certain fictive conventions of narrative in a documentary context. These are predominantly conventions of classic Hollywood narrative, but now transposed to a documentary format. The strategy is clearly one of degree and emphasis not of a difference in kind since documentary seldom if ever escapes the codes of narrative entirely. But for American and Anglo-Canadian documentarists who have traditionally differentiated themselves more rigorously from their Hollywood counterparts than have documentarists elsewhere, this renewed, resourceful use of the codes of classic narrative cinema takes on considerable importance as a rhetorical strategy.

Such a strategy might seemed doomed by its dependence on those very (narrative, realist) codes that work to suppress our recognition of the crisis moment of which we have spoken, of codes that have been subject to considerable scrutiny and attack. But this is to assume that such codes operate in a monolithic, determining fashion. I prefer to stress the possibilities of local fissure or contradiction and the opportunity such moments afford to subvert the frame within which they occur. This may be the work of troubled texts more than troubling ones, but the disturbance to the *'n'est-ce pas?'* of ideological agreement can be effective all the same. The result is to open out onto that amplitude of experience beyond the ideology of unity or wholeness by intensifying the very antinomies, the logical scandals, implicit in narrative.[8] 'In the cinema we sense this break between a story and its presentation every time gaps appear in the events or reversals crop up in the standard conventions of the genre . . . everything, in short, which calls attention to the work of style retards the unmediated flow of illusion and lifts the film experience from the obsessions of the imaginary to the realm of symbolic exchange.'[9] To the obsessions that Dudley Andrew identifies as an impediment to the reception of narrative proper, which we have termed the axis of spectacle, we would want to add our third axis of indexical linkage to the visible, socially constructed world and stress that all three axes coexist in the realist cinema be it framed or labelled for us as fiction or documentary. The symbolic realm never escapes

[8]A fundamental, if somewhat schematic statement of this proposition occurs in Jean-Luis Comolli and Jean Narboni, 'Cinema, Ideology, Criticism,' in Bill Nichols, ed., *Movies and Methods* (Berkeley, University of California Press, 1976). More recent explorations of troubled texts would include Robin Wood, An Introduction to the American Horror Film, in Bill Nichols, ed., *Movies and Methods*, Vol. II (Berkeley, University of California Press, 1985), Tania Modleski, *Loving With a Vengeance* (New York, Methuen, 1982), Dudley Andrew, *Concepts in Film Theory* (New York, Oxford University Press, 1984), David Bordwell, Janet Staiger and Kristen Thompson, *The Classical Hollywood Cinema* (New York, Columbia University Press, 1985).
[9]Dudley Andrew, *Concepts in Film Theory* (Oxford and New York, OUP, 1984), pp. 151–2.

the imaginary one on which it builds, and neither escapes the indexical bondage between sign and referent that marks the cinema as a distinctive medium.

Essentially, I want to suggest that a number of quite successful documentaries have turned to the narrative construction of character for an answer to the question of how to formulate a narrative voice that lends magnitude to the gaps between events. They have adopted narrative (fictive) strategies within a domain and to a degree such that the effect of these strategies derives from a new position, a new set of coordinates on the axes of narrative, myth and indexical reference. A peculiar tension arises that is not unlike the tension sustained by reflexive or deconstructive strategies. These films traverse the other side of the same narrow ridge as experimental works like Michele Citron's *Daughter Rite* where the hybridization of form itself becomes an important signifier of meaning.

Roses in December can serve as the primary example of a tendency with far-reaching ramifications. Other examples include *Frank: A Vietnam Veteran* (Frank Simon and Vince Canzoneri, 1981), *Las Madres de la Plaza de Mayo, Witness to War* (Deborah Schaeffer, 1985), and *A Man Marked to Die* (Eduardo Coutinho, 1984). *Frank: A Vietnam Veteran* adopts the case-history approach that also characterizes the flamboyantly tortured *Mishima* to present a person who lives out his life in accordance with contradictory, self-destructive mythologies he has chosen to embody. *Witness to War* adopts the hagiographic portraiture that runs through *Young Mr Lincoln, Wilson, Dr Ehrlich's Magic Bullet* and other films from classic Hollywood to present Dr Charlie Clements, an ex-Air Force pilot who served behind the rebel lines in El Salvador for a year as a pacifist physician. *A Man Marked to Die* (subtitled *20 Years After*) begins with a screening of Coutinho's unfinished fiction film based on the murder of a peasant leader in 1964 in the man's village to begin an odyssey in which Coutinho traces the multiple fates of the man's wife and their 10 children. *Roses in December* traces the life of Jean Donovan back to her childhood in order to restore meaning to her senseless murder. As such it partakes of the *bildungsroman* tradition that we find in *Julia* or *Coal Miner's Daughter* as the accretions of social, historical determination attach themselves to the human subject whom we encounter.

The primary effect that requires exploration results from the collision of the representation of an individual life, the fabrication of a narrative character and the potential transubstantiation of the body of the person into the imagery of the heroic or mythic. Biography, so often presented as 'A Life', in fact counters the errant trajectory of life with the smooth curve of narrative form. It might more properly be called 'A Story'. Its closure and unity stand at odds to the open-endedness and incoherence of life as it is lived. Documentary operates in the crease between the life as lived and the life as narrativized. It, like the historical fiction, presents the question of how to figure the body, how to structure or present the person situated in history within a text situated as narrative.

Unlike historical fiction, documentary evades the problem of finding itself with a body too many, with an historical personage reincarnated by an actor whose very presence testifies to the gap between the text and the life to which it refers. The problem for documentary is that of one body too few, the need to represent an historical person, an agent of social activity, within a narrative field as a character, an agent of narrative functions, and within a mythic or contemplative field as an icon or symbol, a recipient of psychic investments. The dilemma which André Bazin noted certainly holds true: in order to function within a narrative frame, the historical person must cede his or her historical agency and assume the status of a mythic character whose full trajectory is known.[10] This is only partially problematic for the deceased historical figure but for the living person who is susceptible to the adoption of these very myths as aspects of their own self-presentation, a process Bazin finds at work in Stalin, the dilemma reaches the point of crisis and scandal. To it we may simply add the compounding dilemma of finding individuals represented not only as characters within a narrative but also as mythic personae (be they stars or cultural heroes) within the cinema.

Roses in December, for example, recovers the body of the murdered lay nun, Jean Donovan, in order to reconstitute it as a living person, narrative character and exemplary persona (quite literally: the first scene documents, apparently in newsreel footage, the discovery of the gravesite and the unearthing of the bodies of the four nuns). The partially decomposed bodies unsettle the gaze enormously. They are tangible evidence of a self no longer bound into the imaginary unity of the subject, no longer the agency of action but only the recipient of the actions of others. A terrible objectification manifests itself that raises to another level of magnitude the disquiet that the mythic figure, or even the star and advertising model, can evoke. The absolutely essential, physical body of such myth-bound figures is the living site of a different sort of objectification. Here the body undergoes transubstantiation; it is used to impersonate some other possibility for self-presentation. But how can the self present itself if it does so in the form of a disguise? Like the nude of classic oil painting such bodies are condemned to never be themselves. This is a (mild) form of death, or self-mortification, even if it is for transcendent ends. If the star or model is dressed up rather than laid out; if he or she is made up rather than embalmed, posed or presented rather than interred, and recovered through the fixed likeness of a photographic image rather than exhumed, the treatment of the body is nonetheless disturbingly similar. Mythic figures whom we meet in the flesh may unsettle us in ways similar to an encounter with a cadaver: their bodies represent the place where we expect to locate an abundance of meanings that are, in fact, eerily absent. This is particularly true of stars or models, people whose mythic status depends on

---

[10]See Andre Bazin, 'The Stalin Myth in Soviet Cinema,' in Bill Nichols, ed., *Movies and Methods* Vol. II, pp. 29–40.

their repeated appearance in 'vehicles' rather than on their personal achievements within the domain of the historical. It may be far less true for figures like Dr Charlie Clements or Jean Donovan, whose mythic status derives not from the re-presentation of the body elsewhere but in its political or ethical deployment in history itself. Both forms of the mythic occur along the same axis but in the manner of positive or negative values that tend toward very different conceptualizations of the relation between the body and our psychic investment in its representations.

The success of *Roses* hinges on its ability to sustain the questions of magnitude involving subjectivity and dialectics that its biographical treatment of the individual life provokes. The attribution of character and mythic persona to the Argentine women who marched in La Plaza de Mayo on behalf of their disappeared family members or to Dr Charlie Clements, who hiked into El Salvador with his medical supplies on his back to treat the victims of armed struggle, provoke similar questions. There seems to be a body too few in that an actual historical being must also serve as the plastic material from which the agent or character of their own narrative and the icon or persona of their own myth is constructed.

Roses in December, in dealing with a deceased individual, can only present its central character as a structuring absence that the film must reconstitute as a narrative character (the individualized agent of a series of narrative predicates). In this project it departs quite sharply from the string-of-interviews documentary which attempts to reconstruct a past event, rather than an individual life, and recruits the testimony of participant-witnesses to do so. It is also similar to those fiction films that set out to recover a past life, beginning at a point from which we may ask, 'How did this come to pass?' In this task, *Roses* bears a resemblance to *Young Mr Lincoln*, although it avoids the suggestions of the monstrous dimension to the (patriarchal) hero and begins with the tragic assassination that still lies beyond the concluding horizon of John Ford's film. Still closer analogies are perhaps with *Citizen Kane* (particularly in the stress on the enigmatic, in the use of a largely invisible reporter who travels afar to seek out the insights of those who knew the character, in the multiplicity of voices and evidentiary sources, and in the catalytic, galvanizing force of the moment of death) but *Sunset Boulevard*, *The Power and the Glory* and several other films also bear a close resemblance.

The body – a term that contains the awful ambiguity of being both an agent and an object, an emblem of life and a sign of death – requires reanimation in these films. Its surface must be reinscribed with meaning. But in *Roses* the inscription is meant to attach primarily to the *person*, Jean Donovan, who lost her life in a country whose government feels little compunction about taking it, rather than to the *persona*, 'Jean Donovan', which represents the conversion of the body of the person into a transcendent, mythic image, an image apotheosized in the cinema as the star, that secular deity who represents an idealization of appearances (physical looks, manners, movements, ways of inhabiting space and traversing time with which we may identify).[11] But most significantly, and paradoxically, *Roses* reincarnates Jean Donovan's body as a precarious balance of person, persona and narrative agent that can not be any one of these possibilities entirely. The coordinates at which the film locates the secular trinity of Jean Donovan – person, persona, character – requires the substance of the historical person to provide substantiation for the narrative character and mythic persona.

This peculiar balance derives from the insistence of the cinema upon the presence of the body, its relentless demand of *habeas corpus*. The cinema assigns the photographic image of the body – its appearance as absence – to the locus of narrative agency, unlike the novel which leaves its characters physically unattached to any indexical representation. This assignment simultaneously invokes the third dimension and its axis of the mythic in which the person and the character fuse imperfectly; an excess remains that requires this third axis, the dimensionality of myth, for its manifestation. *Roses in December*, though, does not set out to transform this historical person, Jean Donovan, into that form of cinematic icon we call the star although it must play off this potential, this asymptotic endpoint the film may approach but never reach.

Roses deploys a remarkably full measure of narrative codes in its move along this asymptote. The film never entirely escapes the realm of the indexical to move us into that two-dimensional world of narrative and its fitful interruption by arresting images of the star so well dissected by Laura Mulvey in relation to the represention of women.[12] Instead, we occupy a three-dimensional, conceptual space which, though mediated by a semiotic rhetoric, engages us in a manner decidedly different from the more imaginative realm of the aesthetic or the realm of the vicarious and the pleasures of the simulacrum. *Roses in December* announces its intent to speak about the historical world, most forcefully in its opening scene of (apparently) video news footage recording the discovery of the gravesite. The rich, visual warmth of the site and the calm, loving tones of those who speak about Donovan enforce a disjunction between this past, these remembrances, their invitation to the planes of narrative and mythic ordering, and the harsh reality of her actual murder.

That reality finds powerful expression in the opening newsreel-like footage that begins the film. The graphically clinical nature of the camera's gaze, or stare, disturbs profoundly. The sight of a body pulled out of its grave by ropes only to flop inertly on the dusty ground, the physical

---

[11]See Stephen Heath's essay, 'Body Voice', in *Questions of Cinema* (Bloomington, Indiana University Press, 1981) for a full discussion of the differences among person, actor, agent, character, star and 'figure', Heath's term for a way of representing the linkages among the axes of history, narrative and myth such that an instability results. Another useful discussion of these terms occurs in Barry King, 'Articulating Stardom,' *Screen*, 26, no. 5 (September–October 1985).

[12]Laura Mulvey, 'Visual Pleasure and Narrative Cinema', *Movies and Methods*, Vol. II (Berkeley, University of California Press, 1985).

residue of what had been a human residence, approaches the unwatchable. Such images testify to the problematics of the 'professional gaze'.[13] What ethical (or political) perspective authorizes such a gaze? As Vivian Sobchack notes, 'professional gaze is marked by ethical ambiguity, by technical and machine-like competence in the face of an event which seems to call for further and human response . . . The concern for getting a clear and unobstructed image, and the belief that it is possible to strip that image, that representation, of human bias and perspective and ethicality so that it is 'objective', indelibly marks the inscriptions of the professional gaze with their own problematic ethical perspective in the face of both human mortality and visual taboo.'[14]

Roses in December refuses to endorse the professional gaze, however. Instead, it offers, in the sequences of its own construction, a supplemental, human response that fuses fact and value, body and meaning, healing the breach between self and other which professsionalism or voyeurism opens. *Roses* restores magnitude to what the newsreel footage diminishes. The elegaic structure of the film directs the uncontained excess of that footage, the queasy sense of taboo which it invokes, toward the ethically lived life of a person. Death, the zero point of meaning at the level of the individual life, becomes recuperated within a larger social, political, religious frame that inscribes meaning on this wanton act of obliteration. *Roses* does so without following the trajectory of the mythologizing impulse that remakes the bodies of seven lost astronauts into icons of progress and pioneering spirit, into personae whose historical agency must be arrested so that they can be fixed in the pantheon of American mythology. Instead the film situates the person as an agent in history whose actions are reconstituted in a filmic representation that introduces axes of narrative and myth without lopping off its third axis of indexical reference.

Roses also approaches, without fully adopting, the strategy of a controlling voice that can bring order to the conflicting voices held within the text. This strategy of containment is what gives a film like *Citizen Kane* only the appearance of disorder since the disparate testimonies and evidence are finally ordered by the narrating agency of the film itself, by 'Orson Welles', the *auteur*. *Roses in December* incorporates a number of voices without fully assimilating them to a meaning or theme. Even John

[13]Vivian Sobchack in 'Inscribing Ethical Space: Ten Propositions on Death, Representation and Documentary', *Quarterly Review of Film Studies* (Fall 1984) describes six different visual forms in which the encounter of filmmaker and death or dying can be registered, each bearing a distinct set of ethical implictions. The 'professional gaze' is one of these.
[14]Sobchack, 'Inscribing Ethical Space,' p. 298. See also Michael Shudson. *Discovering the News: A Social History of American Newspapers* (New York, Basic Books, 1978) which argues that the 'professional' or 'objective' code of reportage derives, ironically, from a loss of faith in the givenness of the world in the post-World War I environment. If the world is open to manipulation, better to remain apart from it and report 'the facts' dissociated from values; instead the value of objectivity provides an internal, evaluative code of professional conduct independent of the values that can be assigned to the facts presented.

Houseman's voice-over commentary is held to a minimum and does not provide the riddle-solving equivalent to Welles's final tracking shot into the emblem of 'Rosebud' as it goes up in flames. A heterogeneous mix of authorized voices informs the film and destabilizes the impression of a unified fictive space. Donovan's letters, read by her brother, on camera, and diary passages, read by Susan Stevens in voice-over; home movies of Jean horseback riding, represented in slow-motion with voice-over commentary by her riding instructor; the testimony of friends and parents; contextualizing passages that summarize the history of military repression and violence in El Salvador through the use of stock footage, and material shot for the film, together with press interviews or public testimony by key US officials like then Secretary of State Alexander Haig or Ambassador to the UN Jean Kirkpatrick – all these strands of the film contribute to a plane of logical ordering without achieving a full sense of closure. (Kirkpatrick's claim that the four women were not 'just nuns' but 'political activists' as though this, if true, would be reason enough for summary execution, exerts the kind of undertow that interviews in many of Emile de Antonio's films do: the remark's validity cannot be upheld within the framework that surrounds it; it both relativizes that frame as it nullifies itself.) The radical force of Fredric Jameson's assertion about the nature of history is what this text *figures*, in an inescapably partial way, as a gap between the discourse of governmental figures and the events they try to rationalize away: '[history] is *not* a text, not a narrative, master or otherwise . . . History is what hurts, it is what refuses desire and sets inexorable limits to individual as well as collective praxis.'[15] An excess remains.

Part of that excess is the very question of interior magnitudes which *Roses in December* opens up only to leave unanswered. Narrative fiction can answer more fully to the question of what it feels like to occupy a given body, to present a certain character, to walk the divide between that moment of spectacle which depends on the physical presence of the person and those moments of narrative that rely on the actions of a character. The incarnation of characters by people (social actors) holds us to the surface of subjectivity in that interior states must be displayed on the skin of the actor. But, like the novel, the cinema also has means of engendering subjective states that are more interior. The full weight of the cinematic apparatus can be brought to bear in the constitution of an arresting subjectivity. As Barry King notes, '. . . the projection of interiority becomes less and less the provenance of the actor and more and more a property emerging from directorial or editorial decision. . . . [W]hile film increases the centrality of the actor in the process of signification, the formative capacity of the medium can equally confine the actor more and more to being a bearer of effects that he or she does not or cannot originate.'[16]

One formidable aspect of the generation of an imaginary interiority by

[15]Fredric Jameson, *The Political Unconscious*, pp. 35, 102.
[16]Barry King, 'Articulating Stardom,' p. 45.

the apparatus occurs in the extra-filmic but cinematic discourse about stars. This discourse lends an overarching unity to the disparate roles a star may play by stressing the characterological consistency of the star him / herself. Ironically, the documentary that mobilizes the 'Z' axis of the mythic cannot rely on such a discourse for assistance (unless it is a documentary about a star or similar cultural hero). It may have recourse to the extra-filmic and extra-cinematic discourse that surrounds people whose historical role receives public attention, but, even more suggestively, such documentaries may generate their own discourse about the person in order to lend greater coherence to the character they construct.

A film like *Roses*, then, incorporates two elements that are usually separated between the fictive text and its surround: on the one hand, it represents the codes of social *performance* whereby a person presents him / herself to others, codes closely allied to realist acting codes, and on the other hand, the film generates *testimony* about social performance or life. This evidence of iconic status in relation to history contrasts to what in fiction films remains a function of ancillary but fundamentally cinematic texts or practices such as rituals of imitation or emulation like autograph seeking or the copying of styles of dress or gesture, the circulation of gossip and lore through fan magazines, television talk shows, posters and fan clubs. (The modes of ancillary discourse that have priority in *Roses* include that recruited mix of textual voices described above as well as the subjectivizing strategies discussed below.)

The documentary combination of these two usually cross-referenced but differentiated strategies for the fabrication of the mythic is not a stable one. The change of register and voice fractures 'performance;' it becomes more intermittent and available to interpretation. Subjectivity is rendered less coherent when its origins are so proximate yet diverse; the imaginary unity of character becomes eccentric. Its centre, like that of documentary, lies outside itself, in the historical surround, and in its own enunciative strategies.

Documentary has traditionally taken an ambivalent position regarding interior states of mind – particularly in its *cinéma vérité* mode where the outer surface of the body, including utterances, take on the charged importance of a naturalism – but one of the recurring themes in recent works is their effort to give structure to interiority. In *Frank: A Vietnam Veteran* it comes from the intensely subjective nature of Frank's account in which he speaks of the acts of atrocity he committed in Vietnam and the acts of desperation he then committed back home. In *Witness to War* interiority stems from the use of stock combat footage to which location sound effects are added in an effort to give resonance to the gnawing questions of conscience that finally moved Charlie Clements to refuse to fly US Air Force sorties in Vietnam, to train as a medical doctor and then to hike into El Salvador to do what he could for the victims of war. *No Pasarán* (David Bradbury, 1984) concludes its portrait of the struggle to defend Nicaraguan sovereignty with an ominous, poetic sequence of American C-135s loading and taking off from a jungle airstrip; instead of location sound, these telephoto images of lumbering leviathans accompany an eerie but rhythmic Laurie Anderson song, 'Here Come the Bombs'. In *Las Madres*, as in Michel Brault's French Canadian film, *Les Ordres*, the process of interiorization relies on the recreation of dramatic moments when police officers break into an apartment to effect an arrest. *Las Madres* renders the event in blue tinted, slow-motion black and white photography with the voice-over commentary of one of the mothers of the disappeared, a contrast to the colour photography of the rest of the film.

Roses in December, in sharp contrast to the theatrical version of *28 Up*, does not attempt to elaborate its characters by bullying them; instead it moves toward a more thoroughly subjective invocation of interiority that, like those recreations in *Las Madres* or *Les Ordres*, engage us by means of processes of identification. Specifically, *Roses* offers a reconstruction of Jean Donovan's last hours in El Salvador from her drive to the airport to pick up the other nuns, through their detention at a roadblock, sexual violation and subsequent execution. This sequence, too, relies more heavily on the cinematic apparatus to achieve the markings of interiority than on the performance of actors to re-present the last hours of the four murdered women. We never see any individuated characters or the faces of any actors; all we see, in fact, is a single hand on the steering wheel of their van. What narrative agents there are little more than physical markers of the place of an individuated meaning. The agents' own bodies are strongly deindividuated; they are given no close-ups, no dialogue, no physical movements that can be read as signs of expressivity. They are, indeed, barely visible and only serve to abolish the problematics of a vehicle that would seem to propel itself to its fatal destiny.

A performance as such would be highly problematic, presenting the problem of four bodies too many, of a departure from the indexical compact that grounds the reception of documentary. These nearly invisible actors are little more than what Heath has called 'animated entities' in order to stress the lack of individuation that can be a legitimate feature of the agent/actor as such. Shot in tinted black and white and using dramatic camera angles (most notably a shot from close to ground level as their minibus comes to a stop in a deserted stretch of countryside, a shot as laden with foreboding as the famous moment in *Tabu* when the sailing ship slowly slides into frame), this sequence conveys something of the interior meaning of mission and of witness even as it delivers the body of Jean Donovan to that site at which the film begins and to which meaning must be restored.

The attempt to construct an interior meaning and subjective experiencce propels these films toward the imaginary coherence of actual person and fictitious character in the image of the icon, and yet they also insist on the dispersal of that very coherence. The ground of documentary resides in the relation between character, icon and *social* agent. Here the person acts as an agent in history, not a narrative, no matter how persistently we give meaning to the former by means of the latter. The figuration of this relationship represents a moment of crisis in documentary. The full, ideological coherencce of narrative may impose itself and cast the person into the imaginary mould of the narrative character; the cinematic apparatus for the engenderment of the icon-as-star may dissolve the linkage between the person and the plane of history, or the raw, inchoate flux of history may overwhelm the textual system and subsume the person into the senseless swirl of the anecdotal and episodic.

When held in unstable balance so that we find, as we do in *Roses in December*, that a person takes on the attributes of character (here clustered around the journey as spiritual odyssey and the attendant rituals of both witness and self-discovery) and of icon (here associated with qualities of dedication, devotion, agape love and grace), but also remains situated as an agent within the historical arena to which the stickiness of the film's indexical sounds and images continues to return us, the result undermines the imaginary solidity of the fictive and mythic and confirms the necessary alliance between contradiction and closure in narrative. A resistance occurs. Magnitudes prevail that make the very alignment of person/character/icon seem a violation of the body of the social actor. Those transgressive moments of mythic unity, of the voyeuristic or fetishistic gaze, often wed the star to narrative in the precarious manner of a potential disruption and stoppage of flow. They become all the more transgressive of an historical field that refuses all attempts to arrest it, however momentarily.

The presentation of the person within the three-dimensional coordinates of narrative, history and myth, allows these films (*Roses in December*, *Las Madres*, *No Pasarán*, *Witness to War*, and others) to open the question of magnitudes that exceed any one logic or code, that are, among other things, magnitudes in excess of any discursive frame, that are the stuff to which only praxis can attend. This suggests less the need to accommodate a humanist or phenomenological impulse in the form of the mysterious and ineffable, so much as the need to acknowledge the distinctive power of a utopian (or political) unconscious that employs multiple and perhaps inevitably contradictory means by which to achieve the reconciliation of conflict. In this are located magnitudes that more linear, less dialectical conceptualizations of the personal and the political can only suppress.

Note

An invaluable source of information about Graef's filmmaking is *Nothing But The Truth* (ICA/BFI, 1982) edited by John Wyver. This chapter is based on a review of *Nothing but the Truth* which appeared in *Media Culture and Society* (Vol. 5 No 2) in 1983 and also draws on my discussion of Lukacs and the ideology of realism in *WDR and the Arbeiterfilm* (BFI, 1981) which, in turn, was pre-echoed in my remarks on Graef's *Decision: British Communism* project in the pages of *Comment* in 1978 (themselves cited in *Nothing but the Truth*). However this bibliographical etymology does not adequately indicate my debt to *Nothing but the Truth* and I am pleased to acknowledge here more than the usual reviewer's debt to the work that occasioned the review.

Filmography
One of Them Is Brett, Dir/writer R. Graef, Society for Thalidomide Children, 1964. *The Man From Sotheby's*, Prod/Dir/Writer R. Graef, CBC 1964. *To The Manner Born*, Prod/Dir/Writer R. Graef, CBC, 1965. *Gunter Grass's Germany*, Prod/Dir/Writer R. Graef, CBC/BBC, 1965. *The Life And Times Of John Huston, Esq*, Prod/Dir/Writer R. Graef, CBC/BBC/NET, 1965. *Who Is?* (13 episodes), Exec Prod R. Graef, 5 episodes Dir R. Graef, CBC/BBC/NET/BR, 1966–67. *Why Save Florence?*, Prod/Dir/Writer R. Graef, CBC/BBC/NET/BR, 1969. *In The Name of Allah*, Prod/Dir/Writer R. Graef, CBC/BBC/NET/BR, 1970. *The Space Between Words* (5 episodes), Prod/Dir R. Graef, BBC/KCET, 1972. *The State of The Nation: A Law In the Making*, Prod/Dir R. Graef, Granada, 1973. *Is this The Way To Save A City?*, Prod/Writer R. Graef & M. Dibb, Dir R. Graef, BBC, 1974. *The State Of The Nation: Inside The Brussels HQ*, Prod/Dir R. Graef, Granada, 1975. *Decision* (3 episodes), Prod/Dir R. Graef, Granada, 1976. *Pleasure At Her Majesty's*, Prod/Dir R. Graef, Amnesty International, 1976. *Decision: British Communism* (3 episodes), Prod/Dir R. Graef, Granada, 1978. *The Mermaid's Frolics*, Prod R. Graef, Amnesty International, 1978. *Inside Europe* (5 episodes), Coordinator and series editor R. Graef, Dir (episode 5) R.Graef, Granada/RTB/DR/NOS/SR/WGBH/ZDF, 1977–79. *The Secret Policeman's Ball*, Co-prod/Dir R.Graef, Films of Record for Amnesty International, 1979. *Police* aka *Police: Operation Carter*, (13 episodes), Prod/co-dir R. Graef, BBC, 1982. *Nagging Doubt*, Dir R. Graef, Limehouse/Channel 4. *Fifty Minute Hour*, Dir R. Graef, Limehouse/Channel 4, forthcoming. *Maybe Baby*, Dir R. Graef, Limehouse/BBC, forthcoming. (Filmography 1964–1982 from *Nothing But The Truth*, ed. J. Wyver, ICA/BFI, 1982.) BBC = British Broadcasting Corporation, BR = Bayerische Rundfunk, CBC = Canadian Broadcasting Corporation, DR = Danmarks Radio, NET = National Education Television, NOS = Nederlandse Oemrop Stichting, SR = Sveriges Radio, ZDF = Zweites Deutsches Fernsehen. KCET and WGBH are the identifying letters of two major Public Broadcasting Service stations in the United States of America. The letters are not initials.

7

Seeing is Believing: The Ideology of Naturalism

Richard Collins

All broadcasting systems however organized and controlled have to command the assent of their audiences to their messages. The problem clearly becomes most pressing in relation to messages – the programmes – that are explicitly concerned with presenting reality; the informational programmes of which news, current affairs and documentaries are the most important.

Successive audience research reports mark the decline in confidence of UK television viewers in the trustworthiness of television news. In 1971 the BBC's audience research report noted these percentages of respondents who considered each of five sources to be 'always trustworthy' or 'trustworthy most of the time':

BBC TV 86%   ITN 78%   BBC Radio 74%
Respondents own newspaper   40%   All newspapers 30%

These 'scores' mark a decline in the credence ceded to television's informational programming since the 1950s and a further decline is marked by the 1984 report commissioned by the BBC, *Perception of bias in television news*.[1] The 1984 bias study is not directly comparable to previous reports: it asks different questions and documents different answers and yields results from which it is difficult to generalize confidently. However the following conclusions can, plausibly, be drawn: that the BBC remains the most trusted of television information channels and that audience confidence in the impartiality of television as an information source has declined.

Perception of bias in television news attempted to determine whether viewers perceived television news and current affairs as biased. Respondents regarded television as the most accurate and detailed source of information (they were asked about coverage of three issues: the police, Common Market, unemployment).

[1]M. Collins, *Perceptions of bias in Television News* (London, Social and Community Planning Research, 1984).

	TV	Press	Radio	None/ Don't know
Most accurate source	41%	17%	7%	36%
Most detailed source	41%	25%	6%	28%

There seems no reason to doubt that television remains the information source in which UK consumers have most confidence. Of TV channels:

	BBC 1	ITV	BBC 2	Channel 4
Most accurate	57%	26%	15%	2%

The by-channel 'scores' are curious because the four news and current affairs sources are, essentially, only two. The BBC channels 1 and 2 emanate from the same organization and newsroom (though there are differences in personnel, format and content in BBC 1 and 2 news and more marked differences in the two channels' other informational programming it is essentially the same personnel and apparatus that speaks on the two channels). And Channel 4's news is originated by Independent Television News (ITN) as is that of ITV. Here though there are more marked differences in the two channels' other information programming. The report suggests, plausibly, that 'The view of Channel 4 is unlikely to be based on consideration of its news and current affairs . . . the perception is based on the general image of Channel 4'.[2]

The trust in the BBC (or at least in BBC 1) coexists with a perception of the BBC as the channel most biased in favour of the government. Of the 25% of respondents who thought any channel was likely to represent the government view (i.e. about half thought somewhere in UK television a pro-government bias existed) most thought the BBC to be the most pro-government.

BBC 1	BBC 2	ITV	Channel 4
44%	23%	25%	8%

Though again we find the curious differences in the perception of the BBC's two channels. We have then a contradictory set of perceptions of television as a source of information: of it as more accurate than other media, of the most accurate channel also being that most likely to be biased in favour of government and of different evaluations of the accuracy and bias of information distributed on different channels by the same organization.

The decline (from the 1950s to the 1980s) in trust in television and in the impartiality of the message sources will doubtless have been accelerated by the wider circulation of knowledge about security vetting of personnel and the method of appointment of Governors following the BBC's Board of Governors prohibition of the transmission of the *Real Lives* documentary 'State of the Union'. But television remains the preferred source of information and its message sources – notably ITN and the BBC – are

[2]Collins, p. 5.

generally perceived as preferable to the available alternatives.

In Britain the products of the domestic mass media are the only readily available source of an interpretative paradigm that enables an individual to relate his or her direct experience to the social totality, to the world at large. Whether or not this paradigm and the relations it assigns are believed or not, it remains the only framework in which the day-to-day experience of an individual can be related to the whole. Either its agenda is accepted or the refuser remains in a state of, at best, sceptical agnosticism. Of these domestic mass media the BBC and ITN are correctly perceived as having a less direct connection to one interested party, to capital, than the press (though recent events and the decline in public trust in television suggest that the suzerainty of the state is becoming more apparent and more regularly exercised than before). Hence, I suggest the perceived relative independence of the BBC and ITV earns their statements a degree of trust and credence beyond that generally accorded the press. Secondly, I suggest the aesthetic, or style, of naturalism that governs information programmes earns assent to the programmes' messages. The accumulations of still and moving images in television news, for example, are rhetorical devices that, on the basis of seeing is believing, the camera cannot lie, sustain and authenticate the verbal narrative that alone gives these images coherence. To show an event is to demonstrate its authenticity and the authenticity of the governing voice-over of narration – whether of newsreader, anchor man or woman or interviewer/interviewee. It is the trust invested in the image, the idea that seeing is believing that accounts for the greater degree of trust in television news than in radio news.

This problematic, that of trust invested in the image and the conditions on which that trust is ceded, can be productively considered by examining the work of the most thoughtful and self-conscious of the practitioners of television's dominant mode of informational representation, Roger Graef. Graef is an American documentary film-maker long resident in the UK and is now a member of the board of Channel 4 who defines his own project as that of 'observational cinema' or *'cine-verité'* ('we were observers, not participants, not intruding to control the action as we might have in a conventional documentary'). He has worked consistently with a small group of colleagues who, like Graef, are unusually ready to reflect on and make explicit the bases and procedures of their work, though their characterizations are sometimes interestingly contradictory.[3] Charles Stewart, one of Graef's regular camera operators, pulls the rug from under Graef's customary self-presentation as a practitioner of 'observational cinema'. He states:

When we start to shoot, much of Roger's work is finished.

[3]See for instance Dai Vaughan, *Television Documentary Usage* (London, British Film Institute, 1976) and John Wyver, ed., *Nothing But The Truth: Cinema Vérité and the Films of the Roger Graef Team* (London, Institute of Contemporary Arts and the British Film Institute, 1982).

that is, Graef's work is in the planning and organization of that which is to be 'observed', and Stewart further states:

> Any time we think there's going to be something happening, then we start filming, and when we know it's not going to be interesting we stop filming.

The style of observational cinema or *cine verité* within which Graef works and of which he is a notably skilled and serious exponent dates from its development by Drew and Leacock, sponsored by NBC and Time–Life in the late 1950s and early 1960s to produce a distinctive new product for US network television, and it has its archaeology in the *cine verité* monuments of Vertov and Flaherty and its varied practices in France, the USA, Britain and Canada (Charles Stewart worked with Terence McCartney Filgate, one of the leading documentarists of the National Film Board of Canada.) Graef's work is then a distinctive 'ideolect' within a shared international language.

This truth telling of 'observational cinema' is, I suggest, no less chimerical than the independence of broadcasting institutions. Just as the BBC's independence has a reality, though tightly bounded by unacknowledged constraints like the Treasury's control of the purse strings and the Prime Minister's influence in the appointment of the Governors, so observational cinema's capacity to tell the truth is real but considerably more closely circumscribed than its practitioners believe.

This ideological practice of legitimation has, properly, been the object of attack in an important (dominant in the 1970s) tradition of film criticism and film practice. However the attacks on the 'classic realist text', the naturalization of the status quo and the demand for a modernist cinema in which the device was foregrounded and a critique of the sign mounted, did not customarily make differentiations *within* the practice of what was loosely termed bourgeois realism. Distinctions are there to be made and the central tradition in Marxist aesthetics, initiated by Engels and carried on by Lenin and most importantly Lukacs, distinguishes, within an apparently undifferentiated mimetic tradition, two epistemologies of representation.

For Lukacs, mimetic representations required categorization under two heads: realism and naturalism. Naturalism was simply ideological (and open to the critiques mounted by the anti-realists in British film culture). However, realism was a mode of cognition and representation that could enlighten, liberate and 'adequate the real'. For Lukacs, naturalism, whatever its actual historical productivity (which in the case of Zola or Strindberg could be argued to have been progressive), was based on a false epistemology and thus offered no adequate basis for cognition, no way of satisfactorily knowing the world. Naturalism is distinguished by scrupulous fidelity to the here and now; to the immediate and the apparent. It is an aesthetic that seeks to minimize the mediation through consciousness of the real, in perception and representation. In film theory the classic site of a naturalist aesthetic is in Bazin. In his 'Ontology of the Photographic Image' Bazin states:

> The aesthetic qualities of photography are to be sought in its power to lay bare the realities. It is not for me to separate off, in the complex fabric of the objective world, here a reflection on a damp sidewalk, there the gesture of a child. Only the impassive lens, stripping the object of all those ways of seeing it, those piled up pre-conceptions, that spiritual dust and grime with which my eyes have covered it, is able to present it in all its virginal purity to my attention and consequently to my love.[4]

This strict naturalism is often contradicted in Bazin's critical writings, which approach at times a conception of representation closer to Lukacsian realism than the strict naturalism of his explicitly theoretical essays as exemplified above. Lukacs, though, argues that scrupulous fidelity to the here and now, the immediate and the apparent, is an inadequate mode of knowing. Events, objects, phenomena are chimerical, caught in a process of change and a network of causal relations that require representation if the real is to be fully adequate and understood. Therefore some analytical and constructive activity of human consciousness is necessary for the real to be produced for representation.

> The artistic correctness of a detail thus has nothing to do with whether the detail corresponds to any similar detail in reality. The detail in a work of art is an accurate reflection of life when it is a necessary aspect of the accurate reflection of the total process of objective reality, no matter whether it was observed by the artist in life or created through imagination out of direct or indirect experience.[5]

Whether a particular mimesis is realist or naturalist cannot be determined by the presence or absence of particular formal qualities; rather the criterion is the degree to which the major determining forces in the social totality which fix and produce particular phenomena are represented.

> The work of art must therefore reflect correctly and in proper proportion all important factors objectively determining the area of life it represents. It must so reflect these that this area of life becomes comprehensible from within and from without, re-experienceable, that it appears as a totality of life. This does not mean that every work of art must strive to reflect the objective, extensive totality of life. On the contrary, the

---

[4]Andre Bazin, 'The Ontology of the Photographic Image' in H. Gray, ed., *What is Cinema? Vol 1.* (Berkeley, CA., University of California Press, 1967), p. 15.
[5]George Lukacs, *Writer and Critic*, trans. A. Kahn (London, Merlin, 1970), p. 43.

extensive totality of reality necessarily is beyond the possible scope of any artistic creation; the totality of reality can only be reproduced intellectually in ever-increasing approximation through the infinite process of science. The totality of the work of art is rather intensive; the circumscribed and self-contained ordering of those factors which objectively are of decisive significance for the portion of life depicted, which determine its existence and motion, its specific quality and its place in the total life process. In this sense the briefest song is as much an intensive totality as the mightiest epic. The objective character of the area of life represented determines the quantity, quality, proportion, etc. of the factors that emerge in interaction with the specific laws of the literary form appropriate for the representation of this portion of life.[6]

For Lukacs, the extensive totality of the material world required ordering in the intensive totality of the artistic representation, and the major agency whereby this process of transformation and representation was to be performed was that of 'typicality':

The typical is not be confused with the average (though there are cases where this holds true), nor with the eccentric (though the typical does as a rule go beyond the normal). A character is typical, in this technical sense, when his innermost being is determined by objective forces at work in society. Vautrin or Julien Sorel, superficially eccentric, are typical in their behaviour: the determining factors of a particular historical phase are found in them in concentrated form. Yet, though typical, they are never crudely 'illustrative'.[7]

Both realism and naturalism are mimetic systems or practices of representation but are based on different epistemologies and this distinction between realism and naturalism within the category of mimesis is of great use in exploring the competence of documentary in adequating the real.

I have suggested earlier that if the first of the ideologies that legitimize informational television is that of the apparent neutrality of the originating institutions then the second is that of 'seeing is believing'. Consider the operation of the images in a television news programme; the succession of stills, interviews to camera, location film or video footage that have the rhetorical function of authenticating the governing narrative of the newsreader. The images are unintelligible without commentary and generally consist of no more than public figures entering or leaving buildings, cars or aeroplanes or reporters standing outside factory gates or government offices. The images' significance comes from the context and

---

[6]Lukacs, p. 38.
[7]George Lukacs, 'The Ideology of Modernism' in *The Meaning of Contemporary Realism* (London, Merlin 1967), p. 122.

interpretation provided by speech, yet their presence, the visible evidence they offer of an event, authenticates the carrier of the meaning – the commentary.

Within broadcasting there has been a consistent push towards the refinement of technical equipment so as to minimize the transformation of 'reality' in the process of recording; to reduce what the BBC's *Principles and Practice in Documentary Programmes* (the institution's guide to pro- gramme makers, equivalent to a newspaper's style book) describes as the 'constant obstruction between the producer and his subject'.

'The documentary producer can only create his programme with the aid of a mass of equipment and a whole team of people. Indeed, the equip- ment is a constant obstruction between the producer and his subject, and a great deal of his skill is devoted to presenting his subject matter as if the equipment and the technical processes were not there'[8] The techniques and technologies pioneered in British broadcasting in radio features and in the areas that Norman Swallow[9] called 'Personal documentaries' have become normative over informational (or factual) television.

These technological and stylistic characteristics of television programme- making are symptoms of the passive project implicit in the word 'documentary' or 'recording'. These working practices, the trajectory of technological development and the vocabulary and ideas of informational television, are manifestations of the ideology of naturalism. The concep- tion is of a perfect mimesis, an unstructured recording of an immanent apprehensible reality that is to be achieved by minimizing the interven- tions and transformations specific to the recording process. This ideology that reality is passively reflected rather than actively constituted in the pro- cess of programme-making is the ideology that legitimizes the constituted reality that is transmitted in informational programmes and the chimera that resolves the paradox experienced by TV workers between their active crafts of programme-making – their creation of a spectacle – and their conception of their role as one of non-intervention. *Principles and Practice in Documentary Programmes* uneasily manages the contradiction, insisting alternately on the 'creativity' of the documentary project and the necessity for the accounts of events and relations recounted in informa- tional TV to be an impartial, balanced record. Indeed *Principles and Practice* recognizes that for the desired simulacrum to be achieved a certain active, structuring, creative activity on the part of the programme makers is not only necessary and unavoidable but desirable. The intriguing standard term of TV or film production, 'cheating' (the practice of amending an 'unreal' appearance in things in the recorded format by performing a reorganization of their real relations so that 'unreal' appearance is avoided), does not appear in *Principles and Practice* but the necessary practices involved in constituting the recorded reality are set out. The

---

[8]BBC, *Principles and Practice in Documentary* (BBC, London 1972), p. 7.
[9]Norman Swallow, *Factual Television* (London, Focal Press, 1966).

'innocent eye' of the researcher sees 'What really happens when people go about their daily lives without the knowledge that a television audience is watching. He sees how a man really behaves when he is not putting on a show for the camera', and from that notional reality the producer 'carries out the first of a series of selection processes. He decides broadly what to include and what not to include; he undertakes his "casting" – as vital in a documentary as in a work of fiction, he decides which individuals should take part and which should not. If the subject is a contentious one, he must decide which arguments should be included and which are too trivial to warrant a place.'

He (or she) then directs the shooting stage – 'The director is in fact directing two quite separate things: his camera and his art. On the one hand he is telling cameramen and soundmen exactly what he wants to see and hear. On the other, he is assuming that what he wants to see and hear takes place in front of his camera . . . In practice, most of the things he needs to show are not going to happen in front of the camera of their own accord.'

It is Graef's work that most nearly approximates to the naturalistic ideal that governs the injunctions of *Principles and Practice* and that offers the most serious challenge to the arguments that I am developing in this paper and to the related argument of Robert Tyrell.[10] Addressing the ambiguous zone opened up by the contradictions of naturalist ideology, in a section on 'problems of the documentary' Tyrell argues that informational programmes are governed by contradictions:

> It is not that documentary film-makers are dishonest, they are usually the most earnest and conscientious of men: it is the form itself that is flawed by its own internal contradictions. It purports to show us reality; but what we see is inevitably an illusion. A documentary has to be constructed and contrived. Things have to be included and excluded, time has to be telescoped, space shrunk or stretched, action specially performed. The camera must be there to make the film and its presence must affect the subject in all but the most desperate of circumstances and yet the film-maker is at pains to conceal this fact from the audience.[11]

Graef's film-making, his practice of *cinema verité* or what he prefers to call 'observational cinema' is contrived to transcend the contradictions that Tyrell points to in the documentarists' project and that surface so evidently in *Principles and Practice*:

> The standard procedure for many film-makers seems to be, 'Forget it'. The BBC Green Book on documentaries suggests that you go along,

[10]Robert Tyrell, *The Work of the Television Journalist* (London, Focal Press, 1972).
[11]Tyrell, pp. 27–8.

spend a day or two watching what happens, and then you are suddenly an expert on what's typical. And then you stage what's typical. It implies that you know more about what's typical than the participants do. And what we're saying is that we know all along that we don't.[12]

Graef's claim to respect the internal natural logic of the subject was formulated to resist the suggestion by one of his usual co-workers, Terence Twigg, that their practice was one of:

Proceeding in part to structure your material as is general practice in informational TV. Producing 'films of record'.

Elsewhere he describes his practice as one of producing

Films of record – unstaged. Filmed without lights or interviews and using a minimum amount of apparatus. Our goal is to produce an account of a decision that matters to the people involved and to the public at large, and which is condensed in a manner that the participants will confirm is accurate. To that extent we suggest these films are 'objective' – dangerous a word as that is.[13]

Of the four stages in constituting a documentary itemized in *Principles and Practice* – preparation, shooting, editing and finishing – Graef's practice can be differentiated from the norm in two stages of the construction of the programme.

In 'preparation' Graef's procedure is, as specified above, to eschew the positive and conscious structuring of the programme concept: he does *not* do what *Principles and Practice* enjoins of the director, namely that

He decides broadly what to include: he undertakes his 'casting', as vital in a documentary as in a work of fiction: he decides which individuals should take part and which should not. If the subject is a contentious one he must decide which arguments should be included and which are too trivial to warrant a place.

Rather, Graef's decisions as to inclusions and exclusions, of dramatis personae and argument come principally in the third stage – in editing. *Principles and Practice* specifies that editing ratios:

may be anything from 5 to 25 times the length of the finished film. A shooting ratio of 11 : 1 or 12 : 1 would be quite normal for a major documentary.

[12]Roger Graef, in 'Decisions, Decisions' in *Sight and Sound* 25.1 (1975/76), p. 4.
[13]Roger Graef, in 'Decision', *Granada and Political Broadcasting* No. 6 (Manchester, Granada Television, 1976).

Accounts of Graef's editing ratios vary but cluster around 30 : 1 to 33 : 1. Beyond the ratio of film shot to film used there is little discussion of editing in the published statements or interviews of the Graef team. This suggests, I think, that there is little in this process of constituting the final text to differentiate Graef's work from that of other film-makers in informational TV – an impression that is borne out in viewing the programmes. Vaughan (1974) in his 'The space between shots' says:

> Despite his infatuation with the 'real time' experience – and hence with the eventual extinction of his office – the editor finds himself willy nilly making cuts; firstly to overcome camera run-outs and wobbles, then to eliminate longeurs and repetitions; next to clarify points of confusion created by the earlier cuts; and finally with resignation, to allow the film to take on the form to which it seems to aspire . . . . The way in which 'a slice of life' takes on the quality of being 'about' something.[14]

In the realm of editing the differences between Graef's programmes and the normative practice are differences of degree rather than of kind. Graef's films have a 'dramatic form'; the choice implied in the title of his series *Decision* constitutes a beginning, middle and end to the process with which the films concern themselves and this is so too in his earlier series *Space Between Words*. 'Work' is ended with a mass meeting of workers outside the factory at which the narrative that has been presented up until then is resumed in the account of negotiations given by a shop steward to the shop floor workers. The shift in location from the previous footage shot inside to an outside location clearly signals an end to an episode and the use of the steward's speech to close the narrative is an employment of one of the classic conventions of mystery or detective stories in which the resolving and explanatory function is given to a character and signals the end of the narrative.

So, whilst Graef's cinema does not use many of the familiar techniques of the familiar documentary, e.g. counterpoint montage, the creation of mood by means of music or sound effects, the film's material *is* ordered, it constructs its meaning through familiar formal practices. As Vaughan says:

> The 'Space Between Words' films can be analysed with much the same critical vocabulary as can other films. The differences quarantine themselves in the area where moral uncertainty resides – that of the film-maker's subjectivity. The problems are in one respect worse than those which the BBC booklet evades, for the Mitchell style (*the man not the camera* ed.) left no-one in doubt that what he was seeing was poetry.[15]

---

[14]Dai Vaughan 'The Space Between Shots' in *Screen* 15.1. (1974), p. 80.
[15]Vaughan, p. 81.

It is clear that the procedures involved in producing this effect are no less creative than those of Godard or TV pioneers like Denis Mitchell.

Principles and Practice states that shooting ratios of between 5 : 1 and 25 : 1 are the parameters of normal usage. Graef customarily exceeds a ratio of 30 : 1. His prodigality in the use of film stock enables him to deny himself a number of the established practices in constituting a film and eschew most of the injunctions in *Principles and Practice*. Instead of preconceiving the material to be shot, acted or reconstructed and adding commentary or interviews to explicate any matters that are unclear in the photography, Graef is able to postpone some of his process of selection and constitution of a narrative until shooting and the interaction between subjects and filmmakers begins. Once again, his remarks on the Green Books' ideas on typicality, briefly commented on earlier, are relevant:

> The BBC Green Book on documentaries suggests that you go along, spend a day or two watching what happens, and then you are suddenly an expert of what's typical. And then you stage what's typical. It implies that we know more about what's typical than the participants do, and what we're saying is that we know all along that we don't. But we're going to try to pay some sort of respect all the way through the process to what is actually happening and what it tells us.[16]

Here Graef is arguing *against* a recurrent practice of dressing experience in one of a restricted set of off-the-peg professional paradigms and *for* a discovery procedure in constituting the film's subject (and Graef's sensitivity to the specificities of experience is one of the major elements in his work that differentiates it from the familiar management of subject matter in shooting television documentary).

But Graef's argument implies that it is the participants' perception of the film's concern that is authentic. It is to be sure an implication, not a necessary conclusion to the argument, but Graef's characterizations of his work are rich in implication rather than unambiguous in their conclusions. I will return to this characteristic, but suggest here that the implied authority ceded to the participants' perception does not stand examination. How is the validating perception of the participants formulated and recognized? It is in the nature of Graef's method (and here he's one with standard practice where conscious reflection and construction of the film's content is the prerogative of the recording crew not of the film's subjects) that an orchestrated performance is not mounted for the camera. The subjects – the participants as Graef names them – of the film do not discuss together what is the problem – what is the film's subject or concern. They have no means of formulating a collective view, for often Graef has chosen to depict a relation of antagonism – management and union in 'Work', the two sides in the Korf contract negotiations, the

[16]Roger Graef, reference as for note 12 above.

family that has developed no collective harmony in its own interactions, let alone in its self-presentation to the television film crew and the television audience. The only viewpoint that embraces the situation of the partici- pants is that of Graef for he constitutes that situation, defines its bounds in time and space, peoples it with Mr X and Mrs Y but not Mr Z and witnesses the reflections, negotiations and self-presentations of X apart from Y; Y apart from X, as well as their interactions.

Graef's procedures differ from the normative professional practice he abhors in degree not in kind. His method of constituting a film, his scrupulous endeavour to live out the implications of the documentary- project, differentiate his work from, say, *World in Action, Panorama*, or the news, but the difference is one of style, of achieving a distinctive per- sonal articulation of the same recurrent elements and relations. Graef's project is one of scrupulously performing the naturalist imperatives that govern informational programming, clearly framing 'Steel', 'Rates', or 'Work' by titles, commentary and introduction by anchor man rather than integrating these elements, alien to strict naturalism, with the location- shot, direct-sound kernel of the film. As Dai Vaughan says: 'What we are doing is closer to the nineteenth-century novel. We're treating it as naturalism.'

The limits of this approach become evident in the great baggy, three- decker work on the 35th congress of the Communist Party of Great Britain, 'Decision: British Communism' (Granada TV 1978). Here the viewer was lost among a variety of personae and arguments without adequate 'cueing' by narrator or introduction – the spectacle embraces so much that it becomes incomprehensible.

And a number of the 'invisible' natural rhetorical devices of naturalistic diegetic construction spring to the sceptical eye in Graef's best work, e.g. the framing of the diegesis with an internal narrator/interpreter in 'School', choosing a 'natural' armature for the narrative organization – the nuclear family – in 'Family', the recurrent annual ritual of the local authority budget in 'Rates' and so on. It is clear that the central claim of naturalist aesthetic practice to offer a perfect mimesis, to achieve an unme- diated 'impartial' representation is impossible to sustain. Graef, though within this tradition and more scrupulous in the practice of its norms than others who rest more confidently on its ideology, does *not* claim with André Bazin that:

> Only the impassive lens, stripping its object of all those ways of seeing it, those piled up preconceptions, that spiritual dust and grime with which my eyes have covered it, is able to present it in all its virginal purity to my attention.[17]

Rather, he claims that structuring and intervention are minimized and that

[17]André Bazin, reference as for note 4 above.

the light of events is permitted to shine through when artifice and the processes of constitution and mediation of the subject are stripped away:

> How much we affect the scenes we film is hard to say, but we have never claimed to be filming reality as it would be without us there. All we have endeavoured to do, in devising a unique set of procedures in our film-making – no lights, no interviews, no staging and showing the main protagonists the edited film before transmission – is to attempt to minimize the effect of our presence.[18]

The question is how adequate a basis for cognition, for understanding the world, is naturalism – whether that of Bazin, Graef's more modest aspiration of minimizing mediation so that truth may be recorded and fairly represented, or the strategies of nineteenth century naturalist prose invoked by Vaughan?

The prospect of an extended comparison of Zola and Graef's aesthetic and a few reflections on the Second Empire and Britain's contemporary post-imperial state is seductive indeed, but that *tour de force* can await another writer. But both Zola and Leacock have a shared positivistic fascination with scientific method and discuss their representations in terms of scientific enquiry, and Zola and Graef share a concern with detail. The more than 30 documentaries that Roger Graef has made for British and non-British broadcasting organizations are classic instances of this style and, certainly in the UK, his best known works, the five *Space Between Words* programmes made for the BBC in 1972, the six-part *Decision* for Granada in 1975/1978 and the thirteen-part *Police* series for the BBC in 1981 are the best known examples of the observational cinema style.

Graef is the most scrupulous practitioner of the imperatives of the BBC's *Principles and Practice* who is currently working in British television – Graef more consistently, consciously and thoroughly attempts to reduce the mediations between the subject of his films and their audiences than does any other British television documentarist. Other film-makers like Paul Watson or Angela Pope work in the same manner but not with the same lacerating commitment to a scrupulous recording of events as Graef. To appropriate a category from an aesthetic (and intellectual) tradition to which Graef is firmly opposed he is the 'typical' instance of British television documentary. The aesthetic which has typicality as one of its central categories is realism – an aesthetic which, like Graef's, asserts the primacy of the real but, unlike Graef's, asserts that apprehension and representation of the real is a matter of active selection and organization. 'Realism', as Friederich Engels said in a formulation on which Lukacs's work and much of Marxist aesthetics has been constructed, 'implies, besides truth of detail, the truth in reproduction of typical characters under typical circumstances.' Implicitly, every documentary

[18]Roger Graef, 'The Decision Programme' in *Comment*, 6 Aug, 1977, p. 285.

whether 'observational' or not presents itself as 'typical'. If it did not, what claim would it have on the attention of its viewers? Unless there is a general representative quality to representations their significance can only be of extremely parochial interest. The chief interest of Graef's work is the spectacle it offers of time, intelligence and considerable resources devoted to squaring the circle. It is an exemplary site for the study of the major aesthetic mode of ideological management performed by British television (and, it has to be said, by most other television systems).

Note

The analysis and investigations upon which we base this article relate to two main areas of study, both of which are relatively undeveloped aspects of media research – the study of television documentary form and the study of viewers' interpretations of programmes.

Television documentary form

Here, the 'base' references would be as for the study of documentary film, and they are to be found throughout this volume. A few items of a more specialized kind might be mentioned here however:

Stephen Heath and Gillian Skirrow, 'Television: A World in Action', *Screen* 18.2 (1977), pp. 7–59.

Roger Silverstone, 'The Right to Speak: on a Poetic for Television Documentary', *Media, Culture and Society* 5.2 (1983), pp. 137–54.

Dai Vaughan, *Television Documentary Usage* (London, British Film Institute, 1976).

John Wyver, *Nothing but the Truth: Cinéma Verité and the Films of the Roger Graef Team* (London, Institute of Contemporary Arts and British Film Institute 1982).

Viewer Interpretation

Interest in this area is now developing rapidly, with a number of studies recently completed or forthcoming. The following work can be justly singled out as the most important and influential, as well as the first, of the present phase of research:

David Morley, *The Nationwide Audience* (London, British Film Institute, 1980).

Other relevant studies include:

Rosalind Brunt and Martin Jordin, ' "The Controversial Candidate":
British Television's coverage of the Chesterfield By-election'. Conference paper for the International Television Studies Conference, London 1984.

Justin Lewis, 'Decoding Television News', in Philip Drummond and Richard Paterson, eds., *Television in Transition* (London, British Film Institute, 1984).

8

Documentary Meanings and the Discourse of Interpretation

John Corner and Kay Richardson

Across both its richly various social and technical history and its diverse employment of words and images, 'the language of documentary' has shown an abiding concern with self-effacement. Through whatever devices of naturalization have been available and judged to be stylistically and functionally appropriate, documentaries have regularly sought to present audiences with accounts in which the viewed is to be taken as effectively indistinguishable from the real. Life not only takes precedence over art in such accounts, it frequently replaces it altogether within a discourse and aesthetics of maximum 'transparency'.

Undoubtedly, the particular conventions by which this effect is contrived have been extended and made more subtle by quite recent developments in lightweight television technology. Since documentary television first began to offer viewers a regular 'window on the world' however, these conventions have often been at the heart of discussion and controversy about television's function as a source of popular knowledge and as an 'agenda-setter' on public issues.

But to talk of television's power in this respect – in gaining widespread acceptance of its lucidly 'obvious' interpretations of 'what is going on' – risks begging a number of questions about the *ways* in which programmes are subject to interpretative activity themselves as an integral part of the viewing process. Part of this activity of making sense from what is seen and heard may include not only the attribution of particular motives and intentions to programme-makers, but also the recognition of the different levels at which visual and verbal representations are organized accordingly. In the case of documentary then, whilst the techniques of naturalism may to the film-maker's satisfaction bind together world and 'document' with all the immediacy of revealed truth, the lines of communicative relation with *viewers* may be such as not necessarily to confirm this truth at all but to open up gaps and to render awkward any offered coherence.

In this study we are interested in the way in which a sample group of viewers understood, and responded to, specific sequences in one documentary programme, *A Fair Day's Fiddle*, broadcast on BBC2 in March 1984 but viewed by our respondents on video just before one-to-one discussion sessions.

Our particular concerns thus cut into both the sets of general issues outlined above. We wanted to explore questions of documentary *form*, especially the ways in which the speech and behaviour of the participants in the programme were organized within its mode of address to the viewer and its overall version of 'what was going on'. Here, two aspects of the programme attracted our close attention, due both to their prominence in respondent accounts and to their significance for television documentary more generally. First of all, and of primary interest to us in this article, there were those scenes of 'enactment' in which participants supposedly went through daily routines, with the cameras (and viewer) looking on unacknowledged. These scenes sometimes modulated into sequences of interview response and we have focused on one such scene in our discussion below. The second aspect – again, a staple element of documentary production – was what we termed the 'narratorial function', meaning by this the range of possibilities and effects relating to voiced-over commentary in which some authority for the general guidance of understanding appears to be invested. Again, we have selected one specific sequence for the purpose of our discussion here. In exploring these formal questions, however, we saw it as a primary aspect of our investigation (not just a continuation of it) to research what the forms actually 'delivered' to the viewers. We wanted to get as close as possible to the *interpretative work* which viewers performed by paying the strictest attention to the language of their descriptions and judgements – what did they see happen on the screen? How did what was said seem to relate to what was shown? What bearing did one sequence have on another? What, if anything, was the programme 'trying to say'?

It might be useful for us to proceed by giving a general description of the programme we chose for the study and to offer a very brief account of previous work on audience interpretations of television insofar as this work relates to our own ideas and methods. The analysis of the two sequences selected and the respondents comments upon them can then follow.

A Fair Day's Fiddle – Access Documentary?

A Fair Day's Fiddle was a 50-minute programme made for BBC2's *Brass Tacks* series by BBC North West in Manchester. Its ostensible topic was the various 'fiddles' by which recipients of social security payments on one Liverpool estate supplemented their income. Its chief formal characteristic was its relatively loose structuring as a series of episodes in which various inhabitants of the estate recounted their experiences and offered comments to an off-camera reporter without their contributions being linked or voiced-over by any 'official' commentary. Such commentary was used only in the introduction to the programme – a brief 'scene-setting' passage spoken over long-shots of estate housing and finishing with the remark that 'in this programme, local people speak for themselves about a thriving unofficial economy'.

This 'speaking' occurred within a number of different forms. There were scenes in which participants spoke on-camera to an out-of-frame interviewer. Often the interviewer's questioning was edited out, intensifying the quality of personal testimony, at times close to that of the 'confessional'. There were other scenes in which participants were seen going about 'routine' business (e.g. entering derelict premises in search of scrap materials, welcoming home a child from school, assembled in a group at a friend's house to have their fortunes told, consulting a Citizens' Advice Bureau officer about a debt problem). Sometimes these scenes involved spoken exchanges, thus adding speech 'enactment' to 'enactment' of physical behaviour. This mode of presentation is perhaps pushed to its most dramatized level in a scene where a husband and wife are seen to open the morning's mail and to have a lengthy and emotionally charged conversation about their debts and the possibilities for repayment. A number of devices employed here (e.g. use of held facial close-up during pauses in 'dialogue') seemed to us to construct participant behaviour as 'performance' more intensively than elsewhere in the programme. Where scenes of activity involved one person only, they were usually accompanied by voice-over from the person in shot.

At points, the documentary included contributions from those who worked on the estate (the vicar, the staff of the Citizen's Advice Bureau). In one sequence, it shifted into the conventions of television investigative journalism by having its reporter call on a local moneylender and extract a reluctantly offered series of on-camera answers to questions concerning circumstances which we had heard about in an earlier scene.

For most of its length however, the programme attempts to address its topic 'from the inside', as it were. Access to the 'inside' is through an intimate, cumulative rendering of personal experience – the people of Netherley, in their own homes, speaking for themselves about the difficulties of 'getting by'.

As we indicated above, we were interested in aspects of how this articulation was put together and in the positions of understanding and evaluation which our respondents took up towards it. Together, we saw these as constituting the ground for an inquiry into the *pragmatics* of television documentary form.

Researching Reception

Detailed empirical research on the interpretative schemes which audiences use to understand and assess television programmes is a relatively recent development in mass communication studies. However, in the last few years a number of projects have followed Morley's seminal study, *The*

'Nationwide' Audience,[1] in attempting to explore, either by group or individualized discussion with sample viewers, the various sense which has been made of particular items of output and the range of interpretative resources which the 'sense-making' activity draws on.

Elsewhere, we have discussed theoretical and methodological aspects of these developments in some detail,[2] but it may be useful for us to itemize here the following points, most of which are taken up practically in the ensuing analysis and commentary.

(a) We wanted to find out as much as we could about the primary levels of interpretation at which visual and verbal elements were *understood* rather than simply being concerned to identify *attitudes* towards the material.

(b) This suggested the use of one-to-one discussion sessions which, moving from more open to more closed questioning, allow for exploratory, follow-up points to be made without the problems this can cause in group work. Given sessions of adequate duration (ours were approximately one hour long) it is possible for the conventions of conversational exchange partly to modify the dominant ones of question and answer. At these points, we did not feel constrained from indicating some of our own speculations as to how various items might be understood or from mentioning the views of other respondents in order perhaps to 'trigger' a more focused response and reaction. What might be considered 'leading questions' or 'prompts' in the context of the fixed range of responses in questionnaire method, seem to us to be a useful late stage in sessions of the type undertaken. We felt that the effects of any 'over-prompting' that might occur could be identified and allowed for in the analysis of the recordings and transcripts.

(c) It also suggested a need to pay close attention to respondent's use of language as an indicator of, for instance, variations in the framing, status and perceived intentions used in the construing of items. One part of this close attention was a respect for the particular speech contexts of utterances under analysis. We have followed this through in our presentation by giving some of our transcribed data as continuous exchange rather than in edited chunks.

With these broad considerations in view, we set about the business of recording the accounts of our sample viewers and analysing as thoroughly as we could their commentaries on what they saw and heard.

'The Toy Scene'

This episode involves a boy, his mother, and another woman who speaks about her own child. It begins as enactment: the boy returns from school,

[1]Morley, *The 'Nationwide' Audience* (see prefatory note to this article).
[2]Kay Richardson and John Corner, 'Reading Reception: Mediation and Transparency in Viewers' Accounts of a TV Programme', *Media, Culture and Society*, 8.3 (1986).

8.1.1

8.1.2

8.1.3

8.1.4

8.1.5

8.1.6

greets his mother and runs upstairs to play. She then joins him. When they are together we hear their dialogue, when he is playing alone we hear the two women in voice-over. The naturalism of the scene is grounded partly in the home location and partly upon 'spontaneous' human touches – their hug as he gets home (Fig. 8.1.1): a joke, 'Don't break the bed springs, mum', when she sits down on his bed (Fig. 8.1.3). Before he enters his bedroom the camera is focused upon a toy lying on the bed. He bursts in, grabs it, plays with it for a few seconds of screen-time then moves on to another one (Fig. 8.1.2). His mother comes in and lets him turn the TV on. Some of this action is voiced over by the mothers, who say:

Voice 1   I think I try to make up for being one parent instead of two, and
            I try to get him more to compensate for the lack of a father.
Voice 2   And you feel as if you don't get it you let them down sort of
            thing.
Voice 1   I find the pressure from the school. I mean it's, every week, it's
            he needs trainers for running, he needs pumps for gym, he
            needs a football outfit, he needs shorts for something else. Week
            by week there are more pressures just from the school, I find.

Thus, whilst the verbal track speaks about sports kit, the visual track
shows toys. Toys then become the overt topic, as the enactment gives way
to an interview with the mothers using, firstly, shots of toys they have
bought (Fig. 8.1.4) and, secondly, shots of the speakers themselves (as Fig.
8.1.6). The sequence begins with a list:

Voice 1   This one cost twenty-five pounds fifty. That one cost me
            nineteen pounds. There's another one here for twenty-five
            pounds. There's a thirteen pound fifty one. That cost me about
            seven pounds for the men.

Against the background of a pile of toys, mostly wrapped in plain brown
paper, the camera moves from one parcel / item to another, following the
speaker's pointing hand as she costs each item (See Fig. 8.1.5 for example).

Many respondents speculated that these toys might be Christmas or
birthday presents recently arrived by post from the catalogue (one of the
mothers says she goes into debt in the catalogue in order to buy things for
her son).

This speculation suggests a need to *make* sense of something which lacks
a *given* sense in these 'transparent' terms. It is not obvious why there
should be toys in such quantity, wrapped and stacked as they are. The
possible 'explanations' are all underdetermined textually – including the
nonrealist explanation that the arrangement of the toys was at the request
of the production team.

Certainly, the toys are put to rhetorical use. Unspecified plurality
signifies 'a lot of' toys for one child. Then there is the work done in
constituting that plurality out of individual items, which by implication
gradually increase both the total number of items and the total bill. The
wrapping paper gives them a visual 'sameness' which may play a part in
this incremental effect.

If this is the 'rhetoric of excess' – an idea we wished to explore in relation
to our respondents' accounts – it is underlined later when the 'other'
mother speaks (See Fig. 8.1.6).

He wanted this electric car which was two hundred pounds, but he also
went through the things saying 'I want this' and 'I want that'. I said, 'If
you have the car you can't have all these little things as well'. I wouldn't
let him go without or go less just because I'm on my own.

The mothers' talk is also important in deciding whether they see their expenditure as excessive or normal and whether they are defensive or matter-of-fact about it. One says: 'Well, you can't deny them, can you?', though most respondents thought that children *could* be denied many/expensive toys. But, as we've suggested, it is not perhaps the women themselves who are emphasizing these factors. They seem very open; they speak quietly and evenly – but we don't know what questions they are answering. By the editing out of the reporter, visually and verbally, whilst the speakers address fairly private matters, a somewhat 'confessional' style of unsolicited testimony is produced whether or not the spirit of confession informed the women's remarks when the interview was recorded.

As the scene ends (Fig. 8.1.6, and the remarks about the two hundred pound car quoted above) a television set is seen to be on in the background. The next words to be heard on the verbal track are 'British television . . .' followed by an argument about the social pressure of advertising: 'It doesn't ask me to purchase the product, it dares me not to purchase the product.' This is in a new scene with a different speaker. Nevertheless the thematic continuity is strong and, because of it, the argument about advertising can be read back into the circumstances of the previous participants.

Respondents' accounts

In this section we discuss our respondents' interpretative uptake on the toy scene. The first two lengthy transcripts represent everything that two of the respondents said on this subject. These accounts are revealingly contrastive and the more selective quotation which follows samples the broader range of possibilities amongst respondents who found the toy scene worthy of extended comment. In discussing the long transcripts we point to shifts and inconsistencies of interpretation, themselves very pertinent to our study. This is not possible with the shorter quotations and it must be remembered that these quotes are extracted from accounts just as complex in this respect as those represented in the longer texts.

First respondent

Q Can I just move you on now to talk about another specific scene which one or two people have commented on? That's the scene in which two mothers discuss buying toys. I think first of all it will be useful perhaps if,

R From the catalogue?

Q Yeah that's right, from a catalogue. Can you remember what we see in that scene? It starts off with a little boy, doesn't it?

R Yeah. The little boy comes in from school, gives her a big hug, runs off up to his bedroom. There's a toy ready waiting for him on the bed. This has all been, he's been told to come in, hug his mother, run upstairs. I know because I've seen them make a documentary for *Gaskin** as I told you and so I recognize the fact that that's a script from that, which I might not have done if I hadn't seen one made.

Q   Mm

R   He plays with the toy, he picks it up, he does a face.

Q   Ah, yes, that's right.

R   Doesn't put the nose on. Then he puts that down immediately that he's done the face. He's done as he's been told to do, he's run upstairs, he's sat on the bed, he's played with the toy and he puts that aside, picks up something else.

Q   And then the mothers',

R   Very fabricated.

Q   Mm. And what about what we see subsequently then, when we,

R   The mother comes in and sits on the bed. He tells her not to crease the bed or something. She says 'oh that doesn't matter'. They're trying to keep things natural.

Q   Mm. So its another little scene in a way, rather like,

R   Yeah. And then they go and talk about the toys.

Q   Toys

R   And they show us the price of them.

Q   And what do we see about the, how do we see the toys?

R   There's some in paper parcels, brown paper, wrapped up in brown paper boxes. If they've come from the catalogue that's not really the way they come, they come, I've got a catalogue and they come in a sort of sack, so, but I presume that's to put across that they have actually come from the catalogue. They're all brand new. If they are his toys he's either keeping them very well or they've got replicas of what he owns.

Q   Mm, or some people suggest Christmas on the way or whatever, and they,

R   Yeah, maybe it is. You said the film was made at that time. But there wasn't any sign of Christmas trees or Christmas festivities.

Q   No, that's true.

R   And why would they be in brown paper, they'd be in wrapping paper?

Q   Yeah.

R   But,

Q   And then we hear about the prices of them.

R   Mm. And it ranges from seven pounds to twenty five, thirty odd. And then of course there's the big electronic toy that they have to have, that's two hundred pounds, but if they have the two hundred pound one they can't have the twenty five, seven pounds and all the rest of it, out the catalogue. And their children are going to have these toys no matter what. They're in a poverty trap but they have to have these toys.

Q   Mm. Do you feel that the, at that point the programme or the film at

---

*A drama-documentary broadcast by BBC2 in 1983

that point, never mind about the programme as a whole, portrays their toy-buying as really rather extravagant?

R Yes, they're certainly not looking for sympathy in that scene. In fact they've overdone it, if they've chosen to put those toys out and everything, they're letting you see that, that is putting across a different view. O.K. they're complaining that they're hard up but look here, they're getting all this stuff, they're determined to have it no matter how many bills they run up. So yes, that's giving you the chance to turn against them if you were on their side previously.

Q How do you feel that the mothers sound about it? Do they sound confident or defensive or a bit edgy or embarrassed?

R Defensive with a ring to it, 'Don't dare to try to pass a comment on this, it's nobody's business but ours'.

Q Yes. Do you think that most people would tend to regard that scene as a scene in which a certain extravagance was on display?

R I think, yes, it certainly does show that they wanted to put across that there was extravagance. But I think that the whole film shows how extravagant these people are.

Q Yes, in a number of ways, some of which we've discussed, yeah.

R In a number of ways. And the bloke in the taxi says 'they expect us not to have a video or a car or a television', or everything and he mentions that at the end of the film. And in truth I suppose you wouldn't expect them to have all those things.

Q No

R But I think, it's not so much that you wouldn't expect them to have them as you wouldn't expect them to be priorities, and these people use it as a priority.

Q Yeah.

R Now the gas bill and the electric bill and food in the cupboard and the rest of it. The children's clothes are not a priority. They go down to the social and they get given, the man with the beard again was saying 'the right of clothing our children is taken away from us'. That's not a priority, clothing a child is not a priority, the toys are priority, the television's a priority, drink's a priority. The taxi's a priority.

Q Taxis as well.

The first respondent indicates that the experience of having seen a documentary made informs her perception of the toy scene as 'fabricated'. Her stance allows her to infer production intentions and motivations for programme features – up to a point. 'They're trying to keep things natural' she says about the mother/son dialogue. The talk has been artificially constructed to give the 'natural' effect.

Our general term for interpretations that are intention/motivation-conscious is *mediation reading*; as against *transparency reading* where comments are made about the depicted world as if it had been directly perceived reality. This respondent's account shows some tension between transparency and mediation readings. She takes mediation reading to the point of articulating doubts about the reality-status of programme depictions, saying 'If they are his toys he's either keeping them very well or they've got replicas of what he owns' ('they' quite clearly suggesting the programme makers). The boxes may just be *representations* of his toys. Such doubts do not prevent the respondent from producing transparency readings which go beyond information explicitly encoded in the programme and have judgemental overtones: 'clothing a child is not a priority, the toys are priority'.

This may show that she takes her sense of the real more from verbal testimony than from visual images. But notice also that she says of the scene 'It certainly does show that they wanted to put across that there was extravagance. But I think that the whole film shows how extravagant these people are.' In this mediation reading the idea of the people's extravagance is understood as something 'put across' (by the programme-makers?) and not as an inference derived independently of the programme's authored discourse, as in a transparency reading. The idea-as-shown is *then* taken as truth, without any extra-textual warranting. This suggests either a faith in the veracity of the film's account in this respect or a slide towards transparency reading. The verb 'shows', with impersonal subject 'film', can support either interpretation.

In the passage beginning 'Yes, they're certainly not looking for sympathy in that scene', the pronoun 'they' is used eight times. Sometimes a reference to the participants is indicated, 'they're complaining that they're hard up'; others could be references to the programme makers, as in the opening sentence. Ambiguities of pronominal reference are particularly significant across the initial two sentences, where the first proposes that 'they' were not looking for sympathy whilst the second, in suggesting that 'they' have overdone it seems to imply that 'they' *were* looking for sympathy but have made tactical mistakes. If the pronouns are taken as coreferential, the account is inconsistent – at some level this respondent is just unsure who is aiming for what response. But even if the pronouns are not coreferential the lack of explicitness about this may also be symptomatic of uncertainty.

In this context, it is interesting that the final sentence of the utterance suggests a quite calculated move by the programme-makers to depict the mothers more critically, a move offered as some kind of balance against earlier treatments. Indeed, in the previous sentence, the respondent speaks in the 'voice' of the programme-makers in order to provide a strongly evaluative gloss on what she takes to be their visual undercutting of the mothers 'complaints'.

Second respondent

Q Lets turn to another particular scene now which we've got sort of an interest in I suppose. There's a section in the programme where two mothers talk about toy-buying.

R Oh yeah, the catalogue.

Q Can you just recall what we see, briefly?

R Well, Star Wars, mostly Stars Wars figures, you know, there's about four or five boxes in different,

Q How does it start, can you remember how it starts, that little bit?

R Well, there's a woman, she's a single parent, the kid comes home from school – do you want to go that far back?

Q Well, yeah, run through it like that, yeah.

R The next, he's up on the bed and she's talking, and then she's with another girl, and they're talking about why their children, why should their children have to go without things. It's all about advertising on the television, and, you know, why should their children have to do without because we're out of work? Then she says, 'I get these out of the catalogue and pay so much a week' which again is true, like.

Q And what about the prices of the toys?

R Yeah, twenty seven pounds and fifty, yeah. But that again can give you the impression that, you know, some people would say 'well they can't be that bad off, if they can pay' you know. She might have got one toy then three months later got another toy, but the way she said it then, she seemed to have bought about one hundred and odd pounds worth of toys and then started paying for them, you know, which, you know, it's probably possible, but,

Q Do you think the programme at that point's generally sympathetic to those the mothers, though?

R Well it gives them the chances to air their views, but it doesn't, I wouldn't say it was sympathetic, you've got to draw your own conclusions to that. I mean, a lot of people would probably say 'well they can't be that bad off if they've got them models with thirty pound, forty pound', you know. But I agree with what she says, why should her child go short? And she might be paying for them with, she might be working, you know, on the fiddle.

Q There are some things we don't know, yeah, about that.

R But, obviously, you can't say that, but she says she gets them on the weekly you know, which a lot of people do.

Q I think that's right. There are some kind of technical aspects of the sequence which you could question – again, I'm not saying that I am, particularly, it's passed through my mind. There's the way in which the boxes are all stacked up and the camera goes from box to box, and the way in which they recite the prices. I mean there are ways of doing that and ways of,

R Yeah – you didn't have to mention any prices, did you? But a lot of them boxes were still in brown paper. Was that made just before Christmas, or something(?)?

Q Well I don't know, what do you reckon?

R Well, its in the winter isn't it, looks like it was in the winter. But they're giving you the impression there, when she's telling you the prices of each individual toy, then she says 'I'm a single parent benefit family' and all, I think people will probably, a lot of people'll probably say 'Well, you know, she can't be that bad off'. But then people don't know what she's, she might be missing out on something else. She might never go out, she might never have a drink or you know, I don't know. It's just, them scenes, like that, give you the impression that they're getting enough money, you know, to get these things. They aren't really on such a bad amount of money to live on each week.

Q   In a sense you think they're probably scenes which are open to interpretation (. . . .)

R   Yeah, debate (?), yeah. I mean if someone, if you were talking to a Conservative, typical Conservative like – I'm talking about the people I've seen on television and I've listened to on the radio and that, who've said, 'well there's people in the pubs and there's people . . . .' you know, as if everybody who's on the dole is in the pub everyday. And then if you were talking to someone like that about this documentary they would probably cast something like that up, that you know like 'single parent but she can afford to buy so many toys for him', you know.

Q   So the programme gives enough, well I don't know about enough, but it gives some evidence,

R   of argument, yeah.

Q   to support that kind of,

R   person, yeah. I think it does, in a few things, you know.
Particularly like the pub and the taxi, that would.

The second respondent also shows uncertainty at points in his account, although the general interpretative perspective he employs and his evaluations of what is seen and heard differ from those evident in the first transcript.

For a start, it is interesting how, for this viewer, the scene is perceived to be quite centrally 'about advertising on the television', an interpretation which draws on the comments that bridge across into the subsequent episode (see our discussion above) and uses them retrospectively to organize the significance of the 'enactment and interview' sequence. Use of the comments in this way is clearly part of a sympathetic response to the mothers' circumstances and action ('. . . I agree with what she says'), a sympathy contrasting with the evaluations of our first respondent. But this viewer also regards such sympathy as at least potentially out-of-line with the 'impression' projected by the programme itself, one likely to be uncritically taken up within the interpretations of other viewers (variously, 'some people', 'a lot of people' and, more specifically, a 'typical Conservative').

This feature of interpretative discourse, in which viewers predict the likely interpretations of others, we have called *displaced* reading. It occurred in a variety of forms within our respondents' accounts. Often, as here, it was associated with anxiety about the production of misrepresentations and, in these instances, it was sometimes linked to a perception of the programme-makers' intentions as *manipulative* (i.e. seeking to persuade by covertly strategic management of the programme depictions). Despite his observation that it is 'they' (presumably, the programme-makers) who are behind the 'impression', this respondent does not choose to push the question of production intentions quite so far. Indeed, rather against that line of argument, he remarks that the programme gave participants 'a chance to air their views', suggesting some adherence to a principle of fairness, and cites an aspect of the participants' speech itself as an element in potential misrepresentation ('. . . but the way she said it then she seemed . . .'). Importantly, the question of the programme's own sympathies is regarded as a matter of subjective judgement, of 'drawing your own conclusions' rather than a matter of clear and demonstrable bias or manipulation.

Like many of those viewers we spoke to who, at some point, 'displaced' interpretations on to others, this respondent uses his own social knowledge of what might be 'true' to speculate on what was *not* shown, what we were *not* told and therefore what would not be likely to figure within the understandings and assessments of viewers lacking extra-textual access to the topic of this kind (e.g. 'She might be missing out on something else'; 'she might have got one toy then three months later got another toy'; 'she might be working, you know, on the fiddle').

Comparing the two accounts, we found that the first respondent, despite her declared knowledge of the extent to which the programme is 'fabricated', is untroubled by any sense of possible *mis*representation on this account. In contrast, the second respondent comes to question the *motivation* of programme features (mostly verbal ones) as a result of, so to speak, working 'backwards' from what experience tells him may be misrepresentation or at least ambiguity. He speculates less than the first respondent about the reality-status of programme depictions but both of them, in their different ways, address the programme's status as discourse in relation to the verbal and visual presentation of the toys in the interview phase of the scene.

Other accounts

Other possibilities of interpretation can only be touched on here, with much briefer citation. The first transcript above is not the only one to talk directly about the visual display:

> Well those parcels seemed unwrapped, certain of them, you know. She says 'that one cost fourteen pounds that one cost twenty eight pounds' and you know, it left you a little bit dazed actually because you just saw this pile and not, I mean somethings were open obviously, but there was just brown paper round the others. And then she said something about being in debt in her catalogue and that was interesting actually.

Of particular interest is the idea that the visual element had a *distracting* power, suggesting difficulties in naturalizing the witnessed pile into a perception of the scene as ordinary. As in our first transcript, this respondent's account registers excess and then goes on to react to it personally, 'I nearly died when she said the 200 pound toy but he couldn't have the little ones'; as in our second, the interpretation is displaced, saying it would 'hit home with other people who are struggling to make a living, even working people you know who wouldn't dream of buying that, such an expensive toy for their child'.

We also noted that for some respondents the naturalization problem led to an interpretation of the scene as a failure – an interpretation which is further complicated whenever, as in the first transcript, there are doubts about the programme's intentions:

> And then he's got, I mean I didn't know half of these toys you know, these sort of, spacey-fied things, you know and that cost a hundred and twenty pounds, and that one cost this that and the other. I mean she actually put prices on, I don't know why, you see. Again, I would say that definitely is the weak point in the programme. I mean maybe what the programme was trying to point out is how people, you know, she did actually say that she felt she had to compensate for it. She also did make quite a relevant point, I think, which might have been lost was that an awful lot of pressure comes from school. Now anybody who's got school children knows that this is true, that a lot of pressure does come from school. But I think that point, if they were trying to bring that point over it got lost in all the these, and then her friend talking about a two hundred pound electric car, and things.

Inferring motivation for the listing/costing exercise is here acknowledged to be difficult. Speculation that the pressure-from-school argument is a main point of the scene results in a judgement of failure on the programme's part, referencing the excesses shown. The reference to the scene as 'the weak point in the programme' could mean lack of clarity, or sympathy, or both; furthermore if lack of sympathy is a weakness then it is sympathy rather than criticism which is taken as the programme's actual attitude to its subjects, *or* as this respondent's own preferred attitude. Notice that this account is more *explicitly* unsure of the programme's intentions than is that given in the first long transcript.

In our final set of quotes, the most interesting feature is an apparent shift from an interpretation in which the programme is seen to project sympathy but fails to win the viewers' accord to one in which lack of sympathy is projected; the respondent becoming more motivation-conscious in the process.

> I also got the impression with that that it had been gone through before. But it, I don't know, it wasn't exactly, it didn't gain my sympathy, I don't think, when he went into his bedroom, and he got the brand

new toys and played with about three, or two, and then went and put the television on. I mean they're obviously in the same situation as the other couple, the man and the woman, but the fact that he'd got all these things, it didn't quite hit you as much.

'it didn't gain my sympathy' suggests that it should perhaps have done so. A transparency reading of 'the fact that he'd got all these things' weakened the possible impact of hardship, implied in the comparison with 'the other couple' (previously discussed by the respondent). But later, asked explicitly about the programme's attitude, the respondent says 'it was not trying to get your sympathy perhaps' and the exchange continues:

Q What would you point to as perhaps an indication of a lack of sympathy?
R The way the presents were there, and the woman was actually saying how much they were. And then the other one said something like 'we were going to spend two hundred pounds', or 'he wanted something for two hundred pounds'. I mean it's only afterwards that we know they're from the catalogue and she can't pay the bills, but at that time you don't know that and you just think that the child's had that much money spent on toys.

The account has developed into one where the 'delayed' deployment of explanatory information for apparent excess is a feature of the scene motivated by an unsympathetic attitude on the programme's part.

Looking across this brief selection of comments it is clear that the respondents represented here – and others whose accounts have not been cited – *work* to make sense of the scene, and that in doing so they readily make unfavourable judgements of the mothers' expenditure, though such critical interpretations can take a displaced form amongst those who are predisposed to be sympathetic. Differences between accounts emerge, as we have tried to show, when it is a question of articulating the depicted in relation to the real (particularly at the level of the facts of *this* instance of 'extravagant' behaviour) and of attributing attitudes to the programme itself.

Narratorial forms

The second scene which we want to discuss, albeit in highly condensed fashion, was selected for study because of its prominence both in the accounts of our respondents and in our own programme analysis.

It is the scene which introduces a participant/speaker whose role within the programme is a more extensive one than that of other speakers, involving voiced-over commentary in scenes depicting others and also the linking of certain scenes by in-shot speech.

We were interested in viewers' perceptions of this speaker (who, in reference to the programme's sequence of anonymous participants, we

8.2.1

8.2.2

8.2.3

have termed Speaker Three). Our interest was due partly to the scale of his involvement, partly to the distinctive nature of its visual and verbal rendering and partly to its functioning within the context of the programme's avowed principles of letting people 'speak for themselves'.

First of all, though, it might be helpful to note some of the more salient formal features of the scene in question. Visually, Speaker Three is established as a person through a sequence of shots which allows us ample time to observe him involved in routine, 'incidental' behaviours always, importantly, on his own. These include rolling a cigarette; buying tobacco; walking on estate paths and subways; entering his home and watching television.

The opening shot, of Speaker Three rolling a cigarette against a backdrop of estate blocks (Fig. 8.2.1), runs for several seconds before his voice-over begins. The development of this initial sequence moves from medium close-up to close-up and, as the voice starts to comment on the reasons for 'fiddling' electricity, the face is seen looking out of frame just before a cut to a 'point-of-view' shot of an electricity sub-station. A similar interest in the relatively intimate rendering of the personal – through facial expression, movement and gaze – is displayed in later sequences too. Here, amidst other business, Speaker Three is viewed at home peering through the slats in his window blind (Fig. 8.2.2) and, in a series of extreme close-ups taken from a number of angles, scrutinized with a quite remarkable intensity as he watches the TV news and weather (see, for example, Fig. 8.2.3).

Speaker Three's potential significance for viewers may also be due to his distinctive way of speaking. The following quotation (with stressed syllables marked) shows something of this distinctiveness:

> *Our* fiddles have been *forced* on us,
> Our fiddles are not done for *gain*,
>   or for *profits*,
> Our fiddles are done because it's *necessary*
>   it's necessary for us to *exist*

Here, as elsewhere, Speaker Three makes effective rhetorical use of parallelism, of repetitions with substitution and of elaboration. He speaks quietly but nevertheless this use of parallelism and rhythmically paced delivery gives his speech something of an oratorical quality, unlike the more conversational styles of other contributors.

It seemed to us to be worth exploring how these aspects of the performance and representation of 'selfhood' were registered within the context of the programme's wider scheme of portrayals and accounts. Given the constraints of space, our citation of respondent accounts and our analysis of them must be brief. Elsewhere, we have documented and developed this part of our study more thoroughly.[3] However, enough may be presented here to indicate some of the key variables which we found to be at work. These variables seemed to match up closely with those discussed above in relation to the 'toy scene'. We will present a selection of the responses without intervening commentary and then put forward some observations about interpretative features.

1   Yeah, the man who, he was on his own, always on his own, he'd never got a wife with him. I don't know whether he lived on his own. He was always on his own and they showed him sort of outside with the flats behind him rolling his own cigarette and looking very bleak, and things like that.

2   I think it follows him back into the house and all the time I was aware of the sort of staging of things, you know. And this was a technique that I think that was used quite a lot, you saw the individual and then you saw them in the context of their own house. You follow them into the house and they're talking about squalor and deprivation and poverty and having no money, and then suddenly you see a beautiful three-piece suite, you know, colour TV in the corner, video underneath, and you think to yourself you know this isn't squalor. But your're led into that argument by the camera you know, this kind of incongruity between what's being said and how they're actually living came up

---

[3]Richardson and Corner, *op. cit.*

time and time again. Presumably it was intended you know to raise questions in the viewer's mind.

3   He just, he was like a focus for me on the thing, he drew the whole thing together, it generalized you know it wasn't. Although he was personally affected by it all he could see through that, he could see what the whole system was doing and what his role was.

4   The way the actual unemployed chap was treated, he was given a lot of time. I think he must have been given a lot of open questions, which were then slanted, because he seemed to be railing against things quite a lot, I mean specific things like advertisements, like the status of the unemployed, like the class system, and I'm not sure really whether he was slightly set up to that. He seemed to be given a lot of time to express his grievances, and I think he must've been prompted in some way to talk about these things, on purpose.

Q   What would the purpose be, though, do you think, if he was given lee-way?

   Well presumably, to given an open honest view of how they felt, as unemployed people.

5   I think the film could've been more interesting and still had his point of view come across if he hadn't been interviewed alone. If they'd had somebody with an opposite point of view. I think if they'd had somebody with an opposite or different approach to his point of view, to put his back against the wall where he had to defend his point of view, then that would have held my interest more than him just being given the lead to down-trod everything he thought was against him.

6   He came across as a very strongminded person, I think, I don't think that would have brought so much sympathy. His opinions I think were a bit too strong for perhaps certain members of our society who might be watching the programme, because he seemed to be filled with resentment. Now that's not a bad thing to be filled with resentment, but if you put too much resentment in a programme you're going to alienate certain other sections of the society who'd be watching a BBC programme.

The framings, attributions of motive and evaluations articulated here not only indicate significant differences in the relationship of viewers both to the topic and to the programme but also show certain discursive moves being made as a result of viewer assumptions about documentary conventions and proprieties.

1, 2 and 4 are framed as mediation accounts. In 1, for instance, the 'solitariness' and 'bleakness' are registered primarily as effects of the programme's visual composition, leaving the question of Speaker Three's real circumstances open to a degree of speculation. In 4 the idea of 'treatment' immediately raises the possibility of alternative depictions. Here, the manner in which speech is elicited, as well as its content and duration, is the subject of suspicions concerning contrivance and undue weighting ('slanting', 'prompting'). Interestingly though, the idea of an illegitimate purposiveness at work appears to be retreated from in the follow-up comment, where the production aim at this point in the programme is seen to be (merely) that of obtaining 'an open honest view'. 2 also detects contrivance, though working in a different way for a different end. The respondent here connects the scene with others in noting incongruities between what is said and what is shown. These are seen to follow from a programme strategy of visually 'undercutting' participants' comments. The account involves a form of displaced reading to indicate the potential effectiveness of the device ('and you think to yourself, you know . . .') upon those viewers who, unlike the respondent, are not aware of 'being led . . . by the camera.' And insofar as the programme is assumed to want viewers to remain unaware of any depicted incongruity *as* an editorial device whilst at the same time responding to its cueings, this respondent's reading registers manipulative design too.

For 3 and 5, narratorial functions work to different effect. Whereas 3's uptake strongly registers focus and integration as aspects of the scene, together with a clear measure of agreement ('he could see what the whole system was doing') 5 believes that *adversarial discussion* would have been a more appropriate form for the programme to use. Perhaps connected with this, 5 disagrees with Speaker Three's comments and, as in 4, regards him as being 'given the lead' by the programme-makers.

In 6, adverse evaluation of the strength and nature of Speaker Three's attitudes develops into a criticism of the programme by way of a displaced reading (see discussion above), in which 'certain members of our society' or, more specifically, sections, 'who'd be watching a BBC programme' are potentially alienated by the programme-makers 'putting too much resentment in'. For this respondent, such alienation is registerable as a failure because the programme is assumed to be seeking sympathy for its participants, at least in the scene under discussion.

The scale of the research we undertook was too small for us to correlate interpretative accounts with socio-demographic variables, though not suprisingly respondents with first-hand experience of unemployment tended to have a sympathetic attitude towards the programme's participants, whilst varying in their assessment of the programme's own attitudes. It appears to us that extended survey research on documentary themes and forms, carried out by using the analytic concepts and methods which we have tried to develop here, could provide important insights into documentary television as an agency of public information and knowledge.

We believe that our study brings out some of the key processes involved when the combinatory forms of documentary 'saying' and 'showing' interact with viewers' social dispositions and attitudes. It has to be allowed that our sample audience may have been more inclined to suspicion and questioning as a result of the exceptional conditions of viewing and discussion. Nevertheless, the range of 'mediated' and 'displacement' accounts given, and the frequent tackings between these and the more 'transparent' uses made of screened depictions, seemed to us to open up new perspectives on the transformation of media form into meaning and significance for the viewer.

9

Notes on the Ascent of a Fictitious Mountain

Dai Vaughan

I

A tribe are journeying from their winter to their summer pastures. With goats, sheep and chickens, they travel for a month: the hale, the toddlers and the elderly. Cattle serve as pack-beasts for all their domestic possessions. Of many obstacles which they encounter, the last is a mountain deep with snow.

Film shot in snow is difficult to edit. The near-uniform whiteness, obscuring the topography, blurs also the conventions. If we cut from the front view of a group approaching to the rear view of a group receding, are we showing the same group from two set-ups or two groups from the same set-up? And confusion of space confuses time: is one group passing several points, are several groups passing the same point or are several groups passing several points? How far have we progressed?

Since the mountain crossing takes many hours, the entire tribe cannot accomplish it in one day; and the opportunity has been taken to film it twice, on slightly different routes. One day's rushes emphasize the steepness and treacherousness of the terrain, the other the cold and misery of the people and animals. Partly in order to do justice to both elements, partly to overcome our technical problems, we combine the two sets of material. 'We have created,' says the director, 'a fictitious mountain'.

II

It is disturbingly easy to make mistakes – quite serious mistakes – in our recollection of films. Once, for the purposes of an article, I went to see a film four times in one week. After the second viewing, I had isolated a particular succession of shots which I planned to discuss; but on the third viewing I discovered that I had remembered the episode wrongly, and that there were three extra shots between two which I had thought consecutive. On the fourth viewing, just as a final check, I paid special attention at that point. The three intrusive shots had vanished.

We can, of course, watch a film on a Steenbeck with a notepad in front of us, pausing when necessary, and make sure we get it right. Yet if we view it again under normal circumstances after first seeing it on this shot-by-shot basis, we shall still find we have made mistakes: not in our account of detail, but in our construction of overall mood and even of narrated, diegetic action: not in relation of parts to the whole, but in relation of the whole to its parts. Just as the temporal succession of frames is required for the illusion of movement, so the temporal succession of images is necessary to the experience of a film's meaning. Subdivision may demonstrate the process, but cannot authenticate it.

Rather than become irritated with ourselves and others, perhaps we should accept errors of recollection as indicative of the properties of the medium. Since its grammars are only tentative, and its imagery so lacking in cultural delimitation as to allow wide scope for investment by the viewer, there is perhaps more truth for film than for other media in the observation that no two readers will produce the same text. But for each of us this text has the appearance – and carries the conviction – of a meta-world: a world commentative upon the one we live in, yet itself bearing the aspect of 'reality'.

III

Sometimes it would begin with a general view of a city. Then there would be a few street scenes, busy with black limousines and men in trilby hats. The scope would then narrow to the lobby of an hotel or office building; and finally someone would detach himself from the anonymous populace and hand a card to the receptionist: 'Mr So-and-so's expecting me . . . ' Often, I think, the moment would be signalled by a change in the sound: the fading-out of music, or simply the transition from location effects to studio dialogue. But always, at this point, I felt a pang of disappointment.

This recurrent experience of film-going dates from my teens, or perhaps earlier. Even when I first became aware of it, it seemed to have been with me for a long time. What was the nature of the disappointment? It was not that I did not wish the narrative to start. I had gone for an adventure. But somehow I wanted the narrative to happen without what I might later have called 'theatricality': without any disruption of that casual, eaves-dropping, everywhere-at-once quality which marked the opening establishers. (In the words of the old jibe: 'There are seven million stories in the Naked City! Why did we have to choose this one?')

I should not care to trust hindsight to the extent of saying that what I was looking for was documentary when I continued to hope, at every visit to the flicks, that the moment of disappointment – the almost imperceptible gap to be bridged before the film could be enjoyed – would for once not occur. It may be that what I sought was unattainable because contradic-tory: a story composed of uncomposed elements; something which would attain to narrative significance whilst remaining random; a coherence proposed without artifice: that narration itself should share the referential level of its constituents where these had been staked out prior to it. . . . Occasionally a fiction has come close to satisfying my innocent requirements: Olmi's *Tree of Wooden Clogs*, some of Cassavetes's early improvisations – even *Potemkin*. But what have come closest have been certain states of certain *vérité* productions: not the rushes, yet not the fine-cuts and most certainly not the transmitted versions with their cellophane wrap of commentary and captions and studio presentation, but the films as they stood when their narrative structures had just begun to emerge with the patient chipping away of the surrounding substance, yet were still perceptibly of its density and of its mass.

IV

The women are seated in a great circle, facing inwards, their legs stretched straight before them. Some men are distributing meat to the women: thick hunks of beef, roasted on aromatic twigs, which they carry in the aprons of their robes. . . . This sequence – which did not appear in the finished film – showed one stage in a Maasai fertility ceremony. There was one shot in particular which cried out to be used, since it seemed to crystallize the 'feeling' of the event: a shot along the line, from the women's eye level, in which a man, working his way towards us, handed meat across the stretched legs in a gesture between a deep bow and a genuflexion.

It was, as I eventually recognized, the reverential overtones of this gesture which made it seem so apt. And in a sense, I was not wrong. An essential feature of the ceremony, for the Maasai themselves, was the reversal of social norms in the according of formal respect by men to women. But the fact remains that the Maasai do not bow. In attempting to signify the spirit of the occasion, I was drawing upon connotations of body-language specific to our own culture: and not even our present culture, at that, but rather the recollection, as enshrined in paintings or costume dramas, of a past gestural repertoire: Ralegh laying his cloak down for the Queen. . . .

Of course, this goes for writing too. Anthropologists are not in the habit of insisting that their work be published only in the language of their subject peoples; and every anthropological paper in English is a contribution to *English* literature. But still, English does not operate by mimicking the appearances of its subjects and recruiting these as language for their own representation (with the consequent tacit suggestion of objectivity). It does not, in quite so direct a fashion as does film, taint the alien with familiarity by encouraging us to read back into the pro-filmic those qualities which are in fact the connotatory apparatus of its incorporation into symbolism. That an anthropological paper contributes to its own culture may be obvious to the point of triviality. What is less obvious, and proportionately less trivial, is that every anthropological film, insofar as it relies for its comprehension upon the competencies of our own culture yet conceals this fact behind the referential nature of the photographic image, is as much *about* our own society as about that of its subjects. That which is an inflexion of our own experience is inevitably also an interpretation of it. Parallels do not have to be spelled out. They are spelled in.

V

Like many of my generation, I first encountered cinema when taken to see *Snow White* at the age of four; and, like many children of that age, I spent much of the time with my eyes shut, terrified of the witch. Forty-five years later, finding myself at a loose end in a provincial town where *Snow White* was playing at the local picture palace, I decided to go and catch up on what I had missed. The witch, of course, was *meant* to be scary; but I was surprised to discover how much of this quality came from the imperfect register of the early animation: a constant shimmer which you found yourself trying to stabilize by act of will: in the act of reading the image, willing your own fear to be.

A six-year-old returns from a holiday spent in rural Spain. He describes the slaughtering of a sheep: how they skewered it between the ligaments of its hind legs in order to hoist it up to a beam, then cut its throat and slit open its belly and skinned it. 'Then they hung me up by my ankles and pretended they were going to cut my throat too . . .' I know perfectly well that, had these things been shown on television, he would have been unable to watch them.

When animal slaughter occurs in the rushes of an ethnographic film, there is usually some debate along the lines of:

'We'd better tone it down a bit, or it'll upset the viewers.'
'But why? It's a normal part of these people's lives. There are no implications of cruelty.'
'No, but those still exist as connotations for the viewer. You can't wish them away.'
'Perhaps if it had been shot differently – not so close . . . '

Such debate revolves around distinctions between the 'significance' of an event for its participants and the significance of its record as component in the film text; and those, when the film concerns another culture, are likely to be perceived as relating to the problem of ethnocentricity. But something seems to be missing from the argument.

I too have my limits: things I find too horrible to watch. As with the six-year-old, I suspect that some of these are things I could readily cope with in 'real life', whilst in other instances I imagine the reverse may be true. But at least in these examples, documentary examples, the horror of the images would be recognized as such by others; and differences in response as between pro-filmic and filmic might be assumed to rest purely upon the differing nature of the demands made upon us: in the one case to take action (whether by helping out or by running away); in the other, to construe as meaningful. With fiction, it is different. I have sometimes found myself forced to leave a cinema, not because anything particularly unpleasant was being shown, but because the very activity of animating images which I was not also free to stop, the feeding of meanings into a text which had the physical magnitude to overwhelm me with them, the shriek of feedback as I locked into a tight short-circuit with activities which raced ahead of me, had become intolerable.

The horror of a documentary can lie in our being required to conceptualize (or – if there were such a word – *per*ceptualize) the world in a certain way and being, at least for the duration of the film, powerless to intervene in it. The horror of a 'horror' fiction lies in the fact that the horror to which we are reacting is not in any way pertinent to the pro-filmic but has drawn its compulsion, its power to trap us, wholly out of our own psychic resources.

VI

Magnetic sound can be cut. It would be possible, by excision of a 'no' or a 'not', to reverse completely the sense of somebody's statement. One's first reaction is that this would be unethical, and that any decent documentary editor would refuse to do it. But suppose the person had made what was obviously, in the light of the original context, a slip of the tongue. Should we then leave it be, on grounds of absolute fidelity to the event, or even on the theory that every slip reveals a hidden motivation; or should we alter it to what was 'really' meant?

Even if we believe documentary to be convincingly defined by reference to the viewer's response – the viewer's recognition of the privileged relation between a film image and its pro-filmic source – we are left with difficulties about the nature of the claim documentary makes upon the world.

In the popular press and on television chat-shows, *vérité* films are taken to task for their omissions. An implied claim to 'objectivity' is disputed by obsessive carping about the process of selection and by knowing references to 'the cutting-room floor'. But is the truth of a statement proportional to its duration? Most editors would be insulted at the suggestion that their work consisted essentially of leaving things out. To them, even in *vérité*, what is important is how things are put together. Most people who complain about the way they have been represented by film-makers would surely agree that, in principle, they might find an edited account of an event in which they had participated more accurate, in emphasis and inter-pretation, than the arbitrary totality of the rushes. The question is: does this render the efforts of *vérité* worthless? Does it demonstrate, for instance, that the relation of *vérité* to the prior event is no different from that of a skilled reconstruction?

VII

Imagine two stills from a feature film – a western, let us say. The first, showing a moment of high drama as the baddies descend upon the stagecoach, bears the caption: 'Is this a fictitious event?' The second, which shows a greasy saddle hanging from a peg in a stable: 'Is this a fictitious object?'

VIII

The Jarrow march lasted for 27 days in October 1936. For most of the journey there was good weather; and only on the last day did it rain heavily. Yet the image which has entered our consciousness is of the marchers in their cloth caps and glistening black oilskin capes trudging defiantly and stoically through the downpour. This is partly because the arrival in London was the moment which attracted most newsreel and photographic coverage. But it also reflects our sense of appropriateness: our acknowledgment that a 300 mile slog against deprivation and unemployment was no picnic.

Cinéma vérité was met with detestation by such old documentary hands as Harry Watt; and I think this was because they believed it would leave no room for the sort of selectivity whereby the Jarrow images attain to their proper symbolic potential. They feared the inundation of the medium with *mere* facticity: the reduction of the truth of a moment to the way it *happened* to be shot. They could yet be proven right. But the most striking thing about early *vérité* films, when we look at them today, is the degree to which they revelled in their rough-and-readiness: the bumps, the jerky zooms, the sudden twitches of focus. The pet name for them in the business was 'wobblyscope'. The periphera of slapdash shooting were seized upon and, in no time at all, elevated to the function of eliciting audience-identification with the camera-operator in the urgent search for latent meaning: elevated, that is, to linguistic status. I still remember the excitment of cutting this stuff: of searching for a style which would complement that of the photography. The Vietnam war exists for us in this language as surely as does Agincourt in the language of Shakespeare.

Rapid improvements in camera handling made the world of the late 1970s, as reflected in documentary, a far less zap-happy place than that of the late 1960s. What I am saying is that language abhors a vacuum, and that a medium from which connotations have been expelled will reaccumulate them as quickly as a sterile agar dish accumulates germs. This process is expedited by the holistic way in which the ciné-text operates. I once cut a sequence in which two teachers, seated on chairs facing each other within a circle of their colleagues, engaged in an intense and slightly threatening role-playing exercise. This was in the days when, for cheapness, rushes of colour programmes were still printed in black and white; and the sequence had a brooding, Buñuelian atmosphere of Jacobean furniture and faces watching from the shadows as if trying to stare out through the darkened varnish of old portraits. When we saw the print of the finished film, it turned out that the gloom had resulted from the preponderance of yellow in the light: the furniture was new and shoddy-looking; the watchers were not swallowed in semi-obscurity; and a garish orange-and-red carpet had materialized out of the nether murk. In consequence, the role-playing had lost its concentration and had become an amusement. Nothing had changed in the behaviour or in the dialogue; but to separate these elements out, and to receive the same 'message' as from the sequence in the cutting copy, would have required a conscious act of de-crystallization: a conscious reversal of the act of assigning coherence to film.

IX

It is easy to dislike photographs: not so much when we see them as when we *fore*see them. Glancing through the bus window at the dawn light on the Albert memorial, we can imagine – or imagine we can imagine – exactly what a good colour supplement spread would look like: the dewy grey of the grass, precisely rendered, in muted dissonance with the cuprous stains on the white stone; the figures of the tableaux beckoning and gesticulating to an absent multitude . . . and we resent this reducibility, this predictable accuracy which renders all details equal, denies us the eye's choice of emphasis and disqualifies such non-visual components as the chill in the air or the elusive scent of leaf-smoke. In short, we suspect that the photograph, which seems to posit all other visualizations as subjective and hence discreditable, will negate the experience of 'seeing': will brutalize our perception.

Conversely, we are all familiar with the way in which a glossy picture postcard, which we would normally dismiss as too bland to be expressive of anything, can take on a different quality if it shows a place we are about to visit. We scan the image searchingly. What character of light is represented by this insensitive colour? How would it feel to mingle with that crowd, to sit on that terrace, to look back across those hills? By the shift in the focus of our attention, the glazed surface of the convention seems revealed as transparent. When confronted with an old postcard, in hand-tinted monochrome, where the conventions, though still inexpressive, have shed their facile familiarity, we seek both to reinstate that familiarity – to think ourselves back to when the conventions would have been neutral – and yet to penetrate these conventions to the actuality of what is shown. The 'fascination' of old postcards lies in our attempt to perform these contrary movements simultaneously . . .

X

When Princess Anne fell off her horse at some race or other, the newspaper carried a report accompanied by a photograph: a small oblong comprising dotted and dappled areas in two or three degrees of grey. So irresolute was this image that, even with the clue of the news-item, one found some difficulty in interpreting it. Needless to say, the photo communicated virtually no information *about* its subject, for its rudimentary resources were scarcely even adequate to the job of making her recognizable to a public already familiar with her appearance. Yet the paper had considered it worth printing. Why? Not to demonstrate the existence of someone called Princess Anne; and not to prove that she had fallen from a horse (for there was no horse in the picture); but simply to confirm, as in a host of less extreme instances, the minimal fact of witness: the simultaneous presence of seer and seen.

It is because every photograph bears such witness that photography is widely supposed to have no fictive disposition. But by 'fictive', as often as not, we mean illustrative. (Is a painting by Alma-Tadema in any true sense a *fiction*?) If illustrative photography for fictions has been abandoned by all but the producers of certain picture-romances for the teenage market, there is nonetheless an area in which effacement – or at least attenuation – of the photographic 'witness' is commonplace.

I used to have, side by side on the wall of my cutting room, two photographs, each showing a hand poised over a glass. The first was by Jean Mohr, and was in black and white. The hand was that of a French peasant: stubby, wearing a wedding ring, with a black mark on the thumbnail which was perhaps a blood blister. The glass, over which the hand hovered as if having just put it down, was empty; but drops of apple spirit still clung to its inner surface. A shaft of sunlight, falling onto the table, illuminated the glass from behind and reflected upward onto the man's palm as if his body were glowing with the warmth of the drink; and it linked the gold wedding band with the rim of the glass, and the etching of the glass with the floral pattern of the plastic table-cover. The second photograph, which was in colour, was a newspaper advertisement for a brand of whisky. The tawny drink, in its immaculate tumbler, with the mandatory three bubbles along the meniscus, seemed to glow from within: for the source of illumination could not be determined. The hand, held a few inches above in a gesture inexplicable unless it was that of a customer saying 'When', told us little about its owner except that, since the nails were well manicured and the shirt-cuff spotless, he was not impoverished. In fact, of course, he may well have been impoverished. He was almost certainly a model hired solely for the perfection of his hands – a 'finger artist'. Here, then, was a photograph whose resources were bent to the concealment of its origins. The Mohr might not make us aware of the camera; but it did make us aware of its subject as a moment witnessed, in all the specifics of its detail, by a companion seated at the same table. The advertisement, which on a symbolic level strove towards a similar content (the 'warm glow' of a strong drink), so denied its subject's specificities as to present them as witnessed by no-one: only ourselves, who looked at the advertisement.

There is a similarity here with the classier forms of pornography, which, seeking to distance the model from the sordor of the photographic session, present her not as the contingent object of voyeuristic attention but as 'she who would be desirable *if* she were to enter our world': to present the image not as the record of something seen but as the conjuration of our own wishes. There is, of course, an instability in the concept of 'a photograph which is not of something witnessed'; but it is precisely this instability which advertisement and pornography exploit. The point is not, after all, to posit an ideal; and the purpose of the otherwise puzzling hand in the whisky ad is to ensure that it will not be taken for a painting. Where Mohr gives us a moment aspiring towards universality, the advertisement gives us a universal aspiring to the momentary: a dream aspiring to materiality through the complicity of our vision. Advertisement is the pornography of all our appetites.

When the photograph assumes a temporal dimension – i.e. becomes cinema – the gravitation of the image to its moment as witness may be cheated in the continuous postponement which is narrative. Indeed, we may wish to argue that it is the very instability of the 'non-actuality photograph' which supplies the motive for film fiction. The effacements of actuality in film do not demand the impoverishment of its signs. Since all that is required is that the viewer should suspend enquiry, other means are available: the constitutive grammars of realism. Herzog says of the ship in *Fitzcarraldo*, 'You can see it's a real ship. You can see it's not made of plastic . . .'; yet despite this apparent appeal to its materiality, to its pro-filmic properties, it is in no way the same ship as in *Burden of Dreams*, the film on the *making* of *Fitzcarraldo*: and the difference lies in that the narrative, generated by the images of this very ship, defers beyond the 'End' title any interest in its circumstances. For all its claims to weight, the universe of film fiction has an ontology similar to that of Bishop Berkeley's tree, which exists only while we are looking at it.

Fiction is film's effacement of the fact of witness. Thus when film is used for advertisement, a problem arises: to prevent the instability latent in the 'non-actuality photograph' from being dissipated in the generation of narrative. It is for this reason, rather than because of any difficulty in otherwise identifying the product, that a pack-shot – in effect, a still – occurs at the end of almost every commercial.

XI

A friend, trying to teach words to her two-year-old, was showing him a book with illustrations of animals and birds. It was not a children's book; and the illustrations were wood-cuts, somewhat formalized. The child was unresponsive. Eventually the mother, pointing to one picture, said, 'That's an owl, isn't it?' I saw the child's expression change. He turned back to the earlier pages and, as if now armed with a stylistic key, correctly identified most of the previous images.

Film is neither raw world nor a symbolic description of the world. It is a representation of the world which gains the status of a simulacrum from the trust which our culture accords the photograph. This 'trust' derives from our recognition of the photograph as a trace, an index, of some prior entity. But the indexal property does not in itself entail anything we would acknowledge as adequate representation, as resemblance. A variable-area optical sound track might be called a photograph of a symphony, for it may certainly be an index of one; but it does not provoke in us the conviction that we are in the presence of an equivalent event.

Some people argue that photography is not a language, a code, and that the photosensitive surface has merely stayed the light-waves on their journey from the object to our eyes. But this is no more than is meant by saying that the photograph has an indexal, one-to-one relation with that object. And even if the camera is graphically innocent, our eye is not. The camera is, for example, a machine for replicating the lordly monocular perspective of Versailles; and we know that schoolbooks using perspective illustrations can be misleading to children in whose visual cultures this is not a tradition.

This lack of innocence, or of neutrality, is even more apparent when we look at the moving photograph. The zoom lens, when first introduced into fiction film (I am thinking in particular of Clouzot's *Wages of Fear*), seemed to flout our 'photographic trust' by its capacity to change the size of an image with no effect of parallax. Despite the fact that the human eye alters focus with a zooming action, this seemed 'unnatural'. Likewise colour, until we became used to it, seemed to make things less 'realistic' – more glamorous – than black and white. Our 'trust' had been granted, not to the indexality *per se*, but to this or that manifestation of it at a particular period in the development of the technology; and a change in that technology was sufficient to disorient us.

The disorientation was, perhaps ironically, less severe in documentary, where anything the camera can do (e.g. night filming by infra-red light) is quickly reabsorbed into our reading of the image as actuality, than in fiction, where it is not really supposed to matter how the images were obtained. (Why should we care whether the camera is a neutral observer when what is 'observed' exists only to play its part in the narration?) What is clear, however, is that the realism of the film image is not assured either by nature or by linguistic convention, but requires for its warranty the cultural, ideological and individual contributions of the viewer. And, since this goes for documentary and fiction alike, it is clear too that the problems of documentary and the problems of realism are not the same.

XII

There is nothing in literature strictly comparable to documentary in film. A play made up entirely from the transcripts of a trial might seem to offer an instance of documentary drama. But the fact is that words have no concrete prerequisite. At best, the courtroom drama could attain to a certain para-documentary status to the extent that we chose to *treat* its dialogue as equivalent to that of the original hearing. But to call this documentary would be to blur a clear and important distinction. The dialogue of the play *could* exist without any prior referend, whereas the point about the film image is that it cannot. Only the radio feature, using location-recorded voices and sounds, may truly be said to straddle this divide.

In literature, fiction is defined in contradistinction to fact; and the grey area between them is not so much a no-man's-land as a whole populous continent. In film, fiction is defined in contradistinction to documentary; and the narrow grey area is one not of intermingling but of indecision – indecision as to how a particular text may best be read. Documentary is 'about' the materials of its making; and sufficient of the pro-filmic (or pro-radio) elements must be relevant to the discourse for such a reading to be tenable. Flaherty's films – to take a contentious example – are clearly about the peoples filmed. They may be in some respects lies about them; but that does not prevent their being documentaries. In the case of *Tabu*, however, we may find ourselves switching to the fiction mode: either because we suspect, rightly or wrongly, that the narrative has exceeded any credible relevance to the people performing it; or because we find the narrative closure so hermetic as to render the indexal factor of the images a matter of indifference. It may still be a film about the South Seas; but it is no longer about the people or the objects or the incidents which passed before the camera.

But if film fiction and literary fiction are defined in contradistinction to different things, this does more than require a slight reallocation of the boundary (so that, for example, 'factual fiction' might emerge as a category to embrace such divergent works as *Three Days in Szczecin* and *The Private Life of Henry VIII*): it means that film fiction and literary fiction are radically different in nature, since film fiction inheres in the attempt to disown something which literature does not possess in the first place. To do this, however, is no mechanical matter. Knowing that a panjandrum of ethnographic film was to view one of my rough-cuts, I included in it a matching continuity – a cut on an action – between two shots taken on different days. To my delight, he noticed this and complained about it, saying that such a device would predispose the audience to see the sequence as quasi-fictional. He was right; yet in the end, I decided not to change it. This fictive cut, done first as a bit of a joke, seemed to serve as a point of reference for the other, more disjunctive ones: to draw attention to the fact that all juxtaposition entails selection and construction, the construction of spatio-temporal narrativities being only a special case of this. In other words, I wished to disclaim that innocence on which purists are sometimes inclined to congratulate themselves.

In any case, the construction of spatio-temporal continuities – the 'classic realist' form, where the action defines space and time rather than simply inhabiting them – does not of itself prohibit a documentary reading. We may understand the constituents of a continuity as recurrent events – in which case an action cut will take on the grammatical status of a frequentative – or as having been enacted for the purpose of demonstration. It is true, however, that such usages create a bias towards the fictional; and they do so, paradoxically, because of what they seem to tell us about the pro-filmic. To read a film as fiction is to perceive all its elements as contributing to its statement, as existing *only for* that statement. Everything, including the pointing of the brickwork and the hue of the sunset, is subsumed into discourse. There is no residue of the intractable. And this implies that everything, as in verbal fiction, is subject to authorial control. Conversely, then, anything which bespeaks undue authorial intervention in the pro-filmic (as judged by the individual viewer) may prompt the selection of the fictional mode of response. But the control is not a *component* of the fiction, which positions it as already forgotten.

XIII

Twenty-five years ago, in an article on Robert Flaherty, I quoted from the commentary of *Industrial Britain* the words, 'So these industrial towns are not quite so drab as they seem, for behind all the smoke beautiful things are being made,' and observed: 'But we know perfectly well that "these industrial towns" are a good deal *more* drab than they seem to the camera-man with a good eye for composition.'

I was never happy with this formulation; and it has continued to nag at my mind long after the remainder of the article has evaporated from my memory. The difficulty is that it seems to suggest there is a *correct* balance to be found – hence somewhere a common calibration – between the qualities of photography and the qualities of lives. Obviously there is not. Yet the moment we say this, we are struck by the suspicion that we may be denying the legitimacy of film expression altogether. It is easy enough, when opposing a view we think false (picturesque, sentimental . . .), to offer such a criticism as the above; but how are we to behave if we are *making* a film, and cannot escape the connotatory potencies of our imagery? Do we wish to spend all our lives deconstructing dominant (i.e. other people's) codings? We may, of course, relegate the pictures to the role of testimony to a verbally correct analysis; but this amounts to a refusal to soil our hands with the material in which we have chosen to work.

Most of us do, however undesirable we may think it, read photography as offering something more than bald, factual information about what is represented: as revealing – rather than merely superimposing – something we might vaguely designate 'quality', or at least 'atmosphere'. As we watched the rushes of a Mongolian carpet factory, which had been shot in hypnotic close-up on hands, faces and the richly coloured wools, the sound recordist remarked that he remembered this factory as a bleak, raw, comfortless place. With his comments in mind, I tried to find ways of setting these shots 'in quotes', as projections of a cultivated national self-image in the manner of a poster. But we cannot put everything in quotes. Sooner or later, we must make the decision whether a certain quality of image is or is not appropriate to the matter recorded. Was the close-up shooting of the carpet weavers a proper portrayal of the intensity of their concentration and perhaps also of some level of satisfaction in their work? Again, adjudication presupposes a non-existent scale of equivalence.

The problem is compounded by the fact that some of photography's expressivity is borrowed almost unaltered from its objects. Not all; and never simply. Indeed, there is an irony underlying my opening example in that the images assumed to connote drabness in 1933 were read by myself, in 1959, as having been ennobled by the camerawork (and perhaps, at an intertextual level, by association with Lowry's paintings and the roofscapes of the *Coronation Street* titles). Nevertheless, we do all see the width of a pavement, the weight of a portico, even the slant of sunlight on an allot-ment shed made of old doors, as communicating something of the lives lived in their ambience. No doubt this too is questionable. An old man is digging his front garden. Does he stand for contentment? Perhaps he hates gardening, risks a heart attack with the exertion and is doing it only because the neighbours have complained about his weeds spreading into their plots. Look closely enough, and we shall begin to doubt whether any quality may be attributed to any environment or any life. Yet if we deny that the quality of life can vary according to circumstances, we are left with no reason for wishing to change things. Which is absurd.

It is our constant practice to attribute meanings to experiences we do not share – in a word, to 'sympathize' – and, conversely, externalize our own emotions by investing them in the contingencies of our surroundings. It is doubtful whether film could serve the needs of fiction without recourse to the community of such representations – i.e. as a system whose connotatory complexities were built up purely by overlays of self-reference and intertextual echo. But in fiction it does not matter if we are 'wrong'. With documentary, this question – like others we have touched upon – brings us up against the implacable central mystery: that of the relation of the constructions we place upon imagery to the world on which these supposedly comment, yet which does not exist for us *except* as defined in the operations of the text to which that imagery has contributed.

Again and again we tread the same ground, seeking that slight unevenness which may help us map the buried truth. One more example. In a film I was cutting about a mercurial character, much given to hesita-tion and digression, rarely finishing a sentence before starting another, I came into severe conflict with the director over the extent to which the speech-patterns, in voice-over, should be tidied up for the sake of clarity. The director's position, I think, was that this was not a *vérité* exercise, that we were composing a portrait with filmic materials, that no one portrait could be inherently more valid than another and that to grant priority to

the accidentals of the rushes was perverse. My own position – more difficult to define, for I was certainly not arguing for total non-
intervention – was that we were progressively discarding those very
elements which made the subject an engaging, quirky and likable personality. Towards the end of the schedule, however, the subject visited the
cutting room. I became aware that what I had perceived as 'mercurial'
carried with it something darker, more unmanageable, almost entropic;
and I began to see in the director's compulsion to curb this personality a
fear of disorganization, of loss of control, of the dissolution of that filmic
coherence which director and editor alike are inevitably seeking. Leaving
aside the question whether, in this instance, the director had confused a
threat to his authorial control with a threat to the inner logic of the text, we
are left with the fact that the personality to which I felt responsibility, and
which I hoped to reconstruct in film, was not that of the subject as directly
encountered but that which I had inferred from a reading of the rushes.
And this, moreover, cannot be dismissed as error or misfortune: for it
replicates precisely, and quite properly, the situation of a viewer faced with
the completed work.

XIV

What exactly is the pro-filmic? Fiction does not need to ask, since its only
interest in the pro-filmic is to eradicate it. The documentary impulse
resides in the wish that the distinctive relation of the photograph to its
material pre-requisites should hold for the film text *vis-à-vis* its anterior
world. This is impossible; and documentary has consisted in ways of
concealing this impossibility from itself. These ways have meandered
between two primal strategies. One has been to establish, between the
world and its representation, a purgatorial realm of the putative: of that
which might have happened, or that which nearly did. (In classical
documentary, this would have been scripted in advance of shooting;
in post-*vérité*, it is discovered in the course of refining the material. In
neither event is it to be read as a fiction, since – for one thing – the participants are not enacting it as having happened to people other than themselves.) The other has been to vest the claim to actuality entirely in the
relation of the *elements* to the pro-filmic, and to leave the totality to take
care of itself.

But again, what *is* the pro-filmic? Obviously it is the people and objects
and places filmed. Yet even this may require some qualification if we are to
avoid the tautology: Here is a photograph of someone of whom this is a
photograph. Assuming the subjects are not already public figures, known
from other sources, they must be identified from the viewers' standpoint as
'people to whom operations performed by the text are pertinent'. And
when we move from people and objects to events and actions, the question
becomes more complicated. Must the pro-filmic – as that to which
the viewer is to see the film as referring, and from whose referential traces
the film will be built – be held to embrace such circumstances as the

participants' awareness/unawareness of the fact of filming, or the motivations which might (or might not) lead them to modify their behaviour for the camera? Where does responsibility end?

Despite the formulations I have attempted, I still find difficulty with the idea of a film being 'about' subjects who are ultimately defined for us only through the text of that film. Nobody would be interested in the Turin shroud if the question were simply whether its imprint was truly that of a crucified man. And I am not here discussing the banalities of 'labelling' our material. To believers, I suspect, the shroud takes on holiness from its *own* testimony; and the consequent irrelevance of scientific proof (*dis*proof would be another matter) serves to enhance the eloquence of its majestic linguistic solitude. The Turin shroud would not benefit from a lower-third caption.

Documentary, which to its makers is a window, is to its viewers a veil impressed with the features of the unknowable. The impressions, certainly, are information. We can scrutinize film imagery for details which the original makers overlooked; and we can rearrange shots so as to highlight these details and bring new themes into prominence. And these themes will bear upon the thing first photographed. Documentary, above all art-forms, is not self-referential. It interacts directly – and not just through a presumptive unifying consciousness, whether of author or viewer – with other discourses of knowledge, supplementing and contra-dicting their data. Yet for all that, to construe a documentary as meaning-ful is to consent to the total assimilation of the pro-filmic into its own signification ('its own' in at least the minimal sense that it is not signifying something other). My most revealing reaction, when meeting people who have appeared in films I have cut, is to be shocked that they should say and do things which did not occur in the rushes. The film-maker says to the subjects as perceived by the viewer: 'The limits of my language are the limits of your world.'

XV

All knowledge of the world is a projection of our constructive faculty upon material signals – though these, while they may on the one hand be misleading, can never on the other hand be complete. Documentary is both materialist and voluntarist. Its cathexis is to be found in the convic-tion that 'trusted' images of the world, no matter how these may be mani-pulated, will engage us on a level of direct relevance to this world. But implicit in this idea – of an engagement with the world in the process of constituting its image as meaningful – is the idea that the world's materia-lity is all we have of it, and that its spirit, or meaning, is our ways of interrelating its material and of summoning it before the purposive gaze of consciousness.

Every documentary is a do-it-yourself reality kit.

The mountain is non-fictitious if the viewer deems it so. And to forget this is to lose sight of the essentials of our trade.

Notes on Contributors

Elaine Bell is completing a thesis on realism and television documentary. She is currently employed as a researcher in local government, and is a former Research Fellow in the Department of Sociology and Social Policy at the University of Durham.

David Chaney is Senior Lecturer in Sociology at the University of Durham, lecturing in cultural studies. He is the author of *Fictions and Ceremonies* (Edward Arnold, London, 1979). As well as several articles on documentary and Mass Observation, he has published extensively in studies of popular culture, with particular reference to the historical development of mass cultural forms. He has recently completed a study of spectacular forms of entertainment.

Richard Collins is Senior Lecturer in Film and Media Studies at the Polytechnic of Central London. In 1984–5 he was a Centenary Visiting Scholar at Temple University, Philadelphia. He is the author of *Television News* (London, British Film Institute 1976) and (with Vincent Porter) *WDR and the Arbeiterfilm* (London, British Film Institute 1981). He is an editor of the journal *Media Culture and Society*.

John Corner is a lecturer in the Department of Communication Studies at Liverpool University. He is co-editor of *Communication Studies* (London, Arnold, 1980, 2nd edn 1985) and has contributed a number of articles about mass communications and media analysis to books and journals. He is currently researching aspects of broadcasting policy.

Bill Nichols is Professor of Film Studies at Queen's University, Ontario. He is the editor of *Movies and Methods* (Berkeley, University of California Press, 1976; *Volume 2*, 1986), the author of *Ideology and the Image* (Bloomington, Indiana University Press, 1981) and has written widely on films and film theory in both British and North American journals.

Michael Pickering is Senior Lecturer in Communication Studies at Sunderland Polytechnic. He is the author of *Village Song and Culture* (London, Croom Helm, 1982), which won the 1983 Katherine Briggs Memorial Award. He has also published in the areas of working-class writing and music-hall culture, and is currently working on the topic of autobiography.

Kay Richardson is a lecturer in the Department of Communication Studies at Liverpool University. She is a contributor to the volume *Language and the Nuclear Arms Debate: Nukespeak Today* edited by Paul Chilton (London, Frances Pinter, 1985) and has recently completed a doctoral thesis on sociolinguistic analysis of press language.

Paddy Scannell is a lecturer in the Faculty of Communications of the Polytechnic of Central London and an editor of the journal *Media, Culture and Society*. He has published a number of articles on broadcasting history and is currently working on a social history of British broadcasting.

Roger Silverstone is Reader in Sociology in the Department of Human Sciences at Brunel University, Uxbridge, Middlesex. His previous publications include: *The Message of Television: Myth and Narrative in Contemporary Culture*, (London, Heinemann Educational Books, 1981); *Framing Science: The Making of a BBC Documentary*, (London, British Film Institute, 1985). A book, *Television, Narrative, Rhetoric: Studies in Theory and Method*, is in preparation.

Bjorn Sorenssen is Senior Lecturer in Film at the University of Trondheim, Norway. He has studied film at UCLA and has been Visiting Professor at the Department of Radio, Television and Motion Pictures of the University of North Carolina at Chapel Hill. He wrote his doctoral dissertation on the Norwegian workers' film movement of the 1930s and has contributed articles to Norwegian periodicals and to anthologies on film history, television and literature.

Dai Vaughan has worked as a film editor since 1963, most recently on a six-part series about the Maasai (BBC 2) and on three of the *About Time* series (Channel 4). In addition to analytical articles and short fiction, he has published *Portrait of an Invisible Man* (London, British Film Institute, 1983), a critical biography of documentary editor Stewart McAllister.

176

Index

film theory, linguistic, 48–51, *see also* television
form, hybridization of, 114–22
'Free Cinema', 47

Graef, Roger, ideology, 136–8, method, 132–6, style, 127–8
grande syntagmatique, 91–2
Grierson, John, vii, ix, 47, 65, 71–3

Harding, A.E., 5–6, 12, 14–16
Harrisson, Tom, 37–8, 43–4
Horizon, 86, 87, 101, 103, 'A New Green Revolution', 95–105, *see also* films

iconic status, 120
ideology, 109–11
individualist aestheticism, 34
ITN, 126
ITV, 126

Jennings, Humphrey, xiii, 37–40 *passim*, *Diary for Timothy*, 60–3, *Listen to Britain*, 56–60, and poetic style, 47–51, *Words for Battle*, 51–6

Lyotard, Jean-François, 81–9, 94, 106, *The Post-Modern Condition: A Report on Knowledge*, 82

Madge, Charles, 36–44 *passim*, 63
magazine documentary, 74, 77–9
mass communication, 35–6, 41, studies, 143
mass journalism, 41–2
Mass Observation, xii, xiii, xiv, 21, 26, 32, 36–44
Mass Observation, 37
mimesis, 85–9 *passim*, 108, 128
musical effects, 61–2
myth, 85–9 *passim*, 108

narrative structure, 84–5, 107–8
naturalism, 120, 131–2, 141, Lukacs on, 128–30, Vaughan on, 136, *see also cinéma vérité*
NBC, 70, 128

'observational cinema', *see cinéma vérité*

photography, 67–8, of Jean Mohr, 168–9
photo-journalism, 78

poetic image, 62–3
poetics, xiii, 42
poetic style, 47–63 *passim*
poetry, 51, 59
post-modernism, *see* Lyotard, Jean-François
pragmatics, 142–3
Principles and Practice in Documentary Programmes (BBC), 131–3, 135, 137
pro-filmic, the, 174–5

radio, features, 2–7, 'pure radio', 3, and social documentation, 7–14, *see also* BBC
radio programmes, *Billy Welcome*, 25, *Broadcasting With the Lid Off*, 20, *Canal Journey*, 20–1, *Children's Hour*, 15, 19, *Classic Soil, the*, 21–2, 23, *Coal*, 17–19, *Coalface*, xiv, 16, *Cotton*, 17, *Crisis in Spain*, 5, 23, *Harry Hopeful*, 15–17, 19, 25, *Have A Go!*, 25, 26, *Homeless People*, 26, *Housing Problems*, xiv, 12, *Intimate Snapshots*, 6, *Kaleidoscope*, 3–4, *Miners' Wives*, 26, *New Year Over Europe*, 5, 6, *'Opping 'Oliday*, 12, 21, *Other People's Houses*, 8–10, 24, 25, *Pounds, Shillings and Pence. A Study in Shopping*, 20, *Republic of Austria, the*, 5, *SOS*, 10, *Speed*, 6, *Squirrel's Cage, the*, 6, *Steel*, 16, 20, 23, *They Speak for Themselves*, 21, 23, *Time to Spare*, 10, 24, 25, *Western Land, the*, 15, *Wool*, 17
Radio Times, 2, 4, 5, 6, 10, 26
realism, 34, 111
Reith, Lord, ix, 3, 6, 67
rhetoric, 89–95, 108–9

Selsdon Committee, 65–6
Sieveking, Lance, 1, 3–5, 6, 7
shooting ratios, 135
social realism, 33
surrealism, 39, 112

television, commercial, 80, documentary programmes, 70–80, documentary science, 89–106, formative years, 65–70, language of, 81–5, *see also* BBC, film theory television programmes, *see* films

viewer interpretation, 141–2, 159–60, *A Fair Day's Fiddle* and, 142–9, and mediation reading, 149, and transparency reading, 149, *see also* audience